Between Clan and Crown

Between Clan and Crown

The Struggle to Define Noble Property Rights in Imperial Russia

Lee A. Farrow

DELAWARE

Newark: University of Delaware Press

Associated University Presses
2010 Eastpark Boulevard
Cranbury, NJ 08512

The paper used in this publication meets the requirements of the American National Standard for Permanence of Paper for Printed Library Materials Z39.48-1984.

Library of Congress Cataloging-in-Publication Data

Farrow, Lee A., 1966–
Between clan and crown : the struggle to define noble property rights in Imperial Russia / Lee A. Farrow.
p. cm.
Includes bibliographical references and index.
ISBN 0-87413-887-6 (alk. paper)
1. Real property—Russia—History. 2. Inheritance and succession—Russia—History. 3. Nobility—Legal status, laws, etc.—Russia—History. I. Title.
KLA687.F37 2004
346.4704′32—dc22

2004008123

PRINTED IN THE UNITED STATES OF AMERICA

In memory of Sophia K. Farrow
(June 4, 1997–July 16, 1997)

Contents

Acknowledgments

THIS STUDY HAS BEEN A VERY LONG PROCESS AND, THEREFORE, there are many people to whom I owe thanks. I apologize in advance if I have unwittingly omitted anyone in the following acknowledgments.

I would like first to express my gratitude to the various institutions that made this research possible; these include Tulane University and, in particular, the History Department of Tulane University, through which I received financial assistance from the Georges Lurcy Charitable and Educational Trust and the Selley Fellowship; the International Research and Exchanges Board, which funded a significant portion of my overseas research; and Auburn University Montgomery whose Research Grant-in Aid allowed me to complete the primary research for this book. I should also mention the Interlibrary Loan department of the AUM library, particularly Carolyn Johnson, who has helped me obtain many critical sources.

An earlier version of chapter three was originally published in the *Russian Review* in July 1996. I thank them for permission to reprint the bulk of it here.

There are also many individuals who deserve my gratitude and recognition. During my various stays in Russia, I was fortunate to meet many interesting people and to build some very dear friendships. First of all, I would like to thank my Russian landlady and adopted grandmother, Liubov' Filippova, whose mothering and hot borscht kept me warm and comfortable throughout my time in Moscow. She and her daughter and grandson provided me with a family away from home. Irina Suponitskaia and Valerii Mil'don also made my stay in Russia less lonely and more interesting. On numerous visits to their flat, I enjoyed a delicious meal and stimulating conversation; their interest in my research was, and continues to be, greatly appreciated. I would also like to acknowledge the archivists, librarians and other workers at the Russian State Archive of Ancient Acts (RGADA) in Moscow - Alexander Gamaiunov, Inna Ivanova, and Evgenii Rychalovskii. Many times they went beyond the call of duty to assist me in locating, photocopying, and, on occasion, deciphering documents. Three women at RGADA deserve special mention for their friendship and warmth -Oksana Ponomarenko, Inna Krylova, and Zhanna Vasilievna. These women took me into their circle, inviting me to tea and lunch, including me in their birthday celebrations, and, in general, making me feel welcome. I can not thank them enough for making my days at the archive so pleasant. I am also grateful to the Institute of State and Law in Moscow and, in particular, to Liudmila Lapteva for her assistance. Special thanks also go to those who made my stays in Russia more tolerable and made the Leninka a more friendly place: Claire Gordon, Jim Morgan, David Stone, David Schimmelpenninck, Nikos Chrissidis and Jenni Siegel, as well as Shannon Smith, Andy Day, Chris Nevitt, David Engerman and Sandy Korros. Special commendation goes to Pam Kachurin, who has been a faithful friend, confidant and therapist both inside and outside Russia.

Many colleagues have contributed to the shaping and completion of this study. In particular, I would like to thank the members of Tulane's History Department. I owe special thanks to Linda Pollock and Jim Boyden for their intellectual and emotional support, particularly during the difficult months after our six-week-old daughter, Sophia, died. Words can not sufficiently express my gratitude. I am also deeply indebted to my graduate advisor, mentor, and friend, Sam Ramer, who helped me discover and shape this topic; he has offered me countless hours of advice, careful editing, and thought-provoking discussion and was enormously supportive when personal tragedy prevented me from writing. More than anything, I hope that he is pleased with this book. I would also like to thank several scholars from other universities who have given me professional inspiration and support: Gary Marker, Dan Kaiser, Valerie Kivelson, Eve Levin, Elise Kimerling Wirtschafter, and Paul Bushkovitch. More recently, I have been welcomed by a new group of colleagues at Auburn University Montgomery, both within and outside of my department, who have offered support and guidance during the final stages of this project. Special thanks go to the members of my department who have been a great source of encouragement and have helped me keep things in perspective.

On a more personal level, there are many people to whom I owe immense gratitude and thanks for their support, both professionally and emotionally. From the earliest days, Bobbie Malone, Kevin Fontenot, Pat Harrison, Colleen Slease and Steve Hewitt have been my good friends and cheerleaders. In recent years, I have been blessed with the friendships of Pam Kachurin, Ann Case, Don Wright, Michael Reily, Heather Thiessen-Reily and Karen Racine. These people have provided me with companionship, intellectual stimulation, professional guidance, emotional support and laughter, as well as some memorable "research" trips to Mexico. More importantly, these people rallied around us during the worst of our grief and pain. For this, I will be forever grateful. Since moving to Montgomery, I have been immensely blessed by a new group of friends who has offered encouragement during the completion of this book: Barbara and Wyatt Wells, Michael Fitzsimmons, Steve Gish, Keith Krawczynski, Lee Anna Maynard, and, of course, Susie Paul.

My parents, Adeline and Leroy Verda, have stood behind me throughout this long and somewhat incomprehensible process, as has my brother, Danny Verda and my grandmother, Una Breaux, who passed away in 2000. The extended Farrow family and, in particular, my in-laws, Hank and Marilyn Farrow, also should be mentioned here; I thank them for their support and for giving me the gift of their son.

Finally, I must thank my husband, Ben Farrow. He has been my biggest and most vocal cheerleader and a constant source of love, strength, support and hope. He has tolerated years of poverty, months of separation and numerous bouts of insecurity and temporary insanity, and has withstood them all with admirable humor and fortitude. I can honestly say that I could not have completed this project without him. Most importantly, when our daughter died, he was encouraging, but patient, during the months when I simply could not find the strength to smile. Now, with a completed book, and two more children, we all have reason to smile. Therefore, my greatest thanks must go to Ben, to my beautiful children, Benjamin and Camille, and to our precious daughter, Sophia, who, although she was here for only a short time, changed our lives forever and taught us about what is important in life.

Between Clan and Crown

Introduction

> I am surprised that ancient and modern writers have not attributed greater importance to the laws of inheritance and their effect on the progress of human affairs . . . they should head the list of all political institutions, for they have an unbelievable influence on the social state of peoples . . . in some sense they lay hands on each generation before it is born.
>
> —Alexis de Tocqueville, *Democracy in America*

IN THE LAST QUARTER OF THE EIGHTEENTH CENTURY, THE RUSSIAN playwright Denis Fonvizin wrote with great passion about the "indissoluble link between political freedom and the rights of property," and the necessity for permanent laws of state to protect these rights.[1] Russia's rulers recognized the close connection between property rights and political freedom and sought to use this link to their own advantage, defining the scope and limits of noble property rights through the creation of laws designed to deal with specific property issues: inheritance by sons, daughters, and spouses; alienation of family land and the right of repurchase; and confiscation for crime or debt. Often these laws were contrary to traditional noble practices or contemporary noble preferences; after all, state goals did not always coincide with what nobles believed to be in their best interest. This all-too-frequent disconnect between state ambitions and noble traditions resulted in complaints, noncompliance, and circumvention. Furthermore, the problems these laws attempted to resolve were complex, making it difficult to construct general laws that applied to each unique situation. This combination of noble complaints and legal inadequacies meant that laws frequently needed to be revised and amended.

The nobility as a group, moreover, was far from clear or unified about its own needs and desires regarding land legislation. In some instances, nobles resisted state attempts to restrict landownership within a family. Such was the case with Peter's Law of Single Inheritance, which elicited significant opposition from the nobility and was ultimately repealed after Peter's death. In other cases, nobles chafed under the state-supported power of the clan. Russia's laws of redemption, for example, which gave extended family members the right to repurchase land that had been alienated from the clan, were constantly under attack by noble buyers who resented the insecurity of their new purchase. In fact, as one traces the evolution of Russia's laws on inheritance and property, it becomes clear that opinions changed over time and differed depending on the circumstances of the individuals involved and the nature of the transaction. Understandably, nobles supported laws that met their needs of the moment and rejected laws that interfered with their plans for land disposal or distribution. Despite this overall vacillation, nobles did have one consistent desire, and that was for greater control in the area of property ownership.

Throughout the Imperial period, noble property rights were defined and constrained by two overwhelming forces: the state and the clan. The state controlled property in a variety of ways, restricting ownership, establishing inheritance and redemption laws, and confiscating property for various reasons. To a large degree, at least for the first half of the imperial period, Russian nobles possessed land at the pleasure of the monarch. This was particularly true since Russian monarchs used land to reward faithful service and seized land from those who failed to play by the rules. Thus, the relationship between tsar, nobility, and landownership was a tightly woven and complex one.

The state was not the only influence at work, however. Noble property rights were also constrained by the overwhelming influence of the clan. Though the definition of clan varied depending on the circumstances, one thing is clear—nobles viewed clan membership as important and imbued with certain obligations and rights, particularly with regards to property. In fact, there was a truly familial character to noble landholding in Imperial Russia in which extended family members had a voice in decisions about property that had been in the clan more than one generation. State laws supported clan influence through inheritance and redemption laws which gave preference to family over nonfamily members and restricted an individual's ability to sell or bequeath land. Though nobles often chafed under the influence of the clan, they simultaneously were quick to assert clan privileges when it offered the potential of personal gain.

The numerous constraints on property rights left nobles with an overwhelming sense of insecurity regarding their property and contributed to the view of most nobles that land was transitory and its future was uncertain. This sense was heightened by the peripatetic nature of state service, which kept nobles from establishing roots in any one place and often restricted their ability to purchase land. These circumstances led nobles to engage in short-sighted and self-destructive behavior. Moreover, even those government institutions that were designed to oversee matters of land and inheritance were often rife with corruption and thus offered more potential dangers than protection. This overall instability contributed to a lack of corporate identity within the nobility, which in turn led to cannibalistic exploitation and corruption among its members. These realities, coupled with the trauma of Peter's cultural reforms, perpetuated the problem of noble insecurity well into the nineteenth century. Despite developments in property rights during the eighteenth century, the ruler still had the final word in all matters and the arbitrary whim of the monarch continued to pose a significant threat to noble landowners. Ultimately, state practices and the power of the clan restricted the development of private property rights in Russia to such a degree that even by 1917 one can speak only of limited private property at best.

Discussions about noble insecurity in the eighteenth century naturally lead to the question of the nature of the Russian state. The traditional paradigm of Russian history is that of a dynamic autocracy, transforming culture, society, the economy, and the state. In this state-centered interpretation, the monarch implemented change through the nobility, the first estate of the realm. Thus, historians such as Soloviev, Kliuchevskii, Raeff, and others have viewed the Russian autocracy as the motivating force for change, initiating this change within its most educated and developed social caste.

Within this consensus, however, there are some significant variations. Some historians, for example, argue that, within this paradigm, many of the changes initiated by the crown were, in fact, extracted by the nobility. Thus, important achievements for the nobility, such as the end of compulsory service in 1762 and the Charter to the Nobility of 1785, are seen as concessions that were wrested from the crown.[2] Raeff has challenged this view, arguing that the nobility was but a tool for state aspirations. Though it had assisted Peter the Great and his successors in the transformation of Russian society, it was soon replaced, and to some degree, discarded, with the development of a state bureaucracy. As Raeff puts it: "Through Peter's reforms, the nobility had lost the Tsar as their personal lord; now they felt cut off from the very institution they had helped to establish."[3] Thus, in Raeff's view, the nobility was at best a junior partner in the transformation of Russian state and society. Thus, in contrast to Dukes and others, Raeff has portrayed the state as initiating change for its own purposes.

More recently, John LeDonne has offered another interpretation. LeDonne characterizes the Russian nobility as a "ruling class," distinguished from the rest of the population by its special privileges and aware of its leadership function and unique position.[4] So important was the ruling class that it served not simply as a supportive or collaborative partner to the monarchy, but as the very social base upon which the monarchy rested. The implications of this characterization of the nobility are enormous. According to LeDonne, the ruling class provided "the legitimacy without which no ruler could operate."[5] Thus, state policy was determined primarily by the needs and interests of the ruling class. The monarch, ever conscious of his weak position, granted land and positions as a means of maintaining support: "A convergence thus naturally developed between a dynasty seeking a social base to make its power effective and landowners in need of central government support to protect their holdings, enserf the peasantry, and subjugate the towns."[6]

In contrast to all of these views is the conservative interpretation of Richard Pipes. Pipes has argued the existence of a patrimonial state in Russia.[7] In his view, the organization of the Russian ruler and society strongly resembled Oriental despotism. The autocrat was the source of all law and, until the end of the eighteenth century, there was no recognition of private property. Thus, Pipes argues, the monarch viewed himself as "both ruler of the realm and its proprietor."[8]

Such a discussion of the role of the Russian nobility in society, particularly vis-à-vis the ruler and its insecurity in landholding, leads almost inevitably to the question of whether noble landholding in the eighteenth century can be regarded as real private property. Richard Pipes and George Weickhardt have taken opposite stances on this question. In two separate articles, Weickhardt has argued, placing primary emphasis on legal statutes, that Russian law both protected and promoted the notion of private property. Pipes, on the other hand, has disagreed strongly and has countered that, based on an analysis of inheritance and confiscation practices and other social realities, it is clear that there was no real private property throughout most of the eighteenth century.[9] In evaluating these views, it is useful to pose the question in another way: to what extent, and in what ways, did the nobility acquire more clearly defined and enforceable property rights during the eighteenth century? Although private property may not have been as firmly established in Russia as it was in some Western countries, it seems fair to say that there was some progression, at least on paper, toward greater property rights during the eighteenth century. What that progression meant in reality, however, is a different question.

An examination of Russia's inheritance laws in the Imperial period sheds new light on these complex questions about the relationship between the Russian monarch and nobility, particularly with regards to property rights and their link to political freedom. In Russia, with landholding at the center of the economy and noble concerns of wealth and status, inheritance laws are a useful tool for identifying and interpreting the often conflicting goals of the state and nobility. Even within the nobility itself there were often conflicting aims and concerns, a result of differences of wealth and proximity to the crown and powerful court circles. As Tocqueville observed, inheritance laws have the power not only to determine the fate of the current generation, but the power to control the potential wealth and status of future generations as well.[10] With stakes as high as these, it is no wonder that Russia's laws of inheritance were a frequent source of debate and discussion throughout the eighteenth century and beyond.

There is no thorough study of Petrine or post-Petrine inheritance law, a significant oversight, since Peter initiated many changes in this area. In recent years, some new studies have emerged, both articles and books, but these have focused on more limited topics or other periods, for example, Muscovite dowries and women's property rights and the effects of partible inheritance in Muscovy. Likewise, several historians have produced book-length studies on property law at the end of the nineteenth century and women and the control of property in Imperial Russia.[11] None of these, however, has offered a thorough examination of inheritance and property law during the Imperial period. This study, therefore, serves as a perfect complement to the research that has already appeared in this field and offers more comprehensive coverage of the issues raised by these other works. Moreover, it places the examination of land legislation within the larger context of discussions ongoing in the field of Russian studies, debates about private property, the nature of the tsarist system, and the role of the nobility as a check on the tsar's power.

This study begins with a thorough review of Russia's land and inheritance laws beginning with the pre-Petrine period. For the sake of clarity, I treat these laws chronologically, followed by two chapters that deal with the peculiarities of female inheritance and other special cases not covered by the general discussion. This is followed by an examination of two phenomena critically tied to discussion of noble property rights: redemption and confiscation. Redemption, the legal right by which family members could repurchase land alienated from the clan, contributed mightily to noble feelings of insecurity. Despite its central place in understanding noble insecurity, the subject of redemption has been virtually untouched by historians. I attempt to remedy this with an extensive, archive-based discussion of this complex and unusual legal practice. I also examine in this chapter the state's policies of confiscation. Confiscation, as a punishment for crime or debt, posed a significant threat to members of the nobility, particularly in a system that frequently saw the rise and fall of favorites. Again, despite its importance, this dimension of noble insecurity has been scarcely studied by other historians and, although my book does not exhaust the subject of confiscation, I do offer new insights on this phenomenon through the analysis of little-used records from the Chancellery of Confiscation. In conclusion, I argue that an examination of land and inheritance laws reveals that nobles in Imperial Russia did not conceive of property rights in our modern sense, but rather within the framework of family or clan ownership. Even within this worldview, however, nobles were consistently dissatisfied with the limitations on landownership imposed by the state. Thus, though there is much to be said for the recent trend among Russian historians to view the nobility as an equal partner in a coalition with the tsar, there is more to the story. The Russian nobility may have worked side by side with the tsar in many areas, but Russia's land and inheritance laws suggest that the nobility was an unequal partner at best. This study seeks to demonstrate two things—that noble life, including possession and control of the all-important resource of land, was inextricably intertwined with clan life, and that this often stifling influence combined with the significant power of the ruler to restrict the growth of private property and political freedom.

Terminology

Drawing conclusions about such a complex relationship as power and property, of course, leads a historian into the sticky quagmire of terminology. In particular, terms such as private property, ownership, and property rights open up the proverbial Pandora's box of confusion and potential misunderstanding. Therefore, it is necessary to define our terms carefully.

"Private property," as defined in *Black's Law Dictionary,* is that which "belongs absolutely to an individual, and of which he has the exclusive right of disposition"; moreover, private property is "protected from being taken for public uses."[12] This definition is essentially synonymous with the legal definition of "ownership," which is defined as "the right that confers on a person direct, immediate, and exclusive authority over a thing," that permits the owner to "use, enjoy, and dispose of it within the limits and under the conditions established by law."[13] The key elements in both these definitions are freedom of use and disposal and protection from confiscation by the state. These terms are also distinguished from the legal term, "possession," which is different from "ownership." "Possession" is defined as "the detention and control, or the manual or ideal custody, of anything which may be the subject of property, for one's use and enjoyment."[14] It is a general term that can be prefaced with various adjectives, such as actual, constructive, civil, and illegal. Thus, possession may or may not involve ownership. In this study, then, I will use the term possession in its most general sense and will specify when legal ownership is the important fact. I will argue that Russian nobles often possessed land, but never enjoyed private property because their land was always susceptible to the broader interests of the clan and the intervention of the state. These influences were powerful and pervasive and contributed to the evolution of a relationship between the nobility and its land, and the nobility and the monarch, that was different from that which existed in Western Europe.

The absence of private property in Russia does not mean, however, that nobles had no control over landed property. On the contrary, nobles bought, sold, mortgaged, and bequeathed land on a regular basis and eagerly participated in an active land market. Once nobles acquired land, they did have certain legal rights to it and aggressively defended those rights against neighbors, relatives, and, on occasion, government agencies. It is necessary, then, to acknowledge these legal rights. At the same time, one must also look at the legal restrictions on property imposed by the state and the clan. The picture that emerges is one in which Russian nobles could be said to have limited property rights, what I will call "restricted ownership." This ownership was restricted on two levels—first, in that the state-supported interests of the clan meant that property had a familial quality where immediate family members were often listed on sales and other transactions and more distant clan members had the first right of refusal on land at the time of its sale or mortgage; and, second, in that the ruler could, and did, confiscate property for a number of crimes, most notably treason, which were often broadly defined. Throughout this study, then, I will refer to the "restricted ownership rights" of landowners.

There remains one group of terms that requires explanation. "Property" is the general umbrella term for things, tangible and intangible, visible and invisible, that are subject to ownership. Property is usually divided into two categories: real, defined as land and that which is attached to the land, and personal, which, generally speaking, includes everything other than land, including money, goods, animals, and stocks.[15] The distinction between real and personal property can differ from place to place and has changed over time. In Russia, this distinction was made by the terms "immovable" and "movable." Since I am primarily concerned with the laws pertaining to land, the terms "immovable property," "land," "estates," and "property" will be used interchangeably, and I will specify when I am referring more narrowly to a law or case pertaining to personal, or movable, property.

Finally, the text of this study contains numerous Russian words in transliteration. For the sake of clarity and aesthetics, I have chosen to italicize each word only the first time it appears.

Navigating the Russian Legal System

Russian historians who have worked with legal documents from the Imperial period know what a tricky endeavor this can sometimes be. Primary sources are often vague at best or missing at worst; law codes overlap one another and are difficult to decipher. Even the courts themselves frequently seemed confused about how certain laws should be interpreted. Navigating the Russian legal system was no less complex for Russian citizens who needed to use it. Although already by the Imperial period many in Russian society had come to believe in the importance of law as a basis of government, putting this concept into practice was not always easy. Petitioners might invoke the notion of legal justice in their complaints and requests, but that was far from a guarantee that their cases would quickly and smoothly settle according to those principles.

There were many complications in the legal process that made the smooth resolution of property disputes the exception rather than the rule. First of all, for much of the Imperial period Russia lacked a unified legal code. The basis of Russian law in the eighteenth century was the *Ulozhenie,* a collection of rules drawn from Muscovite customary traditions and legal codes, especially the *Sudebnik* of 1550.[16] The Ulozhenie was compiled in 1649, but no sooner had it been completed than new rules and decisions were being added. These extraneous decrees and resolutions by the monarch and, later, the Senate, mushroomed in the eighteenth century, further complicating the matter since many of these new rules were intended to replace specific rules in the Ulozhenie. Even worse, many of the new laws contradicted one another, while others pertained narrowly to specific cases, creating a precedent, but no clearly defined rule, for future cases. This unwieldy body of laws, decrees, and resolutions was compiled and published as the *Polnoe sobranie zakonov* in 1830, the same year that a new Russian law code was compiled, the *Svod Zakonov.* It is clear, then, that even the most diligent of court officials and petitioners might have found themselves lost in the murky waters of Russian Imperial law.

This situation was further complicated by the fact that there was no single government body that dealt with property disputes in their various forms. Until 1720, the *Pomestnyi Prikaz* was responsible for the administration of various matters of landholding, including registration of changes in landholding and judicial decisions about land and inheritance disputes, both for service and patrimonial land. When the Pomestnyi Prikaz was abolished in 1720, it was replaced by the Votchina College. Since Peter the Great had combined service and patrimonial land into one category of "immovable" property in 1714, the Votchina College oversaw the administration of landholding of all types, including the resolution of land disputes.[17] After 1719, the Justice College was responsible for registering land transfers and collecting taxes on transactions. Matters of confiscation were handled by the Chancellery of Confiscation, created in 1729, and confiscation as a result of debt might also involve the Arrears Chancellery; these two bodies were united in 1736.[18] Sometimes these institutions clashed or contradicted one another in their attempts to settle property disputes. When the rulings of these various institutions proved unsatisfactory, litigants could turn to the Senate as the highest court of appeal. The Senate, created in 1711, made decisions that overrode those of the lower courts and became laws in their own right. When the Senate could not form a resolution, however, the ruler might be called upon to make a decision. Finally, the ruler often issued decrees that immediately took on the force of law. After Catherine's reform of 1775, courts were established on the district- and provincial-level, and the Justice College was abolished; the Votchina College was abolished a decade later. Henceforth, property transfers were registered in the district or provincial level courts, the Provincial Chambers. Still, even with such reform efforts, the potential for confusion persisted. Court officials were given generous latitude in interpreting the law and often came up with very different conclusions.[19]

As if the court system were not complicated enough, the process of establishing and maintaining legal control over one's land was no simple matter either. All land transactions—sales, mortgages, inheritances, redemptions—had to be registered with one of the above-mentioned institutions. This was not as simple as it sounds. Prior to 1775, such transactions had to be registered in one of the two major cities, Moscow or St. Petersburg. This was both burdensome and expensive, and many a petitioner complained of the difficulty of meeting this requirement due to illness, insufficient funds, absence in service, or some other reason. In 1716, for example, Luka Nechaev and his nephew, Mikhail Iazykov, exchanged land with each other, but because of their absence in service they were unable to register their exchange.[20] In fact, nobles commonly sent servants in their stead to file the necessary petitions.

Petitions were a mandatory part of virtually all property transactions. In the best of cases—a straightforward property sale or an amicable division of property between eligible heirs—the participants were expected to petition the relevant institution to have these transactions approved. In inheritance disputes, at the conclusion of the case, when the Votchina College or Senate made a ruling on the division of property, the successful claimants were still required to petition for the land that had been awarded them. Failure to do so could result in a forfeiture of the award. In redemption cases, all other eligible redeemers had to renounce their rights to that property in writing before their relative would be granted the land in redemption.[21] Finally, even widows and widowers who were entitled to a maintenance allotment by law had to petition to claim that property. In 1764, for example, Ivan Ivanovich Samarin petitioned to receive his legal portion from the immovable property of his deceased wife, Praskovia. The remainder of the property was to go to their minor son.[22]

Petitions, moreover, had to be submitted according to specific rules. Beginning with Peter the Great, petitions had to be written on special stamped paper; without it, a petition would be returned. This paper, of course, had to be purchased.[23] Petitions also had to follow a special format, prescribed by law. Each petition had to begin with a title, introducing the petitioner by name, and rank or occupation: "Petition of the wife of nobleman Vasilii, son of Ivan Kazlov, Fekla, daughter of Iakov Chirikov, and in my request are the following points . . ."[24] Following this, the body of the petition had to be presented in sections, or points. In addition, each petition had to be signed.[25] The body of the petition had to contain specific information, including references to the relevant laws where necessary. Petitions omitting these references could be returned. For example, between 1742 and 1744 Natalia Serukhina petitioned the Senate three times requesting her inheritance from her great-grandfather and her aunts and protesting what she believed to be incorrect decisions by the Votchina College and the Senate *Kontor.* Her petitions were returned, however, because Serukhina had failed to specify which laws had been violated.[26] While accidental omissions were tolerated, people who submitted intentionally false or dishonest petitions were punished with a fine, or even confiscation of property. In 1728, for example, the Votchina College warned Agrafina Stepanova that if her petition regarding her husband's property contained any falsehoods, her property would be confiscated.[27] Finally, certain land matters, such as redemption, had a legally defined time frame during which claimants had the right to petition; after this period passed, petitions would be rejected or returned.[28]

The procedure for resolving a property matter depended on the type of land transaction taking place. Land sales required that the participants register the exchange with the proper authorities and pay the required taxes. Participants then petitioned the Votchina College, including a copy of the sale document. If all went smoothly, the land would then be officially registered to the new owner and the participants would be given copies of the College's decision. The transaction would be recorded in the *krepostnye knigi,* or provincial notarial records, under the administration of the *krepostnaia kontora,* or notarial bureau. Inheritance and redemption cases were usually more complicated, involving more individuals and more steps. Even participants in an amicable agreement were required to petition that they had willingly participated in that arrangement, especially if the agreement involved the renunciation of rights by one party. Participants were usually questioned to ensure the honesty and validity of their petitions.[29] In these cases, the courts wanted to be sure that such renunciations were legal and voluntary and, on occasion, amicable divisions of property were altered or overturned. Such was the case in 1764 when some of Anna Iazykova's relatives petitioned that though Anna had been mad (*bezumnyi*) since birth, other relatives had married her off and concluded an amicable division of property with her. The Senate concurred that such an agreement was unacceptable and the amicable division was canceled.[30]

Once an agency like the Votchina College received a petition about an inheritance or redemption matter, the next step was an investigation of the facts. The presiding institution would send out requests to local bodies—the district branch of the Votchina

College, for example—for specific information, such as the number of serfs on a particular piece of property or for copies of certain documents, such as a will, sale, or mortgage. Also important would be a record of the land's history, specifically from which clan it had originated. On occasion, this fact-gathering might require the Votchina College to send officials to the countryside to obtain testimony from relevant people or to question peasant elders. When Stepan Opukhtin died in 1748 leaving behind a wife and eight children and property in various cities, the Votchina College ordered that a lower court official, or *pod'iach,* be sent out to these cities to gather testimony from peasant elders and other selected peasants, as well as the nine claimants.[31] The results of these inquiries would be recorded in the notes of the Votchina College. When sufficient information had been collected, the Votchina College would review the case and make a ruling. All the evidence would be considered—petitions, testimonies, reports from local officials and relevant laws. The written resolution of the case would reflect this, recounting all the circumstances of the case and then explaining the decision in a series of points. The Votchina College would then give the litigants, interested parties, and necessary institutions copies of the decision in keeping with a law of 1737.[32] The successful claimant was then required to request the registration of that land. At that point, the land in question was supposed to be officially registered to the new owner and recorded in the *otkaznaia kniga,* or discharge book. Only after all of these steps were completed was ownership finally transferred.

A quick survey of petitions from the Imperial period indicates that very rarely did a land transaction take place without some complication. The possibilities were virtually endless. In hotly disputed land matters, cases could run on for decades with petitions and counterpetitions, appeals, and new decisions. On more than one occasion, most or all of the litigants were dead by the time the dispute was resolved.[33] Pertinent documents sometimes disappeared as a result of fire or other calamity. The fire of 1737, it would seem, destroyed many important documents and interfered with the quick resolution of many cases. Avdotia Svechina complained in 1741 that although she had petitioned for her mother's property, her case had failed to appear in the Votchina College after the fire of 1737.[34] More extreme, of course, was the case of a female petitioner who in 1775 asked for her husband's property, but could not produce the proper documents because they had all been destroyed during the Pugachev rebellion.[35] Landowners sometimes failed to file the proper petition claiming their property, leaving a complicated mess for their heirs to untangle, or they filed their petitions, but those documents never appeared at their intended destination for reasons unknown.[36] Sometimes, landowners had difficulty filing petitions if they were old, ill, poor, or away in service.[37] Other times, essential participants in a land matter were simply missing, either intentionally or by coincidence. More than one debtor complained that when he, or she, attempted to repay a loan to redeem mortgaged property, the lender was suddenly absent and unavailable to accept the money, resulting in potential forfeiture of the mortgaged property.[38] On occasion, litigants complained about corrupt officials who they declared were preventing the fair execution of some property matter.[39]

Even more often, petitioners complained about illegal and unethical behavior by rival claimants, and here too the possibilities were virtually endless. Competitors for the same piece of land might bribe surveyors and local officials. Rival heirs or redeemers lied in their petitions, misrepresenting their true proximity to the deceased or claiming that female family members had been married with generous dowries and thus should be excluded from inheritance. In other cases, minors or persons with mental disorders were taken advantage of by rapacious family members. Occasionally, dishonest petitioners would simply conceal the existence of other family members entirely, thereby claiming to be the only eligible heir.[40] Finally, all too frequently petitioners reported the use of violence between landowners, especially within families.[41] Nor were the problems over once inheritance decisions had been made; heirs would sometimes complain that their coheirs had taken all of the best land or peasants for themselves or that land had been stripped of its most valuable assets before it was handed over to its new legal owner. In 1736, for example, Sofia Ostaf'eva petitioned the Votchina College complaining that she and her brother-in-law had come to an amicable division of her dead husband's property, however, in the process her brother-in-law had given her the worst and poorest of the peasants who not only could not pay their taxes, but could not even feed themselves. The Votchina College ordered a redivision of the property.[42] Such abuses would result in a whole new set of petitions.

As is clear, the complications in executing land transactions in Imperial Russia were immense, and the acquisition, maintenance, and defense of one's land was no simple matter. Russia's nobles complained about these difficulties in the noble *nakazy* of 1767 and Catherine tried to answer some of their concerns in her Statute on the Provinces in 1775. Nonetheless, problems persisted and laws continued to be misinterpreted, petitions continued to be incorrectly filed, and cases continued to clog the court system. In response, the government repeatedly urged citizens and lawmakers alike to follow the required procedures and appeal through the appropriate channels; the repetition of these reminders would indicate, however, that proper court procedure continued to be a problem well into the nineteenth century.[43]

A Word about Sources and Methodology

When historians try to explain the past, they often have at their disposal a variety of sources and, depending on the nature of the study, some sources will prove more useful than others. In attempting to define legal realities, historians sometimes rely on written laws as an indicator of practice. Moreover, laws are usually indicative of cultural preferences and biases and can reveal much about social relations, economic realities, and the political framework of a country. They can indicate the goals of rulers and lawmakers, and represent the ideal of what should happen in practice. Laws, however, can be disobeyed, either outright or by creative methods of circumvention, and therefore cannot be the sole source in a study of the legal situation in a given country. Legal cases, supplemented by other primary sources such as memoirs, must be used to indicate how the laws were applied in practice. As Cynthia Herrup has noted in her fascinating study of the Castlehaven inheritance scandal in seventeenth-century England, legal cases often illustrate "how completely interwoven are the legal and the cultural."[44] By utilizing both types of sources—laws and legal cases—the historian can attempt to reconstruct a full picture of the legal realities of a certain time and place.

This study is based on a combination of published laws and archival and published primary sources. After a thorough examination of the published collection of Russian laws, the *Polnoe sobranie zakonov* (*PSZ*), to establish the system of inheritance and property law on paper, I reviewed more than 500 "cases" pertaining to issues of property ownership, including inheritance, redemption, and confiscation. The majority of these cases are derived from archival sources found in the records of the Senate, the Votchina College and the Chancellery of Confiscations located in the *Rossiiskii gosudarstvennyi arkhiv drevnikh aktov* in Moscow (RGADA). Other cases have been drawn from published primary sources such as the *Polnoe sobranie zakonov* and collections of Senate decisions, *Doklady i prigovory* and *Senatskii arkhiv.* Since for much of the period under question the law required that land transactions be registered in the central office of the Votchina College, these records pertain to disputes and transactions in many *guberniia* and *uezdy.* Similarly, since the Senate was the final court of appeal, it too dealt with cases from throughout the empire. Consequently, the cases that I have used for this study offer a representative sampling, geographically and chronologically, of the various debates and decisions pertaining to issues of property ownership. Most of my cases, however, come from the eighteenth century because it was during this period that Russia's inheritance laws underwent the most dramatic changes and revisions.

I define a "case" as any distinct instance of property transaction described in one or more primary sources. Thus a "case" might consist of documents from only one source or several; so long as they pertain to the same event, I count them as a single case. Unfortunately, many of the individual case records (*dela*) remaining in the archive are incomplete, containing only a few petitions and some scribe's notes and a final decision. Even more frustrating, the records of many cases—which often dragged on for years and even decades—do not contain any clear conclusion at all. Such cases were still interesting and useful in demonstrating other points, but offered little in the way of conclusive evidence about the implementation of Russian inheritance laws. Finally, because of the incomplete nature of many of these records, there are few that can be described in great detail from start to finish. Sadly, I found no cases that offered any detail comparable to that found in Steven Ozment's study, *The Bürgermeister's Daughter,* or in Herrup's *A House in Gross Disorder.*[45] For this reason, some of my cases constitute as little as a two-page copy of a sale transaction; others are longer and contain more detail. In most instances, the length of the document is not important; a one-page petition requesting dowry registration to the bride is as illustrative of this practice as a fifty-page petition. Moreover, one case will usually contain information about and examples of many different aspects of property and inheritance law. Thus, one inheritance dispute might discuss a widow's portion, partible inheritance between sons, and a married daughter's right to inherit. Given the problem of damaged and incomplete dela, I have attempted to use all of my documents to their fullest potential, citing them wherever they may be used to illustrate a point.

There remains one other frustration regarding the use of these sources. Even those dela that contained a significant number of petitions rarely offered much insight into the feelings and motivations of the participants. On the whole, the petitions follow standard formulas and are devoid of personal narratives. This is not to say that the petitions lack passion, for they certainly possess that in abundance. Noble petitions often express disgust and anger at the behavior of a rival claimant, and petitioners routinely engaged in name-calling. Some documents discuss abuse at the hand of a spouse or in-law, or complain about dishonesty and attempts to conceal legitimate heirs. Many vehemently challenge previous court decisions. Thus, although I found few petitions that waxed sentimental about the holder's heartfelt attachment to the property in question, there is no overlooking the passion and conviction behind these documents. Whatever their motives, those who petitioned to the Votchina College or the Senate about the return or acquisition of land were determined, frequently persistent, and very serious about their claims. Thus, despite their shortcomings, these documents contribute greatly to our understanding of noble culture and values in Imperial Russia.

1
Property and Inheritance Laws in the Muscovite Period

FOR WELL OVER A CENTURY, HISTORIANS HAVE GRAPPLED WITH THE difficult question of how to best define the Muscovite political system. In keeping with the reports of European visitors of the sixteenth and seventeenth centuries, some historians have labeled Muscovy a despotism, emphasizing the overwhelming, virtually unchecked power of the monarch, and pointing to Ivan IV as the greatest example. Others, while avoiding the term despotism, have declared Muscovy's distinctiveness from other European-style monarchies. Many historians have rejected the East-West comparison, arguing that Muscovy was a unique place with a unique governmental style. Finally, there are a number of historians who have emphasized the political power of Muscovite clans, which limited the power of the monarch and resulted in a more collaborative system of government than was apparent to outside observers, Russian or foreign.[1]

Despite these very different arguments about Muscovy, there are some points on which most historians concur; the differences arise over emphasis and degree. Thus, most historians can agree that Muscovy was an autocracy, with a single monarch who wielded a great deal of power which could, on occasion, be used in an arbitrary manner. There is also more or less a consensus on the significance of the clan in Muscovy. On both the social and the political level, the family—and its extension, the clan—was extremely important in determining domestic alliances and power relations. This study seeks to enrich this portrait by discussing the Muscovite service elite with particular regards to landholding. Muscovite laws on property and inheritance reveal a great deal about the nature of the political system and the values that the ruler and the elite deemed important. In examining these laws, it will become clear that Muscovy was a "hypertrophic state,"[2] shaped largely from the top down; that service to the tsar was a central factor in this arrangement; that land, as a reward for service and a means for material and social gain, was of critical importance to elites; and that the extended family—the clan, or *rod*—exerted great influence, not only in the political and social realms, but also legally, through laws that supported their claims to family members' lands.

The Muscovite Service Elite

From its earliest origins, the Russian "nobility" was a heterogeneous and amorphous group. In fact, there was no collective term for "nobility" until that introduced by Peter the Great. By the Muscovite era of the fifteenth and sixteenth centuries, Russian elites ranged from members of the great families and descendants of the former appanage princes to rank-and-file warriors. Between these two extremes were the men who served the prince as administrators or military commanders. Thus, in Muscovite society the definition of "nobility" was far from clear or simple. This confusion was a product of the evolution of the Russian aristocracy.[3]

At the beginning of the fourteenth century, Russia was still fragmented into a number of independent principalities, each ruled by a prince descended in some way from the house of *Riurik*. Each of these princes had his own retinue of servitors and warriors. These men were collectively known as boyars. Some boyars had their own entourage as well. As compensation for service, a prince might grant land to his retainers, either as hereditary land, (*votchina*), or service land, (*pomest'e*). Hereditary land was considered the property of the recipient. Indeed, the prince's servitors enjoyed the right of free departure, that is, the freedom to leave the prince's service in favor of another master without fear of confiscation. In the case of service land, ownership was contingent on continued service and could be revoked if the servitor failed to carry out his duties.

As the princes of Moscow gradually conquered and annexed the other principalities of Russia, they took these defeated princes into their service, either at the Moscow court or as regional servitors. The Moscow princes, however, soon made it clear that whatever the former status of these princes and retainers they were now first and foremost servants of Moscow. As such, they were expected to obey. Moreover, the traditional right of departure that servitors had enjoyed quickly disappeared after the rise of Moscow. Ivan III, for example, treated any attempts to leave as an act of treason, and thus did not hesitate to confiscate land on this basis. This picture was further complicated when Ivan established the pomest'e system more broadly after the conquest of Novgorod.[4] Thus a fundamental conflict in the concept of elite membership had been created: the conflict between nobility of birth and nobility of service.[5]

By the beginning of the sixteenth century, then, the Russian aristocracy consisted of these former appanage princes and their retinues, now all servants of the Moscow Grand Prince. There was still, however, a significant distinction between the princes and the nontitled boyars.[6] This distinction would disappear over the course of the next century, particularly during the reign of Ivan IV the Terrible. In 1556, Ivan established military service regulations for the aristocracy. Although Russian elites had long been engaged in military service, there had previously been no standardization or organization. Ivan's new rules established that each aristocrat would be expected to provide a specific number of horses and warriors based on the size of his estate. These rules finalized a process that was already underway: the expectation that all landowners, of hereditary or service lands, owed service to the tsars.[7]

Only a few years later, following the death of his first wife Anastasia and a serious illness of his own, Ivan came to doubt the fidelity and trustworthiness of the aristocrats at court. With the creation of his *oprichnina* in 1565, Ivan made it clear that he intended to punish all suspicious people by any means he saw fit, including confiscation, exile, and execution. The oprichnina was created as a special institution and subdivision in the Muscovite state with its own separate administration to be staffed and administered in an intensely personal fashion by Ivan himself. It was through this new system that Ivan punished and confiscated the estates of many boyars and princes. These lands were then reissued to his new servitors in the oprichnina.

Historians have differed in their assessments of the oprichnina. S. F. Platonov argued that the result of the oprichnina was that many large hereditary estates were confiscated and replaced by smaller service estates granted to men of non-noble origins. Platonov believed that the oprichnina was created to destroy the political and economic threat posed by the upper aristocracy, the boyars, and the descendants of the appanage princes.[8] S. B. Veselovskii has argued differently that although the oprichnina destroyed the lives of many individuals, it did not attack only hereditary landowners, nor did it significantly alter the existing order of landholding. More recently, Richard Hellie has agreed with this latter interpretation, indicating that the available evidence shows that on the whole more service land was confiscated than hereditary land.[9]

Despite these conflicting views, one thing seems certain. A significant number of princes and boyars perished as a result of Ivan's policies, and substantial numbers of the rank-and-file servicemen saw their power and influence enhanced. This shift was far from complete, but in combination with Ivan's earlier rules about service requirements it marked a crucial step in strengthening the principle of service in the criteria for elite status. By the close of Ivan's reign there was no doubt that service to the tsar had become the prerequisite for advancement. Once the former appanage princes were brought into the service of Moscow, their distinctiveness as aristocrats of birth quickly faded. Though they continued to carry the title of prince and pass it on to their sons, they were forced to share the limelight with members of the nontitled families who had achieved power and prestige through service. Thus by the seventeenth century, the Russian aristocracy consisted of descendants of these two groups.

The tension between birth and service that had been exacerbated by Ivan IV led to the creation of the system of *mestnichestvo.* The mestnichestvo system functioned in Muscovy from the end of the fifteenth century until 1682. Its purpose was to define the status of a family based on the service rank that had been attained by its head, stipulating that subsequent family members who served could only be appointed to those positions that in status and dignity were not below the rank attained by their family head.[10] Thus it sought to create a working compromise between birth and rank as determinants of status. In reality, it did not end the tension between birth and rank, and instead contributed to intense interfamily rivalry and competition and served to fragment the aristocracy. Moreover, it encouraged aristocrats to watch over their kin since the poor service record of one relative could affect the rank of others. The Muscovite princes recognized the potential benefits of this system and consciously used mestnichestvo to keep members of the aristocracy in check.[11]

Mestnichestvo was also a system that underscored the importance of family. Through this system, family and clan ties were not only important traditional influences, they were accepted as legitimate factors in government policy toward elite advancement. Each individual's fate was intertwined with that of his relatives, and not just immediate family members, but also extended members of the clan. The clan and precedence rankings were necessary for social status as well; the source of a servitor's honor was his claim to be descended from a boyar progenitor.[12]

Kinship was also a dominant factor in politics. As Kollmann has demonstrated, Muscovite court politics was largely based on personal relationships, many of them family relationships. Many court positions were hereditary, as was boyar rank. Young men in boyar families had to reach a certain age before assuming boyar rank, but unless their family was disgraced, the promotion was a certainty. Service alone could not open the door to boyar rank. Moreover, once a man became a boyar, his success in that elite group largely depended on the alliances he formed. Often these alliances were solidified through marriage. Boyars aspiring to reach the top of the internal elite hierarchy competed with one another to marry into the royal family. Such ties often cemented a boyar's place within the inner circle.[13]

The centrality of the clan in Muscovite society was also reflected in the laws on property and inheritance. Prior to Peter's law of 1714, all privately held land was divided into two distinct categories—votchina, or patrimonial land, and pomest'e, or service land. In theory, votchina was family land, inheritable and free from service obligation, while pomest'e was tied to service and was not, therefore, eligible for inheritance.[14] In reality, the laws and practices governing these two land types were far more complex and contradictory, blurring the basic distinctions and emphasizing the protection of family members. It is, therefore, impossible to understand or appreciate legislative development regarding land in the eighteenth century without first understanding the evolution of votchina and pomest'e and the complex set of laws that grew up around them.

THE EVOLUTION OF VOTCHINA AND POMEST'E

The origins of the landholding practices that came to be so crucial to the lives of elites in the Imperial period go back to the Kievan era. It was during the tenth and eleventh centuries when individual landownership, or votchina, as a form of land tenure probably first appeared. The available historical evidence suggests that the first large-scale private landholders in Russia were the princes of the Varangian dynasty. These princes were surrounded by retinues of servitors—for example, aides, counselors, and warriors—who served the prince voluntarily and could terminate the relationship at any time. In return for their service, the prince supported and protected his retainers. Initially, this meant that the retainers lived with the prince, sharing in the spoils of his victories. Gradually, with the increasing internal strife of the emerging appanage period, the cost of maintaining one's servitors grew, particularly as war booty increasingly came in the form of land rather than money or other movable spoils. As a result, princes began to reward their servitors with plots of land from their patrimonies with which the servitors were expected to support themselves. The prince still expected his servitors to continue to serve him, yet the servitor was free to terminate the relationship and find another master without losing whatever land he had received. Moreover, when a servitor died, his land would be divided according to his will, or in the absence of a will, it would be divided equally among his sons. This arrangement gave the servitors, who together with local elites became known as boyars, a significant amount of independence. This independence grew throughout the appanage and Mongol periods. At the same time, as the number of princes grew in the appanage period, princely patrimonies grew smaller, until some were no greater than the landholdings of the wealthier boyars.[15]

This threat of an independent boyar elite posed a problem for ruling princes and soon resulted in a trend to dominate and limit the free departure of the boyars. As early as the late fourteenth century, during the reign of Vasilii I, the principle was established that the prince could confiscate the property of a departing servitor if he decided that the boyar had committed treason. During the civil wars of the early fifteenth century, Vasilii II put this principle into practice, confiscating the lands of some boyars who had departed, and forcing others to renounce their right of free departure in order to keep their land.[16] In doing so, he further strengthened the link between votchina and service. This link was made more clear when in the sixteenth century Ivan IV required that all landlords supply a mounted warrior with an extra horse for each 300 *chetverts* of land owned.[17]

As the princes of Moscow gradually changed the terms of votchina land, they also developed another system of reward that was directly tied to service obligation. Beginning in the latter part of the fifteenth century, the Moscow prince began to grant land as pomest'e, or service tenure land. The source of this grant was state land that had been acquired by confiscation or war. Following his annexation of Novgorod in 1478, Ivan III confiscated property there and redistributed it as pomest'e to his followers on condition that they serve him.[18] Subsequent rulers followed the same pattern, so that beginning with Ivan III, who used service land grants as a way of building up a larger army and a larger group of supporters, pomest'e became more common than votchina. Ivan IV further accelerated this process during his oprichnina, confiscating extensive amounts of votchina land and redistributing it as pomest'e. Pomest'e thus became land that was directly tied to a service obligation.[19]

Thus by the seventeenth century there were two types of landholding in Russia—votchina and pomest'e. Both types of land could be acquired in a number of ways. Votchina, as patrimonial land, was transferred from one generation to the next by means of inheritance. An individual could also acquire votchina lands, however, by means of an expired mortgage or by direct purchase, since votchina owners (*votchinniki*) were permitted to sell their votchina during their lifetimes. Men could also obtain votchina as a reward for service. This reward could involve either an outright grant from the tsar or the permission to convert one's pomest'e into votchina.[20] Indeed, royal grants were responsible for some of the largest fortunes in Russia in the seventeenth century. B. I. Morozov, for example, had become the second wealthiest man in Russia by the 1640s thanks to grants of votchina that he received from Mikhail and Alexei.[21] Finally, if a man chose to do so, he could petition the tsar for a grant of votchina land, either as a reward for exemplary service or to rescue him from financial or other personal difficulties. Elites frequently requested that votchina lands confiscated from others be made over in their name.

Pomest′e, on the other hand, was land explicitly granted as a reward for service. There are many examples of this in seventeenth-century legislation.[22] Men could also petition for a grant of pomest′e, whether as a reward for service or simply as an outright request for another man's escheated pomest′e.[23] Despite its theoretical link to service, pomest′e could also be obtained by means of inheritance. Moreover, relatives could petition for receipt of their clan member's escheated pomest′e.[24] A full discussion of this development, with all its contradictions, is thus in order.

The Blending of Votchina and Pomest′e

Despite the legal distinction between pomest′e and votchina lands, in reality, the two types of landholding were becoming more and more alike in practice long before Peter the Great merged them in his Law of Single Inheritance in 1714.[25] In fact, by the sixteenth century it had already become common for nephews or sons to take over a *pomeshchik's* land when he died or became unable to serve, so long as the new holder continued military service.[26] At the same time, pomeshchiki began to attempt to leave their pomest′e to an heir by means of a will. By the seventeenth century this practice was a regular occurrence. Men also exchanged their pomest′e with one another, but until the middle of the seventeenth century a pomest'e could only be exchanged for another pomest′e.[27]

This blending of votchina and pomest′e picked up pace as the seventeenth century wore on. Even the Ulozhenie, which devoted a separate chapter to each type of land, suggests the extent to which this blending was already under way. Although the two types of landholding remained legally distinct, the Ulozhenie permitted pomeshchiki and votchinniki to exchange pomest′e for votchina lands or vice versa. In such cases, the people involved in the exchange were required to petition that these lands be registered to them under their new classification in the Service Land Chancellery (Pomestnyi Prikaz). If this was done, the Ulozhenie ordered that the land be so registered.[28] The Ulozhenie also ordered that the maintenance allotment (*prozhitok*) for wives and children should come from the pomest′e land of a deceased person. That which was left over was to be given into his clan, to those men who had no service land of their own, or to those who had very little.[29] Furthermore, if a son was given his father's pomest'e but then died without ever having been initiated into a service rank, his wife and daughter were nonetheless to be granted a maintenance allotment, or prozhitok, from that land.[30] This tendency was furthered by a law of 1684 that permitted male heirs to inherit pomest'e whether or not they were serving the state.[31] Thus, despite the fact that in theory it was not inheritable, the law encouraged the familization of pomest'e, even when the recipient failed to meet the service requirements of the land.[32]

This blurring of the distinction between votchina and pomest'e was further assisted by the government's practice of allowing individuals to convert a portion of their pomest'e into votchina, usually as a reward for service. For example, in 1667 and subsequent years the tsar granted elites and servitors of various ranks the permission to convert their pomest'e land into votchina land as a reward for their participation in the Lithuanian and Polish campaigns.[33] If this reward was not granted outright by the tsar, then an individual could petition for this right. Thus, there are also laws that grant this privilege in response to direct petitions.[34]

Finally, votchina and pomest'e lands were often treated as interchangeable in laws that threatened confiscation. In 1664, for example, Nikita Ziuzin was exiled to Kazan and his pomest'e and votchina lands confiscated for his involvement with Patriarch Nikon.[35] Later, in 1686, a new law warned that if a person was guilty of either improperly surveying land or accusing a surveyor of such a crime, then that guilty party would be deprived of half of his pomest'e and votchina lands.[36] The two types of land also were named side by side in laws threatening confiscation as a punishment for crimes such as theft or failure to follow court procedures.[37] Finally, failure to appear for service could also result in such punishment. It was ordered in 1670, for example, that all military men of various ranks who had either never appeared for service, or had appeared and then deserted, were to be punished with the confiscation of half of their pomest'e and votchina lands.[38] Evasion of service continued to be a crime punishable by confiscation of votchina and pomest'e lands through the early part of Peter's reign.[39] The reason that these two land types were treated almost as one in laws threatening confiscation is clear: by the seventeenth century, all landowners were required to serve the state in some capacity regardless of the type of land they held. Though votchina and pomest'e were still legally distinct, when it came to matters of the state, the tsar was little concerned about these particulars. Any failure by a landowner to serve or obey the law could trigger confiscation of both types of land. The blending of votchina and pomest'e, then, can be viewed as an indication that service to the state was becoming as important as aristocratic birth in determining political, social, and material success.

Inheritance Rules in Pre-petrine Russia

By the time of Peter's reign, therefore, pomest'e and votchina had become virtually equivalent forms of landholding in practice. As we shall see, Peter would complete this process—first, lumping the two together in a law of 1712, and then blending them legally under the heading of "immovable property" in his inheritance law of 1714. Until then, however, the legal distinction remained, particularly in regards to inheritance. Therefore, legislation prior to the Law of Single Inheritance continued to distinguish between votchina and pomest'e, establishing specific rules of disposal for each. The Ulozhenie of 1649 dedicated a separate chapter to each type, and subsequent amendments to the Ulozhenie also were commonly divided into separate sections. Thus the continuing legal distinction combined with the gradual amalgamation to make a somewhat complex situation in which family members were eligible by law to receive both votchina and pomest'e of various portions and types, depending on their sex and proximity to the deceased. The following discussion of pre-Petrine inheritance laws will unavoidably reflect the complexity of these rules.

Votchina

Votchina existed in three distinct types: family votchina, service votchina and purchased votchina. Family, or clan, votchina was votchina that a person had inherited from another clan member; service votchina was votchina that was granted to an individual for service; and purchased votchina was that which the individual had acquired himself by purchase or expired mortgage. Family and service votchina were governed by the same rules, with an understanding that both were subjugated to the interests of the clan. To some degree, such votchina was considered part of the family patrimony, and thus was placed under greater restrictions regarding its disposal.[40] Several characteristics dominated the rules for the inheritance of family and service votchina in the pre-Petrine period: an emphasis on familization, the primacy of males, and a preference for partible inheritance.

Chapter 17 of the Ulozhenie specifically dealt with the disposal of family and service votchina, and demanded, whenever possible, the preservation of clan lands. The very first article of the Ulozhenie states clearly that hereditary estates are to be inherited by members of the clan.[41] Despite this, during his lifetime a votchinnik was allowed to sell or mortgage family and service votchina, in which case his children and grandchildren had no claim to it. His brothers and nephews, however, if they had not agreed to the transaction, did have claims to the land and could demand to regain it for the clan by means of redemption.[42] A man was not allowed, however, simply to give away his family or service votchina, bypassing his children.[43] Similarly, although a man could sell his family or service votchina during his lifetime, he could not bypass his children, the legal heirs, when it came to inheritance. This restriction likewise prevented him from leaving it to his childless wife by will.[44] In this case, even if the will was witnessed and signed according to legal specifications, it was considered invalid and the votchina was given to his children according to the Ulozhenie.[45] These stipulations guaranteed children their right to inheritance.[46]

Male children generally enjoyed preference in the inheritance of votchina lands and thus were considered the favored heirs to a man's family and service votchina. Upon a man's death, his family and service votchina was to be split among his sons. Daughters were not to inherit in the presence of living brothers.[47] This preference for male heirs had existed for centuries, and can be found in early law codes such as the *Russkaia Pravda*.[48] Moreover, the rule that daughters could not inherit votchina in the presence of living brothers was reaffirmed repeatedly in subsequent legislation, and would often appear in petitions and decisions regarding inheritance.[49]

Sons usually divided their father's votchina between themselves in equal portions, although the Ulozhenie itself only specifies equal inheritance among sons under certain circumstances.[50] A variety of sources, however, indicate that there was a historical tradition of equal inheritance. The Expanded *Zakon Sudnyi Liudem,* for example, recommended equal inheritance to assure fairness.[51] Later, the Russkaia Pravda called for division into equal portions in cases of intestacy.[52] This historical precedent, along with subsequent legislation and a variety of other eighteenth-century sources, suggest that equal inheritance was understood to be the intention of the Ulozhenie's articles on votchina.[53] Thus, almost a century later, when the Votchina College was deciding the inheritance dispute between Ivan Grigorievich Naumov and his first cousin, Ivan Ivanovich Naumov, the crucial question concerned partible versus single inheritance. Although Ivan Grigorievich's father, Grigorii, had been granted the immovable property in question during the period of Peter's Law of Single Inheritance, Grigorii had failed to register the land to himself, thus invalidating the transaction. The Votchina College decided to divide the property between the cousins in equal shares. As their decision notes, "in the strength of the Ulozhenie 16:34 and 17:2 and other *ukazes* before the points it was not possible to register the property to Grigorii alone, since it was ordered to fathers and mothers to divide to children equally."[54]

Although males were the preferred heirs in a family, necessity sometimes led to the inclusion of females. Except for a brief period between Ivan IV's law of 1562 and Mikhail's law of 1628, daughters were considered the legal heirs in the absence of sons, and their children would follow them in this line of inheritance.[55] Daughters too, presumably, were to receive their father's votchina in shares. Once a female family member inherited such votchina lands, she possessed the same rights over that land that a male heir would have had. If the daughters died childless, or if there were no living daughters, however, the order of inheritance reverted back into the male line, to those closest to her father within the clan.[56] The term "closest" is not clearly defined, but in looking at the ukazes of January 15, 1562, and October 9, 1572, which are cited at this point in the Ulozhenie, it appears that "closest" meant the deceased's brother or brothers followed by his brothers' sons, thus inheritance in the collateral lines.[57] This interpretation is supported by the law of June 30, 1676, which stipulated that the votchina of a childless man should be given to his living brothers and the sons of any deceased brothers, since the Ulozhenie says that votchina should be given to the closest in the clan.[58]

A daughter's rights to inherit votchina became more tenuous, however, if she had nephews and nieces, children of a deceased brother. Although a law of 1676 had given daughters the right to inherit along with their nieces and nephews, in 1677 this decision was overturned and it was ordered that aunts were not to be included in inheritance with nephews, citing the Ulozhenie's rule that sisters could not receive votchina in the presence of brothers. The law thus provided that in this situation the property of the deceased should be given first to his deceased son's sons, excluding the deceased son's daughters and sisters, under the argument that the sister cannot inherit in the presence of the brother. The meaning of the law here is, presumably, that the grandson steps into his father's place as heir, thus taking precedence over his aunt's right to inherit. The aunt and her niece could inherit only if her brother and brother's son were dead.[59] This was reaffirmed in 1691, when it was ordered that in the case of a deceased son without male heirs, the property was to be given to the deceased son's daughter and his sister in shares.[60] Thus, it was reaffirmed that sisters in the presence of brothers could not be *votchinnitsi,* even upon the brothers' deaths, so long as there were male heirs. In the absence of male heirs, sisters shared the inheritance with their nieces, the female heirs of their brothers.[61]

Women were also allowed to receive votchina under other special circumstances. Females could, for example, be the beneficiaries of a childless relative. If a childless estate owner died and by means of a will left his votchina to his eligible unmarried nieces, granddaughters, or great-granddaughters, then according to the law those females were to continue to possess those lands on the basis of clan kinship.[62]

The Ulozhenie also dictated specific rules for the disposal of purchased votchina. As far back as medieval times, Russian law had made a clear distinction between votchina lands that had been acquired through purchase and votchina land that had been acquired by inheritance or service.[63] A purchased estate was defined as one that a person had purchased from an alien clan, even if his clan had once owned that land.[64] A wife, even a childless widow, could inherit and have full use of her husband's purchased hereditary estates.[65] The exception was if her husband had declared in his will some stipulation to her possession of the land, for example, that she never remarry, in which case the land would be hers only so long as she obeyed the wishes of her husband's will.[66] Upon the widow's death, if she had not alienated the purchased estates, they were to be returned to her husband's clan.[67] If a man died with no wife, then his purchased estates were to be given to his family.[68] Thus, even purchased votchina was, to some extent, subject to clan interests.

Purchased hereditary estates also had their complications, however, depending on the source of the purchase. Thus the law distinguished between purchased votchina lands that were purchased from other members of the buyer's clan and those that the buyer purchased for himself as a hereditary estate from his own service holdings.[69] If the owner of such estates died leaving a childless widow, she was to receive only those estates that her husband had purchased from his own service lands, and only in lifetime usufruct, without the right to alienate them in any way. Upon the childless widow's death, those lands would revert to her husband's clan. Widows were not to receive clan votchina or votchina awarded for service that her husband purchased from another of his clansmen; such estates were to be granted into the clan.[70] On the other hand, the law stated that any purchased votchina that a man acquired from outside his clan could be alienated in any way he chose, and his wife, children, and family members had no claim on that land.[71] This distinction between inherited land and acquired land would persist throughout the Imperial period.

Pomest'e

Pomest'e, in theory, was service land that was ineligible for automatic transmission through inheritance in the same fashion as votchina lands. Since pomest'e was tied so closely to the obligation of service, one might assume that it could not be retained by those who did not serve. This, however, was not always the case, further testimony to the gradual amalgamation of these two land types. For example, the Ulozhenie ordered that maintenance allotments (*prozhitki*) for wives and children should be taken from the service land of the deceased. This was apparently preferable to parceling out votchina to female family members. Pomest′e that was left over was to be given into his clan, to those individuals who had no service land of their own, or to those who had very little.[72] This rule demonstrates a characteristic of Russian landholding that we have already seen in our examination of votchina: the predominance of clan interests. Rather than parcel out votchina to female family members, the law encouraged the preservation of family lands and ordered the distribution of service lands instead. In the case of pomest′e, it would seem to contradict the fundamental purpose of pomest′e, which was to ensure service to the state. The fact that the law chose to overlook this indicates that clan interests were universally understood to be important, even by lawmakers.

The Ulozhenie dedicated an entire chapter to the subject of the disposal of pomest′e (Chapter 16). The phrasing of many of these articles suggests that by the mid-seventeenth century the normal expectation was that sons would share in their father's service lands after his death. Such transference of pomest′e from father to sons was addressed in a matter-of-fact manner, focusing on specific problems and disputes that might arise in the process. For example, it was ordered that if younger sons were granted their father's pomest′e and their older brothers protested that they were being treated unfairly, then the pomest′e should be divided equally between all the brothers.[73] In other circumstances, if a man fell into foreign captivity and his father's pomest′e was redistributed in his absence, he could petition for and receive those redistributed lands upon his return from captivity.[74] Moreover, the service record of the son no longer determined his eligibility to receive pomest′e. The Ulozhenie stated, "If after the death [of servicemen] their service landholdings are granted to their children who have not yet been initiated into a service rank; and those children of theirs die without ever receiving that service rank," thereby recognizing this as a real possibility.[75] This reality was confirmed by a law of 1684, which explicitly permitted male heirs to inherit pomest′e whether or not they were serving the state.[76]

There were also many interesting complexities and contradictions concerning the disposal of pomest′e to women. According to the Ulozhenie, widows and daughters were to be provided with a maintenance allotment from the pomest′e land of the deceased. In general, the size of the allotment was determined by the rank of the deceased and the manner of his death. The allotment for a daughter was half of that for her mother.[77] Once a woman received such a maintenance allotment of service land, she was permitted to use that land as a dowry.[78] The rules governing this practice, however, were often contradictory.

When a woman married with a prozhitok dowry, her prospective groom was required to petition prior to the wedding that his fiancée's prozhitok be registered to him.[79] In 1706, for example, Fedor Stepanovich Monomakhov petitioned that the widow Maria Kirilovna Balakireva had agreed to marry him with her maintenance allotment of pomest'e in Volodimerskii uezd, which had been granted to her after the death of her husband, Iakim Stepanovich. Fedor requested, and was granted, the right to register that land in his name. In a similar case of 1712, Maria Vasilievna Kalzakova's mother agreed to give her in marriage to Gavril Mikhailovich Kuroedov with the maintenance allotment that she had received from her father's pomest'e following his death. After the necessary petitions, the property was registered to Gavril.[80]

Once a man had succeeded in registering his wife's maintenance allotment of pomest'e to himself, the status of this land became somewhat ambiguous, however. Although it was registered in his name, it was clearly not his for the taking. He might utilize and carry out transactions on her land, for example, but he was still held accountable for it to a certain degree. If during the marriage, for example, a husband exchanged some of his wife's prozhitok pomest'e for another piece of pomest'e land, then upon his death she was to be given that new pomest'e, with any shortfall being made up from her husband's pomest'e, or if there was no pomest'e, from his votchina. She was not permitted to alienate any votchina she received, however.[81]

A woman's rights over her prozhitok pomest'e were not, however, as absolute as they might seem. Several articles in the Ulozhenie suggest that a woman's maintenance allotment of pomest'e, once she married, was no longer entirely her property either. Thus, when a man married a widow or unmarried young woman and annexed her prozhitok pomest'e (now being used as her dowry) to his own pomest'e, then upon his death, his widow was to be given her new maintenance allotment from that pomest'e that she brought into the marriage in an amount based on her husband's compensation entitlements. If the widow's original maintenance allotment with which she entered the marriage was larger than the amount ordered by her husband's entitlement, the balance went to his children. If her original allotment was smaller than the amount now due to her according to her husband's entitlement, then the balance was to be granted to her from her husband's own pomest'e. The remainder of his pomest'e was to be given to his children, or in the absence of children to his clan.[82] In this case, if a woman's maintenance allotment of pomest'e exceeded her husband's compensation entitlement, she actually lost land that she had brought into the marriage.[83]

The determination of a widow's maintenance allotment was an extremely complex matter. Daniel Kaiser has argued that a woman remained essentially an outsider in her husband's family, and her success in obtaining property after her husband's death largely depended on whether she had been able to bear him children.[84] Thus laws often distinguished between a childless widow and a widow with children. This had not always been the case, however. In the Pskov Charter of the late fourteenth century, no distinction was drawn between childless widows and widows with children. All widows were given usufruct of their husband's entire property until remarriage or death.[85]

As a rule, however, Muscovite law did distinguish between the two types of widows, and the laws pertaining to maintenance allotments reflect this. The 1589 Sudebnik declared that a childless widow was due only her dowry and a small monetary compensation for her time in the marriage. This rule was repeated by a law of 1627, with the slight change that a childless widow was now given one-fourth of her husband's movable property in place of monetary compensation. In contrast to widows with children, however, she was not entitled to a maintenance allotment from his service land.[86] This difference was partially erased in the Ulozhenie where it was established that, in addition to her dowry and one-quarter of the movable property, a childless widow could also receive a maintenance allotment from her husband's service land. Her rights over this allotment were unclear, however. The law does not specifically forbid a childless widow from using this prozhitok pomest'e as a dowry. The Ulozhenie was more attentive to the question of childless widows receiving votchina. If there were no service lands or purchased hereditary estates from which to grant a childless widow her prozhitok, then she was to be given a maintenance allotment from her husband's votchina granted to him for service. In this case, it was specified that she was not permitted to sell, mortgage, or give away this land, nor was she allowed to register it for herself as a dowry. In the event of her remarriage, taking of religious vows or death, that votchina was to be given to close members of the husband's clan, who themselves were hereditary estate owners.[87] If a childless widow remained single, her deceased husband's family could request a document from her in which she promised not to ruin the land while it was in her possession.[88]

Despite the abundance of articles that dealt with the provision of widows, there were many oversights. For example, the Ulozhenie failed to state if a *childless* widow could use her maintenance allotment of pomest'e as a dowry in the event of remarriage. Moreover, although the law clearly established that in the absence of sufficient pomest'e, a childless widow was to receive prozhitok from service votchina in lifetime usufruct, with no rights of alienation, it does not clarify whether this same rule applies to widows with children. Despite these shortcomings, the Ulozhenie and subsequent legislation did clearly establish the right of widows and daughters to a maintenance allotment. Thus, if someone petitioned for and was granted escheated pomest'e, and was later found to have concealed the fact that the original owner had a living wife and/or daughters, the latter were to be granted their prozhitok from that pomest'e that belonged to their husband/father.[89] Furthermore, daughters-in-law and their daughters also were to be provided for with an allotment of pomest'e from their fathers-in-law should their husbands die leaving behind no land from which to grant them a maintenance allotment.[90]

Conclusion

In spite of (and in part because of) the abundance of inheritance laws that were issued in the seventeenth century, particularly between 1649 and 1682, there were a host of questions to which there were no immediate or obvious answers. For example, although the provision of widows was treated rather thoroughly by the law, the rights of widowers were hardly mentioned at all. It was only in 1701 that the law stated that a husband was to receive one-fourth of his deceased wife's possessions.[91] This law, however, referred only to movable property, leaving the question of widowers and immovable property to be answered later by Peter the Great.

Pre-Petrine law also contained little reference to the inheritance of a mother's property. According to the Russkaia Pravda, the mother's estate, like the father's, could be willed as inheritance to her children in any proportions she wished.[92] The difference came in the case of intestacy, when it was ordered that the child who had housed and fed the mother received her property.[93] Thus, in case of intestacy, only one child inherited the mother's property, rather than all the sons, as in the case of an intestate father.[94] Later legislation, however, would dedicate little attention to this question; indeed, the Ulozhenie contains no reference at all. Aside from a law of 1677 that stated that a deceased widow's votchina dowry should be given to her sons and not to her daughters, there are no other laws that touch on this issue directly.[95] There were, then, a number of important and knotty legal questions that remained to be tackled by the legislation of Peter and his successors.

Leaving aside the complexities and shortcomings of pre-Petrine inheritance legislation, a close examination does reveal a number of predominant tendencies. First, there was a definite interest in the preservation and familization of various types of land. Votchina, because it was inheritable and often clan land, was particularly subjected to rules that favored clan interests. As the distinction between votchina and pomest'e became blurred, there emerged a tendency to familize pomest'e as well, requiring by law that it pass to sons and clan members before being given to alien clans. Thus, although an individual had some freedom with his land during his lifetime, upon his death the law took over, even to the extent of overriding his will if necessary. Clan interests were a consistent characteristic of pre-Petrine inheritance law.

A second recurrent pattern that emerges is a distinct preference for male heirs. This proclivity was a strong one, excluding daughters in favor of grandsons, and sisters in favor of nephews. It had a long history, reaching its apex under Ivan IV, when daughters and sisters were completely stripped of the right to inherit votchina. This preference for males even included the inheritance of a widow's votchina dowry. The law stated that a deceased widow's votchina dowry should be given to her sons and not to her daughters.[96] The preference for male over female heirs raises an important question about the place of women within the clan. Prior to marriage, though she was not the preferred heir, a daughter was clearly considered part of her father's clan; after marriage, however, her status changed, and her place within the order of inheritance became very uncertain. As we will see, Russian legislation grappled with this problem throughout the eighteenth century, never quite resolving it.

The final tendency that dominated pre-Petrine inheritance law is the tradition of partible inheritance. The nobility had practiced partible inheritance as far back as the Kievan period. By the time of the expanded Russkaia Pravda, it had been incorporated into law as the required practice in cases of intestacy.[97] This practice persisted into the seventeenth century, and though the Ulozhenie does not stipulate partible inheritance in all cases, it was clearly understood to be the recommended, perhaps even required, practice.

Historians have tended to regard the elite preference for partible inheritance as an example of irrational and destructive behavior. More recently, however, Valerie Kivelson has suggested that noble inheritance practices should be viewed not as evidence of shortsightedness, but rather as practical strategies resulting from the social and political realities of noble life. Furthermore, she argues, these practices may suggest how the elite and crown arrived at a compromise to satisfy the needs and demands of both parties.[98] Though Kivelson is correct that the attitudes and behaviors of landowners deserve more attention and examination, the motives for this behavior are open to interpretation. It will be argued here that the nobility's attitude toward its land emerged not from a functioning compromise between crown and nobility, but rather from the profound sense of insecurity that members of the nobility felt regarding their persons and property. Much of this insecurity can be traced to, and saw its height during, the reign of Peter the Great.

2
The Petrine Revolution

> Nothing is so vital to the administration of the state as the firm keeping of civil laws, for laws are written in vain if they are not adhered to or if they are played with like cards . . .
>
> —Peter the Great

WHEN PETER THE GREAT TOOK THE THRONE IN HIS OWN RIGHT IN 1689, no one could have imagined the dramatic changes he would bring to Russia. Peter's reforms were ambitious and far-reaching, and demanded the transformation of both Russia, in general, and the Russian elite in particular. In attempting to make Russia more modern, Western, and "rational," Peter attacked noble privileges and rights in a number of areas. To be sure, Peter was not the first Russian ruler to challenge the traditional role of the autocracy. In the sixteenth century, Ivan the Terrible had struck a blow against the old hereditary landowners through his oprichnina and his standardization of military service, and in the later seventeenth century, Fedor had done away with mestnichestvo. Peter's own father, Alexei Mikhailovich, had brought Western influences to Russia, creating and frequenting the German Quarter in Moscow and using a German doctor and carriage. These were but precursors, however, to Peter's reforms, which sought to transform Russia on a scale never before attempted. The Petrine revolution altered the Russian noble's physical appearance, his personal interactions and the way he cared for his family, threatened his traditional reliance on clan and patronage, and challenged his certainty about the superiority of noble birth above all else. Moreover, it bound him more closely to the state while at the same time reminding him that he was, to a large degree, subject to the control of that state and its head, the tsar. These traumatic changes left the Russian nobility with a tremendous sense of insecurity, one that persisted throughout the remainder of the eighteenth century and well into the nineteenth century.

Peter's reforms attacked the privileges and rights of the nobility in a number of areas and, taken as a whole, challenged the nobility's traditional place in society. To say the least, many of his reforms complicated noble life, particularly those that called for the Westernization of noble life and culture. On January 4, 1700, Peter decreed that noblemen and servitors at court were to wear clothing of European cut instead of the traditional Russian robes. About the same time, he began his campaign literally to change the face of Russia, requiring nobles, servitors, merchants, and townsmen to shave their beards and mustaches under penalty of punishment.[1] Personal appearance was not the only facet of noble life that Peter set out to change. European culture was imposed in other areas of noble life as well. Dress, personal appearance, everyday behavior, social interactions, and societal expectations all changed dramatically, leaving the Russian nobleman "a foreigner in his own country." Women, for example, were released from the *terem* and expected to attend balls and gatherings of both sexes. Foreign languages and knowledge of European habits and customs became important as well. To facilitate this transformation, Peter encouraged a degree of international contact and travel, inviting many foreigners to Russia, while simultaneously sending many young Russian nobles abroad. Over time, the adoption of such elements of European culture became a symbol of status. The result was that on the public and private level, behavior became affected, as nobles struggled to adapt to the changing social mores of the times. As Iurii Lotman has observed, "Play-acting at everyday life, the feeling of being forever on the stage, is extremely characteristic of Russian gentry life in the eighteenth century."[2]

By the second half of the eighteenth century, Peter's Westernizing influence had taken firm root in Russia, and continued to develop under the encouragement of Catherine the Great. Many Russian nobles, both men and women, had become fluent in French, sometimes speaking this adopted language better than their native tongue. Western goods were highly valued and became de rigueur for a proper noble life, as did European styles in clothing, hairstyles, architecture, and garden design. Many noble estates, for example, could boast European architects and offered impressive arrangements of columns, porticos, pavilions, and grottos, all designed to imitate the styles of house and garden design in the West. The interiors of these palaces also owed much to fashions abroad, displaying neoclassical motifs on walls, ceilings, and floors, as well as imported luxuries such as Wedgewood china and Parisian silver.[3] In the early nineteenth century, Alexander Griboedov's Chatsky would register dismay at this overwhelming presence of European influence:

> I hold our North one hundredfold the worse
> Since we have traded all we had—
> Our language, customs, ancient holiness—
> And take on new ways;
> Since we have laid aside our stately dress
> And put on clothes for clowns—
> A tail behind, the front grotesquely cut away
> Against all commonsense, regardless of the weather,
> And awkward when one moves!
> Our faces marred—grey chins scraped ludicrously bare—
> Short coats, short hair, short wits ![4]

The new social and behavioral expectations were not the only developments in the eighteenth century that threatened the status quo for the Russian nobility. Peter's reforms also challenged the traditional expectations that ruled the power hierarchies in government and society. The underlying motive of many of these reforms was the rationalization of Russian life. Thus, Peter attempted to establish rational order in administration by replacing the ancient council of aristocrats, the Boyar Duma, with a Senate appointed by the emperor, and by establishing a network of administrative colleges. His Table of Ranks, an organizational ladder for promotion, was designed to reward hard work and merit above birth and traditional noble privilege.[5] Although ultimately unsuccessful, Peter also tried to establish a code of law. Finally, both Peter's Law of Single Inheritance of 1714 and his Law on the Succession to the Throne in 1722 emphasized the importance of the rational choice of an heir. The Law of Single Inheritance offered parents the right to choose the single heir to their lands, while the Law on the Succession declared that the heir to the throne would be chosen by the current ruler. In both cases, rationality was preferred to tradition. Although many of Peter's reforms failed or were overturned in the years following his death, Peter had planted the seed for a conflict that would challenge the nobility and government alike for the remainder of the Imperial period. This was the clash between the values of legality (a belief in the rule of law) and rationality (decisions based in reason) and the traditional predominance of personal and clan ties.

Historically, Russian government and society had functioned on a very personal level. The noble considered himself a personal servant of the prince or tsar, and frequently appealed to the tsar himself for assistance in personal matters. This idea predominated among the general populace as well. In 1648, for example, the tsar's refusal to continue to accept petitions personally from the people was perceived as a betrayal of traditional Muscovite ways and of the tsar's role as father to his people. The public's reaction to this betrayal was violence and rebellion.[6]

The personal nature of the Muscovite system affected nobles on another level as well. Family and clan ties influenced a noble's status and advancement and dominated his choices about such decisions as marriage and other personal relationships.[7] The personal dimension of mestnichestvo testifies to the importance of family in the definition of noble status prior to Peter's reign. Through this system, family and clan ties were not only important traditional influences, they were accepted as legitimate factors in government policy toward noble advancement. Even in the seventeenth century, however, the first signs of a struggle between legality and tradition can be detected. Following the uprising of 1648, for example, a new code of laws, the Ulozhenie, was compiled. One of its articles stated that henceforth people were to submit their petitions to the appropriate official in the chancellery that had jurisdiction in the case. Petitions were no longer to be submitted to the tsar personally.[8] The system of mestnichestvo also came under fire in the late seventeenth century. The heterogenous nature of the nobility made such a conflict virtually inevitable. While the more influential and successful noble families certainly benefited from mestnichestvo, lesser nobles, whose families had not achieved high rank, were anxious to do away with a system of precedence that tended to frustrate their upward social mobility.[9] The system was abolished by Fedor in 1682.

Thus, the basic tension between the principles of rationality and tradition predated Peter's reign. Peter, however, exacerbated this already extant conflict by imposing revolutionary reforms that touched virtually every aspect of the nobleman's life. By changing the system for determining rank and theoretically eliminating the influence of clan and family, Peter challenged one of the few securities the nobility had in a system that was largely arbitrary and dependent on the favor of the tsar. Moreover, Peter's effort to transform inheritance practices reached deep into the personal lives of his subjects and threatened a status quo steeped in tradition.

The conflict between tradition and rationality grew as the eighteenth century wore on. Subsequent rulers, following Peter's example and looking to the West themselves, persistently sought to introduce greater order to government and struggled to eliminate certain vestiges of the old personal style of monarchy that were considered hindrances to the development of a modern bureaucracy. The problem of direct petitions to the sovereign, for example, arose repeatedly throughout the century and, as a result, Russia's rulers found it necessary to issue decrees on this matter no less than fifteen times.[10] Even Anna and Elizabeth, whose reigns are notorious for the influence of court favorites, tried to compile a new code of law. Efforts at rationalizing Russian administration and government were intensified during the reign of Catherine the Great. Thus, in 1767, Catherine convened the Legislative Commission with the intent of compiling a new legal code. Although, like her predecessors, Catherine failed in this endeavor, her attempt shows her desire to introduce a greater sense of order into Russia's justice system. In subsequent years, Catherine's goals of rationalization would find greater success in her Charter on the Provinces, which reorganized local administration, and her Charter to the Towns and Nobility, which more clearly defined the rights and privileges of Russia's social classes. These reforms, of course, did not mean that Catherine was immune to the temptations of favoritism and arbitrariness—nor had Peter been. Although she fully believed in the correctness and necessity of autocratic rule, Catherine nonetheless strove to make the government institutions and bureaucracy function within some sense of legality rather than by unabashed favoritism and patronage alone.

Despite the efforts of Russia's eighteenth-century rulers—Peter I and Catherine II, in particular—the influence of family and clan ties and the entrenched practices of favoritism and patronage continued to predominate in both private and state matters. Land and inheritance law, for example, still relied heavily on traditional expectations about clan ownership and the right of first refusal. In fact, these concepts were so firmly embedded in the worldview of nobles and lawmakers, who were in essence one and the same, that throughout the Imperial period there was an inconsistent and vacillating approach to questions of individual ownership versus the interests of the clan. That family and clan ties continued to be important considerations in the nineteenth century is demonstrated by Griboedov's character Famusov, in *Woe from Wit,* who describes the prevalence of patronage and nepotism:

> Very few people work with me who aren't relations
> Most of them are my sister's children,
> Or else my sister-in-law's; there's only one exception—
> Molchalin—that's because he is so capable
> But when it comes to putting up a name
> For a nice post, or some small decoration,
> One has to think of kith and kin![11]

These family and personal networks tended to be very strong and tightly bound, so that the fall of one member could have a domino effect. This possibility encouraged members of a network to protect one another to the greatest extent possible. The result was that Russia's rulers often found it difficult to root out corruption or to convince noble officials to prosecute their fellow aristocrats. Catherine II, for example, found that the only way to persuade the Senate to convict offending officials was to appear personally at its deliberations.[12] Thus, the predominance of family and patronage networks also encouraged a great deal of corruption. In reality, what had been considered normal practice under a very personalistic older tradition became classified as corruption with the development of a more bureaucratic environment.

Although family ties and patronage networks could often provide protection and advancement, the personal and unofficial nature of the system meant that there was no real security once a member or members fell out of favor or were convicted of a crime. As the cases of Artemii Volynskii and Ernst Johann Biron illustrate, when the leader of a faction or network fell, everyone associated with him could fall also, including family members or others who had earlier benefited from his patronage and high position. Thus, the eighteenth-century noble was faced with a dilemma. On the one hand, patronage networks and family ties were the traditional means for conducting affairs in society and government, offering nobles avenues for advancement and some protection from the arbitrariness of corrupt officials and the tsar. The very absence of legal values in this system, however, left nobles vulnerable to abuse and without legal recourse. This conflict between the values of legality and rationality on the one hand, and the tradition of personal networks on the other, left nobles with a deep sense of insecurity.[13]

Yet another source of anxiety for Russian nobles was the tension between birth and service, first felt in the fifteenth century with the creation of pomest'e, but considerably intensified by a number of Peter's reforms. After the defeat at Narva, for example, Peter undertook a program of military reform, including the composition of a Military Regulation and the creation of a standing army. In doing so, he made service a lifelong obligation.[14] Peter enacted a number of reforms in 1714 that further bound the nobility to the obligation of state service. On January 20, 1714, Peter issued a decree that stated that any young nobleman who had not received a basic education in math and geography, that is, those subjects necessary for service, would be forbidden to marry. A month later Peter required all nobles to serve in the Guards regiments before advancing into the officer corps, thus making it necessary for nobles to begin serving at a very young age.[15] In 1722, Peter created the Table of Ranks, an organizational ladder of advancement, which listed the fourteen ranks to be attained in the military and civil services. Entrance into service brought personal nobility, while hereditary nobility was attained in the eighth rank in civil service or the twelfth in the military. With the creation of this merit-based hierarchy, Peter made service the compulsory and universal activity of the nobility, the only activity that promised social and economic privileges and rewards. Although the required length of service was shortened after Peter's death, until 1762 all nobles had to serve the state for twenty-five years. Moreover, even after compulsory service came to an end in 1762, the majority of nobles continued to serve the state in some capacity, knowing no other life and having few social and economic alternatives.[16]

The result of these reforms was to elevate the importance of service and rank in determining personal status, putting it on a rival level with noble birth. In reality, the composition of the Russian nobility did not change dramatically in the wake of Peter's reforms. The Table of Ranks did not threaten the legal status of old noble families; it simply gave foreigners and non-nobles the opportunity to become hereditary nobles through service to the state. Even with this possibility, the highest offices continued to be dominated by members of the old nobility.[17] As Brenda Meehan-Waters has demonstrated, "although the Petrine reforms forced younger members of the aristocracy to begin service in the lower ranks and to qualify themselves for high office, their families still held and valued the top positions in government."[18] Those men such as Alexander Menshikov who did manage to rise to high government positions from relatively undistinguished families could only do so through the tsar's personal favor.

Despite the reality that noble birth guaranteed many privileges and offered a quicker path to advancement than service alone, there was clearly an understanding that service rank was a vital factor in the calculation of noble status. Members of the elite recognized that service had become an essential component of nobility, without which a family's status was likely to decline. A number of articles in the Table of Ranks threatened punishment for those who demanded honor and respect above their earned rank. In addition, the Table enjoined nobles to keep certain appearances based on their rank as well. Finally, women were affected by these rules as well, since a woman's place was determined by the rank of her husband or father.[19]

Russian literature reflects the understanding among Russian writers that social status was affected by rank. In *Dead Souls,* Gogol observes,

> For that's how the Russian is: he has an overwhelming passion for scraping up an acquaintance with him who may be but a single step above him in rank, while a nodding acquaintance with a count or a prince is for him a better thing than to be on the most intimate terms with a real friend.[20]

Later in the novel, he describes this scene at a ball:

> The ladies seized each other's hands, kissed, and screamed, as boarding-school misses scream at a reunion shortly after graduation, before their mammas have yet had a chance to explain to them that the father of one of them is poorer and of lower rank than the father of the other.[21]

Both of these quotes are interesting not only for what they reveal about the importance of rank, but for what they reveal about the complexity of determining status within the nobility.

All of the changes described above created an identity crisis for members of the elite, and led to serious questions about the definition of nobility. After the reforms of Peter the Great's reign, particularly the Table of Ranks, the term *dvorianstvo* (nobility) as a legal category comprised all state servitors above a specified rank, including the wealthiest and most politically influential military officers and civil officials, as well as the destitute and propertyless. In theory, all of these nobles, merged into one class by Peter's Table of Ranks, shared the same noble status and privileges. In reality, there were many practical distinctions that existed between old and new nobles, between those who lived in the capitals versus those who lived in the provinces and, of course, between wealthy and poor nobles.[22]

The term "dvorianstvo," then, is very difficult to define, a problem that has not gone unnoticed by Russian historians.[23] Most recently, Elise Kimerling Wirtschafter has shed considerable light on the problem of constructing a definition of the Russian nobility. In her study of social identity in Imperial Russia, she examines the "status honor" of the nobility and makes a number of important observations. She demonstrates that many so-called "noble privileges," such as exemption from the head tax and the right to own serfs, were actually quite limited and ambiguous, and far from exclusive. Such ambiguity made it difficult for the nobility to have a clear and secure sense of its elite status in society. Moreover, the division of the nobility into landed and service elements further complicated any attempt at a clear delineation of nobility and noble status.[24]

The diversity within the nobility and the ambiguity of elite status had other important implications. Nobles of the court and capital lived a life quite different from those in the provinces. They were typically wealthier because of their proximity to the crown, but this very proximity made them more vulnerable: economically, their finances were strained as they attempted to maintain a proper noble appearance, and personally, they were susceptible to court intrigues and falls from favor.[25] Nobles in the provinces had different concerns. Removed from the capital and court life, many provincial nobles lived an existence of limited resources or even poverty.[26] Whereas their brethren in Petersburg and Moscow faced the threat of confiscation for political intrigue, nobles in the countryside were more likely to suffer confiscation for debt. Thus, the Russian nobility in the eighteenth century was extremely diverse, not only in its members' origins, but in their wealth and living standards as well. Not surprisingly, these differences led nobles to view the world around them and, in particular, state policies, in very different ways.

Well aware that the definition of nobility embraced families of diverse lineages, rank, and wealth, nobles were concerned with establishing clear distinctions within this larger category. Throughout the eighteenth century, Russia's elites strove to define their legal and social status more clearly, both by requesting special privileges for themselves and by advocating the exclusion of others from such privileges. In 1730, for example, during the succession crisis, the issue of noble privilege, particularly in regards to property and service, appeared repeatedly.[27] Later, Catherine's committee on the dvorianstvo had considered the possibility of dividing the nobility into two groups, the distinguishing factor being the origin of one's nobility.[28] The noble nakazy of 1767 address these issues. Some of them emphasized the importance of nobles having a monopoly on landholding. Others focused on the definition of nobility. Several nakazy from Moscow province, for example, declared their opposition to the attainment of hereditary nobility through service.[29]

If birth and rank played a central role in determining noble status, there was one other factor that contributed to a noble's personal status that was desired by both nobles of birth and nobles of service: wealth. Wealth in itself did not confer nobility, but it certainly helped one live the proper noble life and participate in the desirable noble circles. As Gogol observed in *Dead Souls,* "The gentry demand cordiality, isn't that so? Of course, one can bury oneself in one's study and never give a ball, but what will he accomplish by doing that? Why, you can't gain anything that way."[30] Likewise, although poverty did not result in a loss of nobility, it clearly affected one's social standing. Priscilla Roosevelt has offered the example of the noble landowner P. A. Shipov who was known, "for greeting people with a degree of cordiality commensurate with the number of serfs they owned."[31] Thus wealth, as a strong determinant of power and social status, was of great importance to the eighteenth-century noble, and land, as the primary means of attaining wealth, was a much-desired commodity.[32]

The ownership of land was thus an important matter and, over time, became central to noble life and noble identity. The ability to possess and maintain landed estates had evolved primarily into a characteristic of the nobility with the development of the military service obligation, though in the years before the Ulozhenie other social groups were not legally prohibited from acquiring or holding land. Beginning with the Ulozhenie, however, non-elite groups were gradually excluded from the ownership of landed estates. Thus, the Ulozhenie ordered that *boiarskie liudi*[33] and monastery servitors were not permitted to acquire hereditary estates by purchase or mortgage. Furthermore, should someone defy this order and be reported by someone petitioning for that land, the land would be confiscated from the first party and given to the petitioner.[34]

The rulers of the eighteenth century were no less interested in controlling the ownership of land. Through his Law of Single Inheritance, Peter the Great had sought to keep land in the hands of worthy noblemen, specifically those who adequately served the state. Only one son was to inherit the family's immovable property, and the noninheriting sons were not permitted to purchase estates until they had proved their willingness to serve the state. Peter's interest in productivity for the benefit of the state applied to the merchant class as well. In 1721 he published a law that permitted merchants to buy whole villages for their factories. Peter advocated this exception, however, only because he believed that merchants were now becoming involved in production of items such as iron, wool, and silk, which were of use to the government. With this interest in mind, he stipulated that villages purchased for a factory were to be considered the property of the enterprise, not the merchant.[35]

In the wake of Peter's reign and the changes that it demanded of the Russian nobility, members of that group were left with a sense of insecurity on a number of levels. One way in which the nobility attempted to combat this sense of insecurity was through its periodic, but persistent, requests for clearly defined class privileges. One of the most important defining privileges that the nobility sought was a monopoly on the ownership of inhabited lands. In the forty years following Peter's death, the complaints of the nobility were answered by his successors in a number of ukazy that gradually granted the monopoly on landholding and serf ownership, which the nobility so desired. On October 25,

1730, for example, a law was passed requiring all boiarskie liudi, monastery servitors, and peasants to sell any immovable property they possessed within six months, under pain of confiscation by the state. Furthermore, it ordered that henceforth, these groups should not be allowed to carry out transactions of sales or mortgages on immovable property.[36] This law, of course, was in part a reiteration of the article in the Ulozhenie; the Ulozhenie, however, had not ordered the immediate sale of immovable property.[37] Merchants, however, were still permitted according to Peter's law of 1721 to purchase inhabited lands for their factories. For some forty years members of the nobility opposed the ownership of serfs by manufacturing establishments. Despite their complaints, the government resisted noble pressure to prohibit merchant and industrial serf acquisition.[38] The noble monopoly on inhabited estates was finally granted by a law published in the last days of Elizabeth's reign. In March 1762 it was ordered that factory owners were not permitted to purchase inhabited lands for their factories until the completion of a new law code. The restriction was repeated by Peter III in August 1762, thereby excluding merchants from the acquisition of inhabited estates.[39]

At the same time that the government granted the nobility a monopoly in landownership, it also reconfirmed significant restrictions on the right of certain nobles to acquire land. In the summer of 1740, Anna prohibited governors, vice-governors, assessors, secretaries, and other government servitors from acquiring land by sale or mortgage in the guberniia or province where they were serving. This rule had in fact been established by the Ulozhenie, but, as the new law emphasized, it had been cleverly circumvented by servitors who bought or accepted mortgages on land using their wives' and children's names. The new law explicitly stated that a servitor was not to acquire such land, whether in his own name or someone else's. The reasoning behind the law provides eloquent testimony to the corruption rampant in the Russian local administration. The law stated that these servitors, often in a position of power, used their offices to extort property from subjects in their jurisdiction, throwing them in jail with thieves and murderers in order to get a lower price or even to have the land given to them outright.[40]

Although the state's goal may have been to reduce corruption and the abuse of power in the countryside, these restrictions had another effect as well. Coupled with the peripatetic nature of state service, this land restriction contributed further to the nobility's general sense of rootlessness. Noble servitors were taken from their homes, rotated throughout the countryside, and forbidden from acquiring property in their new, if temporary, residences. The result was an increased sense of insecurity and vulnerability. This feeling of insecurity explains much about the nobility's behavior in the eighteenth century, both in regards to the ownership of land and to relations between landowners.

Despite the complications and uncertainties associated with landholding, primary sources from the eighteenth century demonstrate an active land market and a strong desire on the part of nobles to acquire land through various means. Although nobles typically acquired land through purchase or inheritance, they also petitioned for confiscated and escheated land. On October 23, 1705, for example, Grigorii Nikolaev petitioned to be granted the escheated land of Vasilii Zeremskii, who had died earlier that year, leaving behind no wife or children.[41] Grigorii was neither alone nor unique in his eager request for land. Most nobles were involved in constant efforts both to obtain more land and to defend what lands they had against rival claims. Moreover, as the empire grew, so did noble landholding. As Ia. E. Vodarskii and others have demonstrated, noble landholding grew significantly in the seventeenth and eighteenth centuries.[42]

Land could also come as a gift from the tsar and, in fact, some of the richest nobles owed their enviable wealth to the favor of the tsar. As one historian observed, it took the old noble families "tens, even hundreds of years . . . to amass several thousand desiatins of land or to accumulate several hundred thousand (let alone millions) rubles in capital, while a favorite . . . could become a millionaire in two years."[43] For centuries, land had been the traditional means by which Russia's rulers awarded faithful and loyal servitors and political allies. At the end of the seventeenth century, for example, Sophia rewarded numerous servitors with grants of land after the 1686 peace with Poland and the Crimean campaigns.[44] In the following years, Peter continued this practice, distributing large amounts of land to court favorites and exemplary military leaders. Anna rewarded her followers in the same way. At the time of Anna's coronation, for example, Prince Mikhail Mikhailovich Golitsyn had been granted villages and settlements taken from the crown lands in Mozhaisk.[45] When Elizabeth took the throne a decade later, members of the Imperial Life Guard who had supported her were rewarded with estates; Adjutant Grunstein, for example, was granted 927 estates, while 258 soldiers of lower rank each received 29 estates. The majority of these estates came from the confiscated property of those arrested on the night of the coup.[46]

Obtaining land, whatever the source, was a constant pursuit of most nobles. The noble nakazy of 1767 reveal numerous requests involving the acquisition of land. Nobles proposed that land belonging to the state or to other classes be made available for noble purchase. Other nakazy called for the establishment of banks in the local capitals where nobles could avoid the expense and trouble of traveling to Moscow or St. Petersburg to obtain small loans.[47] These loans could be used to pay debts, particularly those that involved mortgaged property.[48] The reasons for this behavior are easy to imagine, given the centrality of the land in Russian noble life. Land and estate life were intricately entwined with a whole set of social relations, both between the nobility and its social inferiors and within the nobility itself.[49] From an economic standpoint, the ownership of land was of obvious importance to Russian nobles. The fact that there were many landless nobles does nothing to diminish the truth of this statement. A noble without land had either lost it himself or was the descendant of others who had; in either case, landless nobles were certainly eager to acquire land. While it is true that the concerns and lifestyle of a large landowner would differ significantly from those of a landless noble, we can assume that they shared some basic interests: the acquisition of land, or of more land; the protection of that land from the state and from greedy or uncooperative neighbors; and the ability to sell or bequeath that land freely. Thus even nobles at different economic and social levels undoubtedly had certain concerns in common.

In discussing noble ownership of land, however, it is important to note that we are generally referring to inhabited land, that is, land occupied by peasants. Land without labor to work it had little value. Since the appanage period, the nobility had slowly but steadily gained increasing power over the peasant masses. By the end of the fifteenth century, the government had already begun to impose limitations on peasant mobility, restricting the legal time for a peasant renter to leave his landlord to the two weeks in autumn around St. George's Day. Such restrictions increased in the following century and a half, beginning with Ivan IV's decree in 1580 that peasant movement would be forbidden until the tsar declared otherwise. This practice of "forbidden years" soon became the norm; from 1603 every year was declared a "forbidden year."[50] Later, in the Ulozhenie, the government lengthened the period of time for recovery of a fugitive serf. Thus, by the time of the Ulozhenie, serfdom had been fully established as the backbone of Russian agriculture and the fundamental characteristic of estate ownership.

As the nobles' power over their serfs grew, so did their demands. Nobles typically utilized their serfs for profit, demanding high rents (*obrok*) or forced labor (*barshchina*). The form and extent of this exploitation differed from estate to estate and depended on a number of factors, such as geography, harvest success, and the personality and degree of personal involvement of the noble landowner. Nonetheless, such exploitation was a widespread and accepted phenomenon that found its way into the literature of the eighteenth and nineteenth centuries. In the play, "Nedorosl," by Denis Fonvizin, for example, the character Skotinin comments that he never sues his neighbors, observing, "Anything that I may have lost, due to them, I screw out of my own peasants . . ." His sister replies, "Do teach us, Brother dear, we're no good at it at all. Since we took everything that our peasants had, we haven't been able to screw anything more out of them. It's dreadful."[51]

This close connection between the noble's financial success and his ability to wring money and labor from his peasants meant that the income of the landlord was determined by the number of serfs who paid him in rent or service. In addition, serfs performed a whole range of nonagricultural tasks on the noble estate, serving as carpenters, tailors, and cooks. The serf, then, was not only crucial to the agricultural production of the estate, but to the spending power of the noble as well. For these reasons, the value of an estate, and thus the wealth of a noble, was determined not by acreage, but by the number of serfs living on the land.[52]

Thus, despite the general inefficiency of eighteenth-century agriculture and the overall indebtedness of the Russian nobility, land offered the potential for wealth to nobles. It provided the noble with revenue through peasant rents, and the fruits of the estate kept the noble supplied with agricultural and food products throughout the year. Moreover, the noble could always sell or mortgage land to acquire cash. Thus noble finances depended on the ownership of land.

The ownership of land also had social significance for the Russian nobility. On the most basic level, the ownership of land and the responsibilities and hazards that accompanied it dictated the majority of social relations in the nobleman's life. Owning an estate required the noble to communicate and negotiate with government officials on the state and local level on many subjects: collecting and paying taxes, surveying and settling land disputes. Possession of an estate also usually necessitated contact with, and determined the nature of, a noble's social relations with his neighbors. Often these relationships were tense at best, but even the most amicable relations between neighbors might involve compromise and collaboration on certain territorial and agricultural decisions. Finally, the ownership of land also affected family relationships. While some relatives were undoubtedly drawn to the landowner by the prospect of future inheritance, other family members were reduced to squabbling and even violence over the division and allocation of land. In these ways much of a noble's social life revolved around landownership and bound landowners within certain social matrices.[53]

Estate life also had meaning for the nobility as the model for the proper social order. This order was patterned after the paternalistic nature of the Russian state itself, in which the tsar ruled over and essentially controlled the lives of his subjects. Over the course of the seventeenth and eighteenth centuries the noble landowner gained greater power and control over his subjects, the serfs, acquiring the right to discipline and punish them and to oversee their marriages. A serf owner also had the right, or at least the ability, to take anything he wanted from his serf's property. Although the state set limits on the noble's judicial powers, in fact only the most extreme cases elicited state intervention and most peasants were subject to the whims of their masters, just as the nobles themselves were subject to the whims of the tsar.[54]

In addition to the noble landowner's judicial control over his serfs, many lords demonstrated an interest in guiding and monitoring the social and moral behavior of their subjects as well.[55] This too was patterned after the tradition of the Russian rulers to intervene in the moral and private lives of the nobility. Peter I had dictated both styles of dress and facial hair for Russian noblemen during his reign and had ordered the mixing of the sexes at balls and other forms of entertainment. Subsequent rulers would continue this practice, going so far as to forbid persons in "inappropriate attire" from walking past the Winter Palace.[56] Nobles, then, were culturally conditioned to believe that they had the right to intervene in their serfs' personal lives. Examples of this can be found in the Instructions that some nobles issued for their estates. These Instructions varied in length and content, but on the whole they expressed the noble landowner's desire to regulate the workings of the peasant commune, setting guidelines for recruitment and the protection of poorer peasants.[57] Many of them went so far as to establish rules regarding the proper age and circumstances of peasant marriages.[58] Frequently the landowner's intervention had moral goals in mind as well. The ultimate goal expressed in these Instructions was a more rational and ordered management of estates, one benefit of which would be enhanced productivity and, thus, profits.

Last, but certainly not least, the Russian noble had great interest in the acquisition of land for purposes of enhancing his social status. The link between land and noble wealth has already been well established. It should be added that land and wealth were inextricably tied to power and social status. The most powerful nobles were always the richest nobles, and the combination of power and wealth gave such nobles greater social status and prestige than their poorer brethren. Thus it is no accident that the wealthiest families—the Sheremetevs, the Iusupovs, the Vorontsovs, the Orlovs, the Stroganovs—enjoyed a great deal of social prestige and were also those that were most closely linked to the Russian throne.[59]

Land, then, stood at the center of the Russian noble's economic, family, and social life, and determined to a large degree his wealth, power, and social status. The question thus arises: If land played such a central role in the lives of eighteenth-century nobles, then why is there only scant evidence of sentimental attachment? Or, more directly, why did Russian nobles persist in certain practices, such as partible inheritance, that made the formation of sentimental attachment less likely? We know, for example, that all across Europe during roughly the same period, Western nobilities adhered to a number of different inheritance practices, such as primogeniture, single inheritance, and entail, which sought to minimize the fragmentation of estates.[60] These practices fostered the preservation of family estates and encouraged a sense of attachment and familial continuity regarding these lands. Thus, it was common in Western Europe for noble families to have very close ties to the land, passing family property from generation to generation more or less intact, and attaching the name of the estate to the family name.[61]

In Russia, it has been argued, the situation was somewhat different. Historians have contended that Russian nobles never developed strong attachments to individual estates.[62] Even after the end of compulsory service in 1762, only a small number of nobles used this opportunity to invest substantial time and energy in the management and improvement of their estates. The limited success of the Free Economic Society in promoting physiocratic ideals and agricultural modernization suggests the same conclusion. Although the intended purpose of the Society was to disseminate useful agricultural information, it soon became apparent that very few nobles were interested in actively managing and improving their estates.

It is important to note that there were exceptions to this mercenary view of land. Historians such as Michael Confino and John H. Brown have argued that there were nobles, particularly after 1762, who showed significant interest in and attachment to their estates. Confino argues, for example, that after the abolition of compulsory service in 1762, combined with the opportunities and rights presented by Catherine's reforms of the 1770s and 1780s, noblemen energetically turned to the management of their estates.[63] Brown, of course, cites the case of Andrei Bolotov. Famous for his lengthy memoirs and his participation in the Free Economic Society, Bolotov invested significant time and energy into his estate, constructing elaborate gardens and experimenting with new fertilizers.[64] Edgar Melton also addresses this debate. In his study of enlightened seigniorialism, Melton examines the Instructions of twenty noble families and their attempts to improve the operation of their estates.[65] Finally, Priscilla Roosevelt's study of the Russian estate supports the argument that there were many nobles who demonstrated interest in their estates. She describes numerous Russian country estates and the significant time, energy, and money that were invested to create these lavish retreats. Even Roosevelt admits, however, that the Russians were the last of the European nobilities to pursue estate living as a means of social and personal expression.[66]

The Russian nobility's noncommittal relationship to the land can be attributed to its insecurity regarding person and property. Some of these insecurities originated in state policies prior to Peter, but his far-reaching reforms certainly exacerbated old feelings of insecurity and created new ones as well. These state policies, combined with clan influence, affected nobles' overall outlook on life and, more specifically, their decisions about family and finances. At the same time, the state also often pursued inconsistent and contradictory policies in the eighteenth century: promoting the emergence of a "rational" government based on the rule of law while simultaneously indulging in favoritism; encouraging the growth of an independent nobility, but refusing to grant them all the freedoms and rights that they desired; promoting individualism and individual accountability, while supporting the centuries-old influence of the clan. This confusion in state policy, and noble practices, explains much about the behavior of these two entities in the Imperial period.

3

"Everyone sees the world from his own bell tower": The Law of Single Inheritance and Its Repeal

For nothing sooner destroieth greate houses, than the division of thinheritance, as it appeareth in Germany . . .

—Bishop Aylmer

THE REIGN OF PETER THE GREAT BROUGHT MANY CHANGES TO Russia and, in particular, to the lives of members of the Russian nobility. Peter's transforming vision of Russian state and society demanded many changes from the nobility in all aspects of life—dress, education, service. Peter's vision, however, did not necessarily coincide with the desires and concerns of the Russian people. As a result, the nobility met Peter's extensive demands with varying degrees of acquiescence, resistance, and circumvention. For example, for years Peter struggled against the constant problem of service evasion, threatening harsh physical punishment and confiscation of property. Despite these threats, however, the nobility continued to avoid service whenever possible. Peter invaded noble life in other areas as well, demanding a certain style of dress and a certain level of education from all young nobles.

The culmination of Peter's intervention in noble life came with his publication of the Law of Single Inheritance in 1714, which sought to dictate to parents the means by which they could pass movable and immovable property to their children. Peter, in fact, had begun to delve into the problem of the distribution of family lands several years earlier. In 1712, he published a law ordering that the last living member of a family was not allowed to alienate his family land. In 1714, he elaborated on this issue, and on the more general question of the inheritance of children, in his Law of Single Inheritance. This law was considered by many nobles to be an infringement on their ability to provide for their family members and protect their families' political and social interests. From their point of view, the new law went directly against their concerns for family preservation and the future of their children. Peter's Law of Single Inheritance, therefore, is another important example of how Peter's dream for a rational and productive society came into direct conflict with the dearly held traditions and concerns of the Russian nobility. It also illustrates the vital concern that members of the eighteenth-century nobility had for the material well-being and social standing not simply of themselves, but of their families.

The Law of 1712

On January 23, 1712, Peter the Great issued a law that prohibited the last surviving male of a clan from giving or selling his inherited immovable estate to individuals outside the clan, either during his lifetime or by means of a will.[1] Instead, he was required to bequeath it to a female within the clan, but no further removed in degree than granddaughters. Beyond that point, the land was to be considered escheated and was to revert to the state.[2] The law of 1712 reaffirmed the traditional tendency of Russian land legislation to protect the interests of the clan even at the expense of the individual. According to this law, individual landowners were forbidden from exercising the full rights of ownership over their land, being restricted instead to very specific channels of disposal, namely to female clan members. Although women may not have been the preferred recipients of clan lands, this law established that they were preferable to non-clan members. The purpose of the law was to keep land within a family until the very last possibility of an heir had vanished; thus, a landowner who was the last in a family could not alienate the property in any way to non-clan members. Presumably, the hope was that an eligible male heir might be born in the meantime; if not, then a female heir would have to do.

The law of 1712 had extraordinary longevity and left a mark on virtually all land transactions of the eighteenth century. An examination of sale documents from the eighteenth century reveals that the seller was expected, either by law or custom, to include a statement declaring that he, or she, was not the last member of his or her clan. On January 24, 1732, for example, Nastasia Vasilievna Bobrishcheva-Pushkina sold immovable property in Krapivenskii uezd for fifty rubles to Marina Petrovna Esipova. In the copy of the sale transaction it said, "not the last in my clan I Nastasia . . ."[3] Thirty-one years later the same formula can be found in a sales transaction between Matrena Grigorievna Miachkova and Nikolai Leontev Voronin. Matrena Grigorievna, "not the last in her clan," sold immovable property in Kolomenskii uezd on April 23, 1763, to her relative, Nikolai for fifty rubles.[4] There are many examples of sales transactions that contain these words "not the last in his (her) clan . . ."[5] Indeed, the formula can be found in documents pertaining to the sale of factories as well. Thus on July 1, 1773, the widow Avdotia Matveevna Navrozova, with the permission of the Colleges of Manufacture and Justice, sold one of her deceased husband's silk factories in Moscow uezd to Ivan Pankratevich Kolosov. In the sale document she testified that her children, Elizaveta and Matvei, for whom she was acting, were "not the last in their clan."[6] Finally, the assertion that a party was not the last in his or her clan also appears in mortgage documents. Thus on March 23, 1730, Semen Iakovlevich Ilin borrowed twenty rubles from State Councillor Fedor Vasilievich Naumov, for which Ilin mortgaged to Naumov his immovable property in Tulskii uezd. In the mortgage agreement between the two men, Ilin stated that he was not the last in his clan.[7]

Finally, the law of 1712 is of great importance because of its terminology. This law is the first instance in which Peter used the term "immovable property," thus failing to distinguish between votchina and pomest'e. It was an important step in the amalgamation of the two land types. This ukaz of 1712, however, did not combine votchina and pomest'e in the full legal sense that the law of 1714 did.[8]

The Law of Single Inheritance

On March 23, 1714, Peter the Great published the Law of Single Inheritance, establishing new rules for the transmission of family lands and property. In doing so, Peter sought to ensure the conservation of noble estates and the protection of the peasantry's taxpaying ability. Peter argued that his goals provided for the long-term benefit of the Russian state and the Russian nobility alike. The nobility, as we shall see, did not share Peter's view that the law would benefit them. Instead, they viewed the law as a threat to their vital interests, and by opposing it in various ways they demonstrated a considerable capacity to disobey the monarch and the law. In 1731, after seventeen years of noble complaint and noncompliance, Empress Anna Ioannovna repealed this controversial piece of legislation.

It is worth asking why this particular law should have elicited such a negative response. The Law of Single Inheritance would seem to fit easily enough into Peter's general pattern of legislation. It was, in fact, just one of many laws designed to bring about Peter's dream of a rational and productive society. Despite some recalcitrance, the nobility had supported or acquiesced in most of Peter's reforms, so the intensity of its opposition to his inheritance law is all the more noteworthy.

What distinguished the Law of Single Inheritance from most of Peter's other legislation was the scope of its attack on noble family interests. With this law, Peter went into the nobleman's home and dictated to him how he was to provide for his family and bequeath his ancestral lands. Many nobles considered this an infringement on their ability to provide for family members and protect their families' political and social interests, and thus saw Peter's new law as unjust and immoral. Family preservation was critical to eighteenth-century Russian nobles, who still relied heavily on clan and family connections to establish and maintain political and social status. Thus members of the nobility opposed Peter's law because it undermined their ability to develop and sustain these clan and family networks.

Peter's Goals

Peter's law begins with a short introduction that sets forth his motives in establishing a new rule of inheritance. His first justification of the law was that "the division of immovable estates among children after the father's [death] is of great harm to our government, both to the state interest and to . . . families."[9]

Peter's use of the term "immovable" was significant, eliminating the distinction in landholding, which had existed for centuries.

Peter argued that partible inheritance was a harmful practice in three ways. His first stated concern was with its impact on the state treasury. Providing for the treasury was Peter's first interest and was certainly the thread that tied all of his concerns together. Under Peter, there arose a new idea of the state as an autonomous entity with its own interests and goals.[10] This can be observed in the introduction to the law where Peter repeatedly referred to the "government interest." In order to provide for the government interest and to pay for Peter's numerous reforms and projects, the payment of taxes had to be of primary consideration.

Thus the first point in Peter's introduction expressed his belief that the equal division of family estates threatened the peasantry's ability to fulfill its duties to both the state and the landlord; he wrote that "from such division there is great harm to the state treasury, and destruction to the base peoples." When fathers divided their land in this way, the portions their sons received were often quite small. In an effort to support the lifestyle in which they had been raised, these sons tried to squeeze as much as possible from their serfs.[11] Peter was convinced that abolishing partible inheritance would ameliorate this problem of sons attempting to live beyond their means at the expense of the all-important taxpaying peasantry. That the taxpaying ability of the peasantry was one of Peter's main concerns is affirmed by his actions in 1719. In January he complained to his governors that some landowners so overburdened their peasants that they were forced to flee. The resulting depopulation caused the tsar's treasury to suffer. Later that year, in December, Peter instructed the Board of Revenue that, "nobody should be burdened more than is proper, for otherwise the oppressed poor will leave their farms and eventually the revenue will decline and the weeping of the poor will call down the wrath of God on the whole state."[12]

Peter's second motive in promulgating the law was to stem the decline of noble families. The nobility had practiced partible inheritance as far back as the Kievan period. By the time of the expanded Russkaia Pravda, it had been incorporated into law as the required practice in cases of intestacy.[13] This practice persisted into the seventeenth century, and though the Ulozhenie does not clearly require partible inheritance in all cases, it was clearly understood to be the recommended, perhaps even required, practice.[14] Peter believed that the continued division of noble estates would result in such poverty that, "the great family, instead of glory, will be peasants, as there are already many examples in the Russian people."[15]

There is disagreement among historians as to whether partible inheritance had the negative effects that Peter perceived. A number of historians have argued that Peter's assessment was correct, presenting evidence of splintering estates to support this theory.[16] More recently, Valerie Kivelson has argued that, while partible inheritance did result in the splintering of estates, the economic effects of this process were mitigated by the acquisition of new property by each generation.[17] To some extent this was true; undoubtedly, noble children did acquire new lands. The problem was not just that estates were divided between children, but that *each* estate or village was divided. No amount of new acquisition could alleviate the problem of this kind of fragmentation.

There was, however, another practice that occasionally could have helped to stave off the splintering of estates. This was the conscious choice by nobles, supported by Russian law, to divide estates "to one place." Typically, when a landowner's property was allocated between his sons, each son received a portion of each estate, thereby fragmenting not only the man's holdings in general, but each individual estate as well. It was this practice of dividing each estate that made partible inheritance particularly destructive. The ruinous effects of this practice could be minimized, however, if each landowner's property was apportioned "to one place," meaning each son receiving a whole estate, or as close to that arrangement as possible. There is evidence that this type of division did occur and was supported by Russian legislation. In 1725, for example, a supplement to the law of 1714 permitted individuals who had divided immovable property before the Law of Single Inheritance to redivide it "to one place" if they so wished. Furthermore, this type of division could also be employed in accordance with the Law of Single Inheritance regarding the division between a widow and the single heir.[18]

It is unclear just how frequently this arrangement was utilized, but archival evidence demonstrates that it was not a rare or exceptional occurrence. Surviving spouses, for example, commonly received their share in one location; this arrangement was described in petitions and primary sources as dividing land "to one place." Indeed this arrangement had been supported by the Ulozhenie. Thus in 1766, Nadezhda Ivanovna Chirikova received her designated widow's portion "to one place" in Velikolutskii uezd.[19] Moreover, family members frequently would settle inheritance divisions by amicable agreements; on occasion these agreements would include requests that the property be divided "to one place." In 1728, for example, Ivan Likharev's widow, Avdotia, and his daughter, Vera, petitioned to have Ivan's land distributed in such a way that Avdotia would receive her share in one place and Vera, as the single heir, would receive her share in one location. By the time the matter was settled, however, the Law of Single Inheritance had been repealed and the practice of partible inheritance restored. Still, Avdotia and her daughters—for now her younger daughter Natalia was included in the division—opted to divide the property "to one place." Later, in 1763, after Avdotia's death, her two daughters petitioned to divide her property in the same fashion.[20]

Despite these possible avenues for forestalling the fragmentation of noble estates, the testimonies of eighteenth- and nineteenth-century Russians suggest that partible inheritance continued to have detrimental effects on noble families. In his response to a questionnaire of the Free Economic Society, for example, Andrei Bolotov bemoaned the splintering of noble estates and the conflicts that often accompanied such division. Moreover, he was troubled by the agricultural disadvantages of this type of landholding, specifically citing the resulting inefficiency in plowing, sowing, and harvesting. In the next century, Alexander Pushkin condemned partible inheritance even more severely. Pushkin complained about the fragmentation and mortgaging of property, and identified the repeal of the Law of Single Inheritance as a historical mistake, arguing that the progressive splintering of estates had robbed the country of a real nobility and contributed to the Decembrist rebellion of 1825.[21] Whatever the severity of this problem may have been, Peter believed that partible inheritance was a harmful practice and enacted this law with the hope of ending the erosion of noble family wealth. He was certain that once his law was in effect, "families will not fall, but . . . will be unshakable through glory."[22]

Finally, by ending partible inheritance Peter sought to transform the nobility's attitude toward state service, and more broadly toward work itself. Peter maintained that the nobles, "having their free bread . . . do not serve in any use to the state without force . . . but find any evasion and live in idleness, which . . . is the mother of all evil affairs."[23] Peter presumed that his inheritance law would allow the sole heir to become an officer who could afford to prepare for service without overtaxing his peasants, and at the same time permit and indeed compel the noninheriting sons to choose other professions. With this concern in mind, Peter declared in his law that those sons who pursued careers in trade or the clergy should incur no dishonor for themselves or their families.[24]

The Body of the Law

To achieve these various aims, Peter composed a law comprising sixteen articles that established extensive regulations concerning the inheritance of property, under the classifications of "immovable," such as land, peasant households, and shops, and "movable," a category that had long existed in Russian law and included such items as clothing, jewelry, household goods, and livestock.[25]

The first article of Peter's law established that immovable property was not to be sold or mortgaged, but was to be left to someone in the clan in the manner described in Article 2. This second article is the one from which the law derives its name, for it set forth the rule of single inheritance. It established that a father's immovable property would pass to one son, or in the absence of a son, to one daughter. Movable property would be distributed among the remaining children of both sexes. If the parents did not designate the single heir, then the law prescribed that the immovable property would pass to the oldest son and movable property would be shared by the other children in equal parts. Peter urged parents to make these decisions; in Article 5 he stated that "it is necessary for fathers and mothers to write wills in advance and to apportion the movable property into shares."[26] Peter's later emphasis on individual ability in the Table of Ranks suggests that he hoped that parents would choose the child they thought most capable of managing the family estate. Although this intent is not clearly stated in the law itself, the overall character of Peter's legislation suggests that Peter preferred this selection of an heir to involve some degree of rational choice, in the same fashion that he later transformed the law of succession to the throne. Viewed together, these three pieces of Petrine legislation demonstrate Peter's desire to promote an emphasis on individual ability.[27]

There are numerous examples of how this "single heir" article functioned in practice. Ivan Prakofevich Nepenin, for example, owned immovable property in Lutskii uezd that he and his brother had received from their father prior to the points of 1714. In 1721, Ivan Prakofevich died, leaving behind two sons, Ivan and Trofim. Since Ivan Prakofevich had neither named an heir nor carried out any divisions between his sons prior to his death, the Votchina College determined in 1727 that his elder son, Ivan, was to be the single heir of the immovable property, in accordance with the Law of Single Inheritance.[28]

Not all cases were so simple, however. Often, years after the fact, inheritance decisions hinged on whether divisions had taken place "in the points" or after the law's repeal. In November 1750, for example, Princes Peter and Sergei Ivanovich Repnin stated that on February 10, 1714, prior to the execution of "the points," their grandfather Prince Anikita Ivanovich Repnin had made over his pomest'e and votchina in various cities to his sons, Ivan, Sergei, Vasilii, and Iurii. However, because the Law of Single Inheritance ordered that all transactions carried out in January or February be redone according to the new law, Anikita's division had been set aside. Thus, in 1726, in compliance with the new law, Anikita wrote a will naming his eldest son, Ivan, as his single heir. Upon Anikita's death, Ivan received this property and possessed it until his own death, at which time it passed to his sons, Peter and Sergei. In January 1750, their cousins petitioned the Votchina College, basing their claims for their share of this property on the will of February 1714. Peter and Sergei argued that their cousins had no claims to Anikita's immovable property because of the rules of the Law of Single Inheritance; furthermore, they emphasized that their cousins' father, Vasilii, had received his share of the movable property and had never filed any petitions or complaints. Although it is not clear how this case was resolved, the dispute provides an excellent example of how the Law of Single Inheritance could remain at the center of a contested inheritance long after its repeal. Moreover, these examples and many others disprove the argument of some historians that Peter's Law of Single Inheritance was never practiced.[29]

Although Peter's preference may have been for the rational choice of one son as heir, a close reading of the law makes it clear that in lieu of that ideal situation, Peter was not so concerned with which family member received the land, but rather that the estate remain both undivided and within the family. In the latter respect Peter's new law was not such a radical change from previous legislation. As we have seen, Russian inheritance law had long favored the interests of the clan over the individual. Peter had indicated his intent to continue in that vein with his law of 1712 about the last member of a family.[30] In the single inheritance law of 1714, Peter modified his earlier law to provide that in cases when the last surviving member willed the family estate to a female member of the family, her husband and his heirs were obliged in perpetuity to attach her family name to theirs.[31]

Several articles of the Law of Single Inheritance address this problem of keeping land within a family. For example, Article 3 provided that a childless landowner should will his immovable property to a family member of his choosing. His movable property could be left either to family members or to individuals outside the family. In the absence of a will, his immovable property would go to one person in his family, in the closest line, and his movable property to other family members in equal portions. In the same vein, a later article established that should a childless widow die, remarry, or join a convent, her husband's immovable estate was to be returned to his family, while her dowry was to be returned to her family.[32]

This provision for the return of land to the deceased's clan was not in itself new.[33] Peter's law, however, was not only interested in returning the land to the clan, but also in keeping it intact. Thus the rules for the return of immovable property were quite specific. When the husband's land was returned to his family after the death of his childless widow, it was to pass not to one of the *kadety* (noninheriting children), but to one of the heirs in the family, preferably the closest in relation to the deceased. This is in contrast to the rules of the Ulozhenie by which land was intentionally given to those relatives who were landless or whose holdings were very small. The widow's dowry was to be returned to her family in the same manner. Their movable property, if there was no will, was to go to the closest of their respective family members in equal portions, excluding, of course, the heir who received the immovable property. These stipulations demonstrate

Peter's determination to prevent kadety from inheriting estates, even by indirect means, while at the same time preventing the single heir from receiving more than his share of the overall estate by forbidding him from inheriting movable property.[34]

Several portions of the law illustrate Peter's anticipation of circumvention and noncompliance. Two articles in particular were designed to discourage the illegal transfer of land. Article 12, in contradiction to Article 1, permitted the sale of property if absolutely necessary, but imposed a charge intended to prevent the nobility from relying on this to continue the former practice of equal division. In addition, the law provided that any attempt to resell this land to kadety would result in confiscation in favor of the person who reported the illegal sale. Article 13 also sought to prevent kadety from obtaining their father's estate; it declared that mortgaged immovable property could only be redeemed by the legatee, not by one of the noninheriting children.

As these articles suggest, Peter was aware that his effort to abolish equal inheritance would encounter opposition. Convinced that the law was essential for the preservation of a strong, propertied nobility and the overall well-being of the state, he was determined to implement it as fully as possible. One of the last articles declared the law effective as of 1714; land divisions carried out in January or February of that year were to be redistributed according to the new law.[35] However, parents who had already carried out inheritance divisions could redistribute their property according to the new law, if they wished, even if the first distribution had taken place several years before.[36] Several days after the publication of his new law, on March 27, 1714, Peter issued an ukaz to his governors, instructing them to execute the new law. In January 1719 he again commanded his governors to enforce the new order of inheritance strictly and to watch for illegal land divisions.[37]

Peter's abolition of partible inheritance was accompanied by a concern for the welfare of all noble children, and the law contained several articles designed to protect the kadety. For example, Article 4 required the heir of the estate to preserve the inheritance of his siblings until they reached maturity—age eighteen for males and age seventeen for females. In the interim, the heir was expected to feed, support, and educate his siblings. When his siblings reached maturity, the single heir was to give them their inheritance in full, not deducting any of the expenses incurred in their minority. Similarly, another article stipulated that, until the single heir reached twenty years of age, and until the kadety reached the age of eighteen for males and seventeen for females, they could not enter into legal transactions, and therefore no "letters or records should be believed, which appear before these years."[38] Furthermore, kadety should not be compelled to marry at an early age; the age of consent for men was twenty and for women, seventeen. These articles are significant for several reasons. First of all, they had the important effect of raising the age of majority required for entry into legal agreements, including marriage, from the age of fifteen established by the Ulozhenie.[39] These articles also demonstrate both Peter's recognition that depriving kadety of partible inheritance made them vulnerable to additional hardships, and his consequent effort to shield them against further disadvantage.

Provisions for Women in the Law of Single Inheritance

One dimension of the Law of Single Inheritance that largely has been overlooked is the way in which it altered the rights of women in regards to the ownership of land. Several of the articles already discussed mention women in relation to other issues, for example, distribution of a childless landowner's property and protection of kadety. Other articles addressed the problem of female inheritance rights more directly and endowed women with significant independence. For example, an unmarried woman acquired the right to choose where she wanted to live after the death of her parents. Once she turned eighteen, if the unmarried young woman no longer wanted to live with her brother, the heir, she had the right to take her portion of the movable property and leave, having expressed this wish in the presence of witnesses. However, she retained the right to live with her brother until marriage, or even permanently, if she did not marry.[40]

A similar independence was extended to women in several articles regarding provisions for widows, whose status had always been a controversial question for the Russian state. It will be recalled that by the close of the seventeenth century a widow was entitled to receive a maintenance allotment from her husband's service land together with the return of her dowry, to the degree to which that was possible. She also might receive some of her husband's purchased estates. A widow was not to receive any of her husband's family or service votchina, and if she did for some reason, such as a shortage of pomest'e from which to provide her with a prozhitok, she was forbidden from alienating that land during her lifetime. In addition to her immovable allotment, a widow could expect to receive one-fourth of her husband's movable property.

The Law of Single Inheritance significantly altered the allotment for widows and resurrected a principle of women's property rights that had existed in medieval law. Peter's law gave a childless widow all of her husband's immovable property for her use until she died, remarried, or took religious vows, at which time the land returned to her husband's clan.[41] She was not permitted to alienate this land. This article, however, referred only to the property interests of childless widows, an oversight that Peter corrected in a supplementary article of April 1716. According to the new article, widows of both types were entitled to one-fourth of their husband's movable and immovable property as a life portion, to be considered "possession in perpetuity."[42] This included the right to use that property as a dowry in a subsequent marriage. A woman's rights to this one-fourth portion ended with her death, when it returned to her husband's clan. The remaining three-fourths of the property was to go to the children, or, in the absence of children, to the husband's clan, according to the rules of the Law of Single Inheritance.[43]

The new rule posed several problems. First, since Peter had combined votchina and pomest'e under the name of "immovable," widows were now allowed to receive a larger portion of their husband's land than under Muscovite law, which now also legally included patrimonial estates. Second, as Brenda Meehan-Waters has noted, many men in eighteenth-century Russia married more than once, often to women much younger than themselves; thus, a life portion of one-fourth to a young widow meant that the stepchildren of this widow frequently had to wait many years to claim this property.[44] Moreover, since a widow could use her one-fourth portion as a dowry in a new marriage, a large portion of the family estate was left in nonfamily hands. In 1726, for example, Maria Divova agreed to marry Boris Shcherbatov with a dowry that consisted of her dowry property from her first marriage and her one-fourth portion that she received after her second husband's death. Both Maria and Boris petitioned that the property be registered to Boris, her third husband.[45]

Peter's Law of Single Inheritance further augmented women's property rights by an article regarding the control of dowry lands. This article reaffirmed a principle of early Russian law: the concept of the dowry as the sole property of the woman. The expanded Russkaia Pravda, for example, confirmed that a woman could choose the heirs to her property among any of her children. Several centuries later the Pskov Charter stated that, upon a woman's death, her husband would gain usufruct of her property until remarriage or death, at which time it returned to her family.[46] As Ann Kleimola's research has shown, this idea persisted into Muscovite times. Although the husband may have acquired the use of his wife's dowry during their marriage, it was always perceived as "a kind of separate account for which he would eventually be held responsible."[47] The Law of Single Inheritance reaffirmed this principle, providing that husbands had no control over the immovable property that a woman brought to the marriage as dowry. Specifically, the article stated that the single heir chosen by the father would only receive the father's immovable estate; the mother's dowry land was to pass to her children under separate arrangement.[48]

This reaffirmation, however, had mixed implications, for although Peter's law restored greater property rights to women under some circumstances, it curtailed those rights when it came to the question of daughters receiving immovable property by dowry or inheritance. The question of dowries was closely tied to the question of inheritance since in previous centuries a daughter had often received her inheritance in the form of a dowry.[49] Often this share included land. The disadvantages of giving land to a daughter who would later marry into another family were recognized as early as the reign of Ivan IV. At that time, it was ordered that dowries should be constructed from land granted for service, not patrimonial land. Furthermore, the law prohibited the inheritance of votchina by a daughter, even if her father's will expressed such a wish.[50] In the Ulozhenie, this desire to keep patrimonial lands out of daughters' hands was clearly stated once more. Only in the absence of sons were daughters to receive patrimonial lands, either as inheritance or dowry. Many families respected this rule. In 1703, for example, Fedor Koliupanov petitioned to have his bride's dowry registered in his name, stating that the property in question was pomest'e in Epifanskii uezd given to her by her brothers.[51] Nonetheless, as Valerie Kivelson has shown, there were numerous cases in the second half of the seventeenth century in which fathers divided their property equally between their children, both male and female.[52]

The Law of Single Inheritance addressed this concern over the alienation of family lands in several ways. First, it reiterated the long-standing legal preference for male heirs. More importantly, Peter used his new law to bring the debate over dowries to its natural and extreme conclusion. Failing to distinguish between votchina and pomest'e, Peter ended all concerns about what kind of land to give daughters as dowries and simply forbade the use of land dowries altogether. Henceforth, daughters were to be given dowries comprised of movable property only. Thus, when in 1715 Aleksei Aristov requested that his new wife's land dowry be registered to him, he was sure to specify that the land had been given to her in inheritance in 1713, before Peter's law.[53] This, of course, was yet one more attempt by Peter to stop the fragmentation of noble lands. As in the case of single inheritance, the new rule for dowries posed a problem for many parents and indeed, was one of the many complaints the nobility had against the law.[54] It also made a daughter's chances of obtaining a portion of her father's land even more remote.

Noble Reaction to the Law of Single Inheritance

The nobility's reaction to Peter's law was overwhelmingly hostile. From the moment it was enacted the nobility despised it and tried by various means to avoid complying with its letter and intent. The ways in which they did so testify to the nobility's considerable capacity to resist the full implementation of autocratic edicts.[55] For example, fathers would write into their wills a fabricated debt to their noninheriting children, which would then have to be paid upon the execution of the will.[56] Parents also illicitly sold portions of their land, and divided the money received equally among their children; in other cases, the land would be resold to the nonheirs.[57] Peter tried to stop such practices by an ordinance of April 14, 1714, which declared that a kadet who had earned money with which he wanted to buy an estate could do so only after a period of service: seven years in the army, ten in the civil service, fifteen in trade or in a profession. But a kadet who did none of these things could never buy land, "even unto death."[58]

The nobility's opposition soon made it necessary to augment and elucidate the new law of inheritance. In 1725, Catherine I published a supplemental ukaz that sought to clarify certain murky areas in Peter's law. For the most part, the law of 1725 defined the line of inheritance in specific, problematic situations, something the Law of Single Inheritance had failed to do. For example, the new law specified what should be done if a man died leaving two sons, and then the eldest son, and legal heir, died without ever having registered his father's land to himself. Who should inherit in this case: the heir's son or his younger brother? The law determined that the elder son had one year to register his father's land. If he died after that year without having done so, then the land was to be given to his younger brother. If, however, he died before the year had passed, then his son should inherit the land whether he had registered it or not.[59] In keeping with the male preference, however, the rules changed if the decision involved a deceased heir's son and sister. In this case, the male child received the immovable property, whether his father had registered it or not, regardless of the amount of time elapsed.[60]

Regarding female children, the law of 1725 addressed another interesting question. The law determined that if a man died leaving only unmarried daughters, then his immovable property should go to the eldest daughter and the movable property be split evenly between the others. If some of his daughters were married, however, then the immovable property was to go to the eldest unmarried daughter, and the other unmarried daughters were to divide the movable property between themselves. The married daughters in this case were to receive nothing since they had presumably entered marriage with dowries from their father. Ultimately, however, if there were only married daughters, then they would receive the property according to the Law of Single Inheritance, the eldest receiving the immovable property and the others receiving the movable.[61] As we shall see, this dilemma of the married daughter as heir would arise again and again in the course of the eighteenth century.

The law of 1725 is also significant for its discussion of the inheritance of a mother's property, a subject that Muscovite law had not often addressed. The law of 1725 declared that a woman could bequeath her property to whomever she chose, even excluding the single heir whom her husband had chosen. The wording of the law presumed, however, that the chosen heir would be a son. It stated that a mother was free to change her mind about her chosen heir and "to name as heir someone from her other sons."[62]

None of these clarifications did anything to answer the concerns of the nobility or mollify their initial opposition to Peter's law. In fact, the only concession that the law of 1725 made to the nobility was to reduce the lengthy service required of kadets before they could purchase immovable property. According to Catherine's ukaz, henceforth kadets were permitted to purchase estates immediately upon entering military or civil service.[63]

This concession was not enough to satisfy the nobility, however, and only five years later, in the succession crisis of 1730, the nobility resurrected the question of inheritance in the projects they submitted to the Supreme Privy Council. Eight of the twelve projects that were composed during this period, reflecting the concerns of over 1,000 noblemen, included requests for a reconsideration of Peter's law.[64] The project of Mikhail Matiushkin, a military and political figure who helped to draft the Table of Ranks, for example, called for a reexamination of the issue of "inheritance of immovables and about the last in a family." This sentiment was echoed by the Dmitriev-Mamonov project.[65] Three other projects—the Grekov project, the Sekiotov project and the Alaberdeev project—stated their desires more clearly and called for the "setting aside of primacy in inheritance."[66] The Cherkasskii project, so named for one of its signators, Prince Alexei Mikhailovich Cherkasskii, recommended that inheritance matters be decided according to the Ulozhenie.[67] The "Outline" submitted to the rank-and-file nobility took this request a step further, arguing that "the seniority rule in matters of inheritance should be abrogated and complete freedom given to the parents, and, if there are no parents left, the inheritance is to be divided in equal shares."[68]

The nobility opposed the law for several reasons. Russian nobles had a strong sense of duty and responsibility to their families. Parents felt it was their responsibility to provide for their children—all their children—but Peter's Law of Single Inheritance forced them instead to favor one child, leaving the others to find their own means of support. This was a troublesome prospect for young nobles since there were few economic and institutional alternatives to landholding that were both realistically available and socially acceptable. The younger sons of Russian nobles did not usually enter the clergy as was the tradition in Western Europe. Landholding was the most common source of income for Russian nobles, particularly since "official salaries were too small to live on even if paid regularly, and trade was out of the question."[69] Peter's law was problematic not because it gave widows a large percentage of a family's property, but because it simultaneously deprived younger children of what was commonly perceived to be their fair share of the family's assets. To members of the nobility, this abandonment of some children seemed not only unfair, but immoral. In this vein, the Senate report of 1730 spoke of partible inheritance as "commanded by divine law." Major Mikhail Danilov, an artillery inventor and memoirist, wrote that the "inequality between children disturbed the tender parents' hearts." Their persistent efforts to provide for all of their children attest to this feeling. So widespread was the dislike for this law that a phrase arose to refer to the unfortunate souls who had been born during the years this law was in force—"he was born in the points."[70]

A strong sense of familial responsibility, however, does not by itself explain the nobility's opposition to Peter's law: political and social reasons figured as well. It was crucial for noble families to have as many well-connected family members as possible. Nancy Shields Kollman and others have demonstrated the importance of family and clan ties in the lives of the Russian nobility.[71] Partible inheritance allowed more sons to adopt the status of noble landowner and exert influence in the government and society. But sons were not the only protectors of family interest. Daughters and widows also weighed heavily in this equation. Like women of the planter class in the American Old South, noblewomen in eighteenth-century Russia were status-bearers for their families.[72] Thus it was important for the nobility to provide well for its female members. Well-dowered daughters and widows of substantial means could achieve good matches, which could in turn further a family's political and social interests.

Finally, we must consider one other possible reason for noble discontent with Peter's law. Under Muscovite law, a landowner was restricted in the disposal of his property in many ways, but he was permitted during his lifetime to sell or mortgage his immovable property, so long as he obtained the approval of his fellow clan members. Peter's law attempted to halt the sale and mortgage of immovable property altogether. This must have seemed an unfair limitation to men whose lives were so closely bound to the use of land as a means for acquiring and maintaining social status, wealth, and good marriages for their children. The possession of land, with all its incumbent insecurities, was essential to reaching these goals. Thus Peter's law threatened to thwart the efforts of nobles to attain wealth and status on many levels.

In discussing noble opposition, however, one should note that not all nobles viewed the Law of Single Inheritance in the same way. Because they could cope more easily with the changes Peter's law demanded, providing their younger children with cash and other movables, the wealthier members of the nobility did not oppose the law as vehemently as the poorer members. Indeed, through the beginning of Catherine II's reign some nobles continued to call for the reintroduction of single inheritance.[73]

The Law's Repeal

With Empress Anna Ioannovna's accession to the throne in 1730, the nobility's complaints against single inheritance were finally answered. On December 9, 1730, a Senate report advised Anna that inheritance decisions should be determined according to the old Ulozhenie. It argued that "it is not only natural but also commanded by divine law that fathers reward each of their children with equal shares." The report went on to discuss the methods that fathers employed to circumvent the law, concluding that the law had merely created "hatred and quarrels among brothers and drawn out litigation involving substantial losses and ruin for both sides." On occasion, these disputes had led to violence, where "not only brothers and close relatives but even children beat their fathers to death."[74] Moreover, even when parents abided by the law there were often negative results: "Grain, horses and animals are considered as movables and given to the younger brothers and sisters," the report contended, "and just as the heir's village cannot survive without grain and cattle, so the younger brothers' grain and cattle will perish without the villages."[75] By this practice, the land was stripped of its most valuable assets, bringing ruin to all parties involved.

The Senate report also specifically cited those aspects of Peter's law that dealt with land portions for women. It indicated that the Law of Single Inheritance's stipulation that all dowries should be paid in cash was undermining the law's primary purpose of preserving noble estates. The report observed that fathers with insufficient cash "have nothing to sell other than villages. For that reason villages have begun to pass out of the hands of the family." The report also acknowledged the nobility's dissatisfaction with the new rules for the maintenance of widows and called for the creation of "new rules for the compensation of wives and daughters."[76]

In March 1731, after seventeen years of noncompliance and resistance, Anna repealed Peter's law, calling it "contrary to God's justice" to deprive some children of their inheritance. Although Anna's law set aside Peter's mandate of single inheritance, it nevertheless retained important aspects of Peter's legislation. Most important in this regard was Peter's merging of the concepts of pomest′e and votchina into one category of immovable property, now to be known simply as votchina. At the same time, the law of 1731 made some significant adjustments in the rules of inheritance pertaining to widows and daughters. Thus, although the basic principles of inheritance law derived once again from the Ulozhenie, Anna's law also embodied important new departures.

The new law, for the most part, revived the rules for inheritance rights of sons that had been established by the Ulozhenie. There were, however, some important differences. Although Anna's law stated that parents were to divide their property equally between all their children, what this actually meant was the equal division of property between all sons, for daughters were to inherit a different specified portion in the presence of living brothers. Moreover, widows and daughters received their portions first (see figure 3.1). For example, when Stepan Opukhtin died in 1746, he left behind a wife, Tatiana, and eight children, two of them from a previous marriage. Tatiana, her children, and stepchildren petitioned the Votchina College for the division of Stepan's immovable property, which lay in various uezds. In 1748 the Votchina College decided that after Tatiana and her daughters received their legal portions, the remainder was to be divided equally between the five sons.[77]

When there were no daughters involved, the property was simply divided between sons. For example, when Nikita Pavlov died

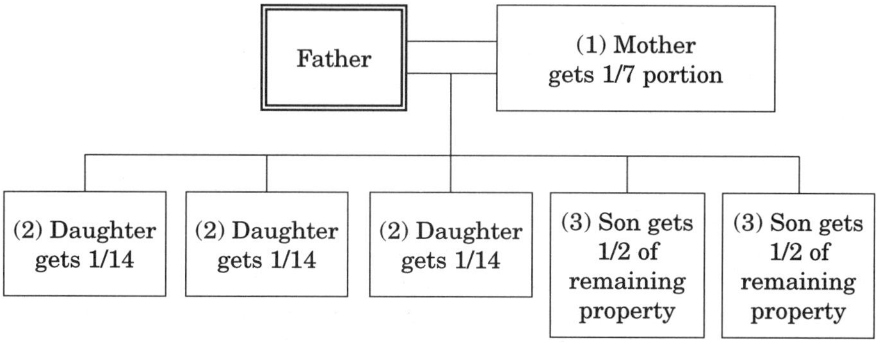

Figure 3.1. ***The Law of 1731***

intestate in 1723, he left behind property in Vladimirskii and Zubovskii uezds to which he had never assigned an heir. Had Nikita's land been settled at that time, his eldest son, Ivan, would have received all of the land. For some reason, however, the division of Nikita's property was not settled until the late 1760s, by which time the new law of inheritance was in force. Thus, in accordance with the new law, the Votchina College decided that the land should have been divided between Nikita's three sons, Ivan, Andrei, and Vasilii. Since Ivan and Andrei were already deceased, it apportioned their respective thirds to their widows and children.[78] When male relatives were the legal heirs the same rule of equal division applied. Thus, the Votchina College ordered in 1732 that the immovable property of Alexander Divov in Moskovskii, Galitskii, Kinishemskii, and Vorotynskii uezds, which he received in 1718 from his father, Filit, should be divided in half between his cousins, Ivan Titov Divov and Feodul Petrovich Divov, once Alexander's widow, Maria, had been given her legal share.[79]

The Law of 1731: The Allotted Portion for Widows

The inheritance statute of 1731 made significant changes in the inheritance provisions for widows and daughters. The most important concerned the widow's legal portion, which had been set at one-fourth by Peter's decree of 1716. This law had referred to a widow's portion as "possession in perpetuity," but had also stipulated that it return to the husband's clan upon her death. In the statute of 1731, Anna reduced the widow's portion to one-seventh of her husband's immovable property, but reemphasized that this portion was her "possession in perpetuity." The new law gave real meaning to this phrase by giving a widow the right to sell or mortgage her portion and to appoint heirs.[80] Later legislation would underline this new right by emphasizing that the one-seventh allotment of a surviving spouse should go to that person's clan upon his or her death, so long as the widow or widower had requested the portion prior to death.[81]

Anna's law had a significant impact upon women's property interests. Essentially this arrangement deprived the children of one-seventh of their inheritance permanently in exchange for their receiving the remainder immediately. Moreover, this one-seventh now included both family and acquired land. Presumably, this arrangement was more tolerable to noble children now that they were no longer deprived of their father's land. It was presumably preferable to women as well, who now had the explicit legal right to sell their widow's portions, a right which it seems they exercised on a regular basis. In 1756, for example, the widow Pelagia Volodimirova Bezobrazova sold the allotted portion that she had received from her husband in Zubovskii uezd to Under Lieutenant Aleksei Talyzin and his heirs for thirty rubles.[82] Moreover, in agreement with previous law, a woman could use her allotted portion as a dowry for a second marriage. Thus, in May 1732, Maria Kondrateva, the widow of Vasilii Maslov, petitioned to have the allotted portion that she had received after Maslov's death, along with the immovable property she received from her father, registered to her new husband, Ivan Mikhailovich Pavlov, Leibguard of the Semenovskii Regiment.[83] Finally, a woman could use her legal portion as a dowry for her daughter, as Marfa Spasiteleva did in 1763, granting her daughter Avdotia immovable property in Belozerskii uezd, a portion of which she had received after the death of her first husband.[84]

The right to an allotted portion, however, was not the exclusive domain of women. Husbands too were entitled to a one-seventh portion of their deceased wives' immovable property. Husbands were for obvious reasons no less interested than wives in obtaining their legal portions of their spouses' estate. In 1755, for example, Matvei Danilovich Zubov petitioned for his allotted portion from the immovable property in Vologotskii uezd that had belonged to his deceased wife, Irina Mikhailovna. He further specified that the property remaining after his portion should go to his son, Mikhail.[85]

The new rules established by Anna's repeal law of 1731 were also significant because they determined the pattern for widow's rights for the remainder of the eighteenth century. After that date, there was no significant legislation that altered the allotments guaranteed by Anna's law.

The Law of 1731: Provisions for Daughters and Dowries

The law of 1731 also made significant changes concerning the inheritance and dowry rights of daughters. Under the new law, daughters were entitled to an inheritance of one-fourteenth of their father's immovable property, or half of the widow's share, in the presence of living brothers. Thus, when a man died, his widow would receive one-seventh of his immovable property, his daughters each one-fourteenth, and his sons would divide the remaining property equally between themselves. In the absence of sons, daughters would inherit the property and divide it equally.

A daughter's right to a share of her father's property was strongly upheld in subsequent years. In 1740, for example, the Senate heard the case of an unmarried girl, Natalia Golovina, concerning the division of her father's immovable property. When Admiral and Cavalier Golovin died, he left behind his wife, Maria, his daughter, Natalia, and two sons, Ivan and Alexander. On March 28, 1740, the Votchina Office decided to give Maria her widow's portion and divide the remainder in halves between the two brothers. Natalia received nothing. Natalia appealed this decision, and the Senate supported her claim, ordering that the property should be divided according to the law of 1731, which stated that "parents are to divide their property between their children, and daughters in the presence of sons are to receive an amount equal to half of their mother's share."[86] The significant fact in Natalia's case, however, is that she was unmarried. As we will see in a later chapter, Anna's law failed to specify if married daughters were also to receive a one-fourteenth share. This question would trouble lawmakers for the remainder of the century as they tried to decide if a daughter's dowry was an advance on or a revocation of future inheritance rights.

The law of 1731 also made a significant change concerning the granting of dowries. Peter's Law of Single Inheritance had prohibited the granting of landed dowries to daughters, creating particular hardship for nobles whose wealth was tied up primarily in land and serfs. The dissatisfaction of many nobles on this count was expressed in the Senate report of 1730 that advised Anna to repeal Peter's law. The report argued that the Law of Single Inheritance's stipulation that all dowries be in cash tended to undermine the law's primary purpose of preserving noble estates by forcing fathers with insufficient cash to sell villages in order to establish a lawful dowry. Anna's law of 1731 repealed this notion and ordered that dowries were to be granted as before, according to the Ulozhenie. However, this new freedom was almost immediately limited by a law of November 1731, which specified that dowries of immovable property could not include family property, but could only be composed of acquired property.[87] Primary sources indicate that with the repeal of Peter's law, nobles returned to their traditional practice of giving land dowries to their daughters or sisters. In 1750, for example, Peter Sheremetev agreed to give his sister Ekaterina a land dowry from his own personal property in Nizhegorodskii uezd upon her marriage to Aleksei Urusov. Similarly, in 1752 Mikhail Neliubov married his daughter Irina to Iakov Barantsov with a dowry of his immovable property in Livenskii uezd.[88] Significantly, Anna's law did not specify the amount of a proper dowry, leaving room for yet another legal debate in subsequent years.

Anna's repeal law of 1731 brought an end to one of Peter's most notorious and hated pieces of legislation. Only Peter's overwhelming authority had kept the law alive, and when he died, the law died soon after. Overturned only six years after Peter's death, the Law of Single Inheritance did not achieve its primary goals. It failed to create a new pattern of inheritance concentrated on one child, and instead succeeded only in angering the nobility and forcing its members to find creative methods of circumventing the law. Moreover, the law failed to create a pool of young nobles compelled to enter trade or other professions, for although these children were removed from the business of landholding, they were still required to serve the state. As the Senate report noted, "all children of the nobility, both heirs and kadety, start their service in the army or navy in the lowest ranks. The kadety see this as a double misfortune. They are deprived of their inheritance while serving for a long time as a soldier or sailor."[89]

The law's lack of success may be attributed to several factors. Kliuchevskii suggested that the law failed because it was poorly framed. It is true that the law was occasionally unclear and contradictory; for example, the beginning of the law prohibits the sale or mortgaging of family estates, whereas a later section permits such actions in cases of necessity.[90] Peter also failed to anticipate the problems that the Russian definition of "movable property" would pose for the successful enactment of his law. This reason alone, however, does not explain the law's failure. Many of Peter's laws were ambiguous and poorly framed, but no more so than many Muscovite laws. Thus the law's lack of success must be attributed to other factors. Clearly, Peter did not fully anticipate the intensity and breadth of the opposition that would arise from the law's enactment. Members of the nobility felt strongly about their duties to their families and proved more obdurate and creative in their opposition than he had anticipated. Their adherence to partible inheritance was derived from concerns about family preservation, the lack of economic alternatives for their children, and the loss of political power and social status for their families. Moreover, the absolute nature of Peter's law—prohibiting nobles from selling or mortgaging property of any sort during their lifetimes—was exceedingly extreme.

Despite the eventual repeal of Peter's law, most historians recognize that it did have one significant result—it ended the legal distinction between pomest′e and votchina. Anna's repeal law of 1731 upheld this important change. But Peter's law had another important result that has rarely been noted: it furthered female interests in landholding. Peter's law reaffirmed the principle that a woman's dowry was her own property, preserving a right that offered women a significant potential for independence. Anna's law took this further, once again permitting parents to give land dowries. In addition, Peter's law paved the way for improved allotments for widows, establishing the concept of "possession in perpetuity." Anna built on this in her repeal law and added the right of free disposal. Thus, although Peter's Law of Single Inheritance was short-lived, it did have important long-term consequences for other inheritance legislation in the eighteenth century, Anna's repeal law being just the first example.

4
Fool's Gold: Property Legislation Under Catherine II

> You should know that if your government became a republic, it would lose all its power and the land would become the prey of anyone who cared to seize it.
>
> —Catherine the Great

WHEN CATHERINE THE GREAT ASSUMED THE THRONE IN THE SUMmer of 1762, it was the beginning of a long and eventful reign, one that drew from both the cultural and imperial ambitions of Peter the Great and the liberal ideas of the Enlightenment. By all accounts intelligent, hardworking, and well read, Catherine envisioned many reforms and changes for Russia during her reign. In particular, Catherine placed special attention on legal reform and strove to create a legal monarchy that could better meet the needs of society. Not surprisingly, many of the thorniest issues in these attempts concerned the nobility—its service obligation, the education of noble children, and its rights over property.[1] Although some of Catherine's plans never came to fruition, such as the Land Survey and her project for a new law code, many others did make an impact; her Charter of 1775, for example, completely remodeled local administration in Russia, and her Charter to the Towns and the Nobility in 1785 organized the urban and noble estates.[2]

Catherine's desire to improve the state of the law in Russia and her understanding that the nobility was essential in this transformation necessitated that she dedicate much attention to questions of land and inheritance legislation. Although many important issues had been addressed in the reigns of Anna and Elizabeth, a number of complex inheritance questions remained to be answered. The nobility recognized these gaps and regularly vocalized its complaints about land and inheritance issues, requesting greater rights over land, greater clarification of certain thorny inheritance problems, and protection from confiscation and corruption in the countryside. Catherine recognized the importance that land and inheritance issues had for the economic and social well being of the nobility, and addressed them at length in her Instruction of 1766 and in subsequent legislation, most notably the Charter to the Nobility of 1785. Although the Charter to the Nobility is perhaps the most well known and most acclaimed reform of Catherine's reign, it was by no means the only legislation pertaining to land and inheritance. On the contrary, Catherine's long reign is rich with primary sources that discuss, debate, and, occasionally, resolve various landholding and inheritance problems. These sources offer the historian a fascinating view of both the expectations and desires of Russia's noble class and the goals of the state, as well as suggesting how these two visions clashed.

The Committee on the Freedom of the Nobility

In attempting to understand the issues that were of the greatest concern to Russia's landholding class, it seems sensible to begin by listening to the voices of the nobles themselves. There are numerous instances during Catherine's rule when members of the nobility were invited to express their views on a number of matters. The first such opportunity occurred quite early in Catherine's reign and was instigated by the Empress herself. In the summer of 1762, immediately upon assuming the throne, Catherine was acutely aware of the tenuous nature of her position on the throne following the overthrow and murder of her husband Peter III and her own decision to rule as Empress rather than regent for her son Paul. In an effort to win broader political support within the nobility, she considered the idea of creating an advisory council of nobles, approaching her chief advisor Nikita Panin with the idea. In answer to Catherine's request, Panin drew up a proposal for a noble council of between six and eight members that would have substantial influence in the realm of legislation. The council would not have legislative powers of its own, but neither would the sovereign be able to enact new law without the council's approval. The general spirit of Panin's proposal was aimed at the establishment of legality and the elimination of favoritism. Certain rival factions at court, however, among them the Orlovs, saw Panin's project as an attempt to limit not only Catherine's absolute power, but even her choice of advisors. In the end, Catherine shared their fear and set aside Panin's project in December 1762.[3]

It was not long, however, before the Empress created another opportunity for members of the nobility to express their views on various issues. In February 1763 Catherine set up a commission to examine the question of the nobility 's freedom from compulsory state service, as laid out in Peter III's Manifesto of 1762. The commission consisted of the same people whom Panin had recommended for the advisory council. Although Catherine had asked the Commission to discuss the question of noble service, its members clearly had other concerns in mind as well. Since only two proposals survive—those of Count Alexei Bestuzhev-Riumin and Mikhail Vorontsov—we have a somewhat limited view of the Commission's interests. Yet these proposals, along with Panin's critique of Bestuzhev-Riumin's ideas, offer interesting insights into the concerns of Russian nobles in the mid-eighteenth century. They also present a preview of some of the issues that would appear in the noble nakazy of 1767.[4]

In his proposal, Bestuzhev-Riumin addressed a number of important issues, such as the definition of nobility and the monopoly on landownership. He proposed, for example, that nobility should only be acquired as a grant from the crown, not through the Table of Ranks. Moreover, only nobles who had served should be able to own settled estates. Bestuzhev-Riumin also sought to delay any order for a nobleman's arrest, the confiscation of his property, or his exile until the case had been heard and proof of the crime presented. Panin, however, disagreed with Bestuzhev-Riumin, arguing that even non-nobles should be able to purchase estates if they had served. Mikhail Vorontsov's proposal presented some interesting suggestions as well. Vorontsov recommended that titles should be attached to landed estates, which would in turn be added to the family's name. Moreover, he argued that noble estates should be protected from fragmentation.[5]

In the end, the Commission presented Catherine with a number of recommendations. First among these was the need to distinguish between Russia's "old nobility" and those who had achieved their status through the Table of Ranks. Moreover, the Commission recommended that the nobility be guaranteed certain privileges, including a monopoly on the ownership of inhabited estates, exemption from corporal punishment, freedom from confiscation except for debt, and the right to establish entails. When Catherine received these suggestions in October 1763, however, she set them aside. Thus, the Commission's recommendations came to naught.[6]

Despite the Commission's ultimate failure to bring change for the Russian nobility, there is much to be derived from this episode. Few though they are, the individual proposals and the final suggestions of the Commission illustrate the concerns that were foremost in the minds of at least a small group of Russian nobles. Most important among these concerns was the desire to establish a clear definition of nobility and noble status and to limit access to this elite group. In addition, members of the Commission were also concerned with establishing guaranteed privileges for members of the nobility. Many of these desired privileges were directly linked to issues of landholding. Thus, the Commission's recommendations included requests about the ownership of inhabited lands, creation of entails, and protection from confiscation. Because the Commission was composed of some of the most influential Russian nobles, their interests and concerns regarding land were somewhat different from those of the provincial nobility. Nonetheless, as the noble nakazy of 1767 reveal, the general concern with issues of landholding and the desire for greater rights to and over land was one that a large majority of the nobility shared. In this sense, the fears and concerns of the Commission regarding ownership and confiscation were representative of issues that were important to the nobility at large.

The Legislative Commission

Each of Russia's rulers in the eighteenth century had attempted to compile a new law code, yet none of these attempts had succeeded. Catherine also recognized the need for a new and comprehensive law code, and began to work toward this goal as early as 1764. Reading Russia's own laws as well as philosophical texts from Western Europe, Catherine began to compose instructions and guidelines for the codification of Russia's laws. The final text filled some twenty-two chapters, containing 655 articles. Borrowing heavily from such Enlightenment figures as Montesquieu, Diderot, and Cesare Beccaria, Catherine's guidelines, called the *Bol'shoi Nakaz,* or Great Instruction, set forth her ideas not only about Russia's legal needs, but also its needs in regard to the manner of government.[7] Catherine declared that the large size and diverse nature of the Russian Empire made absolute monarchy the only fitting form of government. She made a point of distinguishing Russia's absolutism from Montesquieu's definition of despotism, but was firm about the need for a central and strong authority figure. Thus, she emphasized that "The Sovereign is absolute; for there is no other Authority but that which centers in his single Person, that can act with a Vigour proportionate to the Extent of such a vast Dominion."[8]

Catherine's Great Instruction also addressed the question of noble inheritance at length. The Empress stated that the laws of inheritance should be based upon the principles of civil or political law, not natural law. She further explained,

> The natural Law enjoins the Fathers to nourish and educate their Children, but does not oblige them to make them their *Heirs.* For Instance, a Father who brought up his Son to some Art or handicraft Trade, by which he can earn his Bread, may enrich him more by that Means, than if he should leave him his small Property, which might only serve to make him idle and lazy.[9]

Thus, to raise one's children "is an *Obligation* of the Law of Nature; but to *give* them their Inheritance, is the *Regulation* of political or civil Law."[10]

One might infer from Catherine's discussion of civil versus natural law that she was opposed to the practice of partible inheritance and favored single inheritance. As her discussion of inheritance continues, however, the opposite proves to be true. Catherine goes on to criticize Roman law for allowing the bequeathal of land by will, and declares that this practice led to an enormous division between rich and poor. The result was that, "many Shares of Land *centered* in one Owner; and some Citizens had *too much,* while an infinite Number of others had *nothing,* and by that Means became an *insupportable* Burden to the Publick."[11] She concludes her discussion of inheritance with the following declaration:

> *My* Opinion in this Affair inclines more to the Division of Property; as *I* esteem it *My* Duty to wish, that every one should have a *Competency* sufficient for his *Livelihood.* Besides, Agriculture, by this Method, will arrive to greater Perfection; and the State will receive more benefit from several *Thousands* of Subjects, who enjoy a *moderate* Competency, than from a few *Hundreds* who are *immensely* rich.[12]

With her Great Instruction complete, Catherine was ready to initiate the codification process. Despite her belief in the need for absolutism in Russia, she nonetheless possessed a desire to involve her subjects in the governmental process to the greatest degree possible. Thus, unlike her predecessors, Catherine chose to involve representatives from Russia's various social classes and government institutions in the process of drafting a new law code. On December 14, 1766, the Empress issued a call for deputies to be chosen for participation in the Legislative Commission. Each government institution was to choose a deputy, as was each registered town. The nobility was to send a representative from each district, and the *odnodvortsy,* state peasants, and free peasants were each to send one deputy for each province. Moreover, as an incentive for attendance, deputies were to be paid a salary. These deputies were instructed to bring with them nakazy, or lists of the needs, complaints, and suggestions of their fellow estate members for consideration by the Commission.[13]

The Commission was convened on July 30, 1767, with great pomp and magnificence by Catherine herself. The first working session took place on the following day, with some 460 deputies in attendance. As requested, these deputies, and those who appeared later, brought with them nakazy from their local constituencies. In the end, there were hundreds of nakazy compiled and collected by the Legislative Commission. The nakazy were not to be presented to the Commission in toto, but were to be reviewed by a special committee. In fact, none of these plans came to fruition. The Commission was bogged down by various delays and by the overwhelming task of reviewing Russia's previous legislation. In December 1767, the Empress moved the Commission to St. Petersburg. It resumed its work in the capital in February 1768, but still saw no great progress in the following months. The Commission was in the process of reading and discussing the existing laws on landed property when it was prorogued by Catherine in mid-December 1768 due to the imminent war with Turkey.[14]

Although the Legislative Commission failed in its goal of codifying Russia's laws, the materials gathered by the Commission contain a great deal of useful information for Russian historians. The nakazy, in particular, enumerate the concerns and opinions of various segments of the Russian population. Most interesting for our purposes are the nakazy of the Russian nobility.[15] These nakazy have their flaws as source materials, of course. Many of the nakazy are short and lack depth or detail, and occasionally they so closely resemble other nakazy that one suspects a bit of copying may have taken place. Moreover, the nakazy tend to focus on local problems, with very little commentary on larger issues of state government or administration. Finally, most of the issues discussed in the noble nakazy relate to the ownership, distribution, and protection of property in some way. This is no surprise given the fact that all of the noble deputies were landowners. It does, however, mean that the nakazy represent the interests of Russia's landowning nobility, leaving out the concerns of those nobles who were landless.[16]

Leaving aside these limitations, the noble nakazy offer the historian a great deal of insight into the attitudes and concerns of the nobility on a variety of issues. Despite the brevity of some nakazy, there are others that are lengthy and informative, describing various problems and concerns of rural life and offering possible solutions. Nor does their provincial character diminish their usefulness as sources. The local issues that the nobles addressed take on larger significance when it is remembered that noble landowning was, in many ways, the basis of Russian social and economic life.[17] Finally, it is also important to remember that the nakazy reflect the opinions of the nobility prior to their exposure to Catherine's Instruction. Thus, we can assume that these nakazy accurately portray the interests and concerns of members of Russia's noble landowning class in the second half of the eighteenth century.[18]

The noble nakazy cover a wide range of topics. Many nakazy, for example, called for a more clearly established definition of nobility. Several instructions from Moscow guberniia argued that hereditary nobility should be obtained only as a grant from the monarch. Moreover, there were also requests to distinguish between the different types of nobility.[19] The noble nakazy also complained about the restrictions on cutting certain types of wood, the procedures for carrying out a lawsuit and the problem of corruption.[20]

The majority of noble nakazy, however, dealt in one way or another with issues of land and landholding. These requests and complaints, despite their many variations, demonstrate the central role of land in the life of the Russian noble. Thus many noble nakazy called for greater freedom and opportunity in the acquisition of land, while others complained about the insecurity that nobles faced in the possession of their land. Both of these concerns reveal the nobility's interest in creating a more secure notion of private property. Finally, the nobility also addressed issues of inheritance, redemption, and the legal portions of widows and daughters. Collectively, these nakazy reveal a great deal about the issues dearest to noble hearts, most of which were related to land, inheritance, and noble status.

The close tie between the ownership of land and noble wealth and status meant that Russian nobles were naturally interested in the acquisition of land. Thus, many noble nakazy expressed a desire to obtain land that currently belonged to others. The largest landowner in Russia and the most obvious possible source for land acquisition was the Russian government. Thus, many noble nakazy proposed that government lands be made available for noble purchase. The nobilities of Kadom, Kerensk, Nizhnii Novgorod, and Pskov, for example, requested the sale of lands held by the Economic College.[21] Other nakazy, such as those from Kineshma, Likhvin, and Odeov, requested that state forests be made available for use.[22]

This desire for more land extended to the property of other social groups as well. Some noble nakazy, such as those from Kasimovskii and Temnikovskii uezds asked for permission to purchase immovable property from Tatars.[23] Others focused on the lands of the odnodvortsy. Many of the nakazy expressed the desire to strip the odnodvortsy of their land and make it available to others.[24]

Accompanying these requests, numerous noble instructions also asked for a monopoly in landholding. This request took various forms. Nobles of Iaroslavskii uezd directly asked that land ownership be limited to the nobility. Similarly, several of the nakazy from Kazan guberniia proposed that the nobility should be given command over their land and distinguished from other groups by this right.[25] The Belgorodskii nobility, on the other hand, addressed the problem from a narrower point of view. They expressed concern about noble women marrying non-nobles, thereby opening the possibility for their common husbands to obtain a portion of their land at the time of death. The Belgorodskii nobility asked that in such a case a woman's property not be allowed to leave her family.[26]

The availability of land, however, was only one facet of noble interest in land. The nobility was also concerned about the procedures for settling disputes, and registering and carrying out transactions involving land. Numerous noble nakazy complain about the slowness of the local courts and the confusion and abuse that often resulted when cases dragged on for months or even years.[27] The nobles of Riazhsk uezd, for example, complained about the slowness of the Riazhsk Voevoda Chancellery: "Consequently many wronged parties are deprived of the proper legal suits and satisfaction; and offenders, seeing the procrastination and red tape of the said court, proceed to oppress their brethren still further in various ways . . ."[28] The Kostroma nobility expressed a similar complaint, but also offered a possible solution:

> Extremely great delays and losses are caused to the nobility and their peasants, on account of the slowness with which injured parties obtain justice . . . The Kostroma nobility humbly propose that in every township there be elected by vote of the gentry a commissar . . . and the commissar would provide quick and just investigation and judgment in all quarrels arising between neighbors . . .[29]

Nobles were also frustrated by the procedural difficulties of registering various land transactions. Thus many noble nakazy suggested that the government should allow land transactions of various sorts to be registered on the local level. They complained that the current law, which demanded that nobles travel great distances to register land transactions at the Votchina College in Moscow, was a great inconvenience and resulted in considerable loss of time and money. The nobility of Kazanskii uezd, for example, complained that Moscow was 800 versts away, a considerable distance to travel particularly for those with little property or for widows who needed to register possession of their one-seventh portion. The result was that many people simply possessed land without legally registering it, a practice that later resulted in disputes and confusion when sorting out inheritance divisions.[30] The Kazan nobility was not alone in its complaint; numerous other nakazy offered the opinion that land transactions, wills, and simple inheritance divisions should be carried out on the local level, for the sake both of efficiency and of expense.[31]

The security of property was another concern that is clearly enunciated in the noble nakazy. Thus many noble nakazy complained about the frequency of theft and violence in the countryside. Noble groups throughout Russia described how unscrupulous landowners regularly committed a variety of agricultural offenses against their neighbors. These included acts of sabotage and petty theft and the outright seizure of land, livestock, and agricultural produce. Landowners also on occasion shifted landmarks, permitted cattle to trample or consume another's crops, or illegally chopped wood from commonly held woodlots.[32] In fact, the illegal cutting of wood is the offense mentioned most often in the noble nakazy.[33] As the nobility of Belgorodskii uezd noted, these crimes often resulted in disputes and even murder.[34] Thus, many of the noble nakazy requested that the government take action to bring an end to this disorder in the provinces. The nobility of Penzenskii uezd, for example, asked that soldiers be sent out to assist local authorities. Other noble nakazy suggested harsh punishments for offenders, including the loss of noble status.[35] These requests all suggest that the nobility suffered from a lack of security of property, a weakness of which they were aware and sought to remedy.

Noble insecurity regarding property appears also in complaints about Russia's rules of inheritance and the complex and fragmented nature of landholding in the provinces. The Russian nobility had practiced partible inheritance long before the reign of Peter the Great and, except for the seventeen years that the Law of Single Inheritance was in force, continued to adhere to this practice in the eighteenth century. As will be recalled, when a landowner's property was allocated between his heirs, each heir—whether wife, daughter, or son—received a portion of each estate, thereby fragmenting not only the man's holdings in general, but each individual estate as well. It was this practice of dividing each estate that made partible inheritance so destructive. By the 1760s, as many nakazy testify, consecutive generations of such divisions, not to mention sales and other transactions, had resulted in a tangled mess of interspersed landholdings and conflicting claims of ownership.[36]

Many nobles found that these circumstances led to great difficulties on a number of levels. In his response to a questionnaire of the Free Economic Society in 1766 for example, Andrei Bolotov noted that such fragmented holding made efficient plowing and harvesting impossible. The nobility of Arzamasskii uezd expressed a similar complaint in its instruction to the Legislative Commission. Addressing the conflict between large and small landowners from the viewpoint of the former, the Arzamasskii nobility complained that large landowners were hindered by their smaller neighbors without whose permission they could not carry out the simplest tasks, such as chopping wood or building a mill.[37] The nobility of Mikhailovskii uezd shared this sentiment, stating, "Nothing is so destructive of village life, nor is less conductive to the increase of agriculture and the preservation of wood supplies, than the common ownership of one village by many lords."[38]

Since the root of this fragmentation was the repeated division of family estates by each generation of owners, the Legislative Commission thus became the occasion for noble commentary on the question of partible versus single inheritance. Some thirty-five years after the repeal of Peter's Law of Single Inheritance there were still conflicting opinions on this issue. The nobilities of Bolkhovskii and Putivlskii uezds, for example, bemoaned the fact that generations of partible inheritance had resulted in increasingly numerous and smaller portions.[39] The nakaz from the Lukhovskii nobility echoed this complaint, adding that the shares received in inheritance were often too small to support the heirs.[40] The nakazy from Mikhailovskii and Poshekhonskii uezds offer a solution to this problem, namely, that each heir should receive an entire village as his share of the inheritance.[41] Such criticisms of estate fragmentation, however, did not mean that all nobles were ready to abandon partible inheritance. The nobility of Maloiaroslavetskii uezd, for example, asked that fathers and mothers be allowed to divide their immovable property to sons in as equal portions as possible, after granting a share to both their single and married daughters.[42]

Perhaps the most interesting requests on this issue were those that called for the establishment of some form of single inheritance. The nobility of Moscow uezd, for example, asked that landowners be granted the right not to divide their property in inheritance.[43] There were also calls for the right to establish entails. Entail as defined in Western Europe was an arrangement by which land was preserved intact by placing it beyond the control of any one generation, forbidding sale or any other form of alienation. Such a system restricted the freedom of successive heads of the family in favor of the perpetual interests of the clan. Peter's law had not required entail, since it had not attempted to restrict property beyond one generation. Now, years after the repeal of Peter's law, some nobles were suggesting that even single inheritance was not enough to stave the decline of noble families. Thus the nobilities of Ryl'skii and Pereslavskii-Zalesskii uezds asked to establish entail in the Western European sense.[44]

It is useful to contemplate why after the vehement opposition Peter's law encountered in the early part of the century some noble factions would now be calling for the establishment of entails. Addressing this question, the historian V. I. Briullov argued that family ties in the upper echelons of Russian society had significantly weakened by the middle of the eighteenth century. As a result, the obligatory distribution of family property among all children was now thought by many to be both restrictive and unreasonable.[45] There is another possible explanation as well. Because they could cope more easily with the changes Peter's law demanded by providing their younger children with cash and other movables, the wealthier members of the nobility had not opposed the law as vehemently as the poorer members.[46] The same distinction might be made about the requests in the noble nakazy. Of the hundreds of nakazy presented to the Legislative Commission, only a few—primarily those from the Moscow area—called for the establishment of entails. It can be assumed that these nobles could afford to provide for their younger children by other means.

Although there may have been conflicting opinions on the issue of partible versus single inheritance, most of the noble nakazy agreed on one thing—that the laws of inheritance needed clarification. Some nakazy, such as those from Simbirskii and Moskovskii uezds, asked for a general clarification of the current inheritance laws. Others, such as the nakaz from the nobility of Alatorskaia *provintsiia,* requested that the rules of inheritance pertaining to the rights of male versus female heirs be more clearly defined.[47] There were also, however, some very specific complaints regarding the current laws of inheritance.

One of the issues that arises most frequently in the noble nakazy was the allotment of the widow's, or widower's, portion. The complaints were varied and often conflicting. It will be recalled that according to Anna's inheritance law of 1731, a surviving spouse was entitled to one-seventh of the deceased spouse's immovable property, to which was added the right to sell, mortgage or bequeath that portion.[48] This one-seventh portion, in fact, meant one-seventh of each separate property. Thus, as we have seen, this type of division could pose serious problems for the other heirs. Since the surviving spouse had the right to sell this land, an alien enclave could be created in an estate owned by the deceased's children.

Members of the nobility certainly recognized the potential hazards of the one-seventh portion and therefore offered a number of suggestions, often distinguishing between those surviving spouses with children and those without. The nobility of Dankovskii uezd, for example, proposed returning to the practice of previous law, by which a surviving childless spouse received all of the movable and immovable property until death (or, presumably, remarriage), with the restriction that it not be sold, mortgaged, or alienated in any other way. Surviving spouses with children would be granted the same right, with the distinction that upon remarriage they could take their allotted portion with them into the new marriage. Other noble nakazy echoed this suggestion as well, although occasionally with some small variations.[49] The Novosil'skoe dvorianstvo, on the other hand, recommended a different formula. According to their proposal, childless widows and widowers were to receive one-fourth of the immovable property and one-half of the movable property, with no stipulation about death or remarriage. However, they requested that the immovable property be granted "to one place," thereby eliminating the possibility of alien enclaves.[50]

While many nobles were apparently willing to grant surviving spouses all of the deceased's immovable property, or at least a larger portion than the law of 1731 had stipulated, many other nobles sought to restrict the allotted portion for widows and widowers. The nobility of Tambov, for example, presented a plan that combined the restrictions of the laws of 1714, 1716, and 1731. It suggested that surviving spouses be granted a one-seventh portion according to the law of 1731, but only until death or remarriage. Several other noble nakazy suggested more extreme restrictions. The nobilities of Arzamasskii, Kerenskii, and Karachevskii uezds all proffered that under certain circumstances surviving spouses should be granted cash in the place of an allotted portion of property. The Kerenskii nakaz, for example, argued that this arrangement would be more beneficial when the allotted portion was too small to maintain the recipient. The nobility of Karachevksii uezd, on the other hand, was willing to grant surviving spouses usufruct of all of the deceased's property until death or remarriage; at the time of remarriage, however, the widow or widower would have to take the allotted portion in cash.[51]

The noble nakazy to the Legislative Commission also addressed the question of parents inheriting from their children. Under Russian law parents were not considered the heirs of their children, even in cases where the children died without issue. In such cases, the nearest relatives of the child from their own or subsequent generations—brothers or nephews, for example—would inherit. By the 1760s the nobility had clearly decided that this arrangement was unjust. The nakazy almost universally presented the same scenario: parents often gave their children land, or bought land in their children's names, only to be deprived of this property when their children died childless. Thus, noble nakazy from all regions of the realm requested that parents be the first heirs of their childless children's property.[52]

The settlement of a woman's dowry upon her death was also given significant attention in the noble nakazy. The primary issue of concern here seems to have been the question of how much of a childless woman's dowry should be returned to her family at the time of her death. The nakazy indicate that some nobles believed that the determination of this amount depended on the length of the marriage. The nobility of Verkhnelomovskii uezd, for example, complained that at the end of marriages of ten or more years, the family of the deceased childless woman would frequently demand the value of the dowry from the husband according to the dowry list, despite the fact that over the course of the years many of the items could have been used up or even sold.[53] The nobility of Belevskii uezd echoed this complaint, emphasizing that when the dowry lists were originally drawn up, the bride's family often overestimated the value of the individual items. This fact, combined with the natural wear and tear that took its toll on dresses and other personal dowry items after many years, meant that many husbands were forced to pay sums far beyond the original or current value of the dowry items.[54] This was particularly true if the wife had sold some of her dowry land during the marriage. Thus, the nobility of Sudislavskii uezd put forth the idea that a wife should not be allowed to sell immovable property without her husband's permission.[55]

The noble nakazy reveal that familial discord and the control of property was also a matter of some concern. The nobility of Kolomenskii uezd, for example, complained about wives or husbands who, after leaving their spouses and living elsewhere, then claimed their one-seventh portion upon their spouse's death. The nakaz declared that those who abandoned their spouses should thereby forfeit their claims to property and inheritance.[56] The noble nakazy also addressed the problem of disobedient children. Thus the Kerenskii nobility proposed that a daughter who married a close relative without her parents' permission be deprived of the right to inherit from her parents. Moreover, the nobility of Karachevskii uezd requested that noble daughters who married non-nobles also be deprived of their inheritance.[57]

Finally, in addition to all of the specific complaints and suggestions that the noble nakazy put forth, many nakazy also made general requests for full ownership and control over their land, including the freedom of disposal. As previously mentioned, both the Simbirsk and Kazan nakazy requested that the nobility have command over their land and be distinguished from other groups by this right.[58] Many other nakazy asked for freedom of disposal. The nobility of Dankovskii uezd, for example, asked for the freedom to divide their property among their children and heirs as they wished, but suggested equal division if the parents failed to make such arrangements.[59]

The Response to the Noble Nakazy

Despite the fact that the Legislative Commission never managed to compile a new code of laws, the noble nakazy raised a number of significant issues pertaining to land and inheritance, many of which would be addressed in the remaining years of Catherine's reign. The first major step toward addressing the complaints of the noble nakazy came in Catherine's Charter for the Administration of the Provinces of the Russian Empire, promulgated into law in November 1775. The Charter on the Provinces introduced a number of significant changes in the organization of provincial administration. It established the basic structure of local and judicial administration in Russia, which would last until the reforms of 1864, and the territorial division, which would last until the early twentieth century. The existing guberniia were redivided into fifty new guberniia roughly equal in population. Each guberniia was subdivided into uezdy, and the old intermediate unit, the province, was eliminated.[60] In addition to a governor, each guberniia was to have a surveyor, uezd courts, superior land courts, and chambers of civil affairs to resolve property disputes. In effect, these various bodies took over the function of the Votchina College. Henceforth, these district courts could handle all matters concerning land possession, including various transactions and inheritance arrangements. Thus, the requests of the noble nakazy that local institutions carry out land transactions were answered. Moreover, the Votchina College was abolished five years later.[61]

Not all of the nobility's complaints saw such resolution, however. Many of the nobility's concerns remained unanswered until well into the next century. In 1773, for example, the Senate addressed the question of whether parents could be the heirs of their children. The case involved Praskovia Ovtsyna who, upon her son Avram's death, attempted to take back the property that she had given him in order to grant it to her other child, Avdotia. Avram's wife Anna and daughter Elena, however, challenged this move. The Senate decided that although the law of 1725 granted a mother the right to change her mind and reassign her property to another child as heir, this decision had to take place while the child was alive. Moreover, Avram had an heir of his own who was now entitled to that property.[62] This case, then, differed somewhat from the pleas of the nobility in 1767. It demonstrated the legal strength of legitimate heirs. It was only in 1823 that parents received the right to inherit from their childless child.[63]

In the years following the disbanding of the Legislative Commission, the state attempted to respond to other inheritance questions, though often addressing only part of the issue. For example, although the basic laws of inheritance stipulating equal division remained in force throughout the nineteenth century, there were several instances in which the law actively supported efforts to stave off the fragmentation of estates. In 1776, for example, the Senate supported the division of the property of Lev Treksin between his heirs "to one place."[64] More significantly, in 1774, Catherine permitted the first entail to be created for Count Zakhar Grigorievich Chernyshev. Chernyshev requested that his land remain forever indivisible, passing to his eldest son, then to his eldest son's eldest son, and so on down the line. In the absence of an eligible male, a daughter or other close female relative could inherit. Chernyshev's primary motive was to assure that his land never left the Chernyshev clan. Thus, if a female inherited, she and her heirs were obliged to adopt the family name and the coat of arms of Count Chernyshev. In subsequent years, Catherine created other entails in response to the specific petitions of a few wealthy noblemen, but general guidelines were not established until 1845.[65]

The Charter to the Nobility of 1785

Perhaps the best known example of Catherine addressing the needs and concerns of the Russian nobility was her legislative charter of 1785. Over the years, historians have dedicated much discussion to Catherine the Great's Charter to the Nobility. At the very least, most historians have described it as a landmark in eighteenth-century legislation, which addressed many of the nobility's desires and complaints.[66] Others have credited it with establishing a fundamental change in the perception of the nobility's role in society. Robert Jones, for example, has argued that the Charter to the Nobility initiated a shift in emphasis from state service to estate ownership. Jones bases his argument on the Charter's stipulation that each nobleman was to be enrolled in the nobility of the guberniia in which he owned an estate, thereby excluding landless nobles from membership in provincial associations and from their corporate activities. On the other hand, a noble landowner who had never served was eligible to enroll and participate in his local association, though his participation in its affairs would be restricted.[67] Finally, Richard Pipes and others have regarded the Charter to the Nobility as the first instance when Russian nobles were granted true rights of private property over their land.[68]

Although the Charter to the Nobility was unquestionably an important piece of legislation, the question of its accomplishments bears reexamination. A more balanced judgment of the Charter would focus on two points: that the Charter drew largely upon previous law, and therefore, was not entirely an innovation, and that many of its provisions were far less generous than they may appear at first glance. Moreover, it should be stressed that the Charter hardly answered all of the nobility's demands.[69]

The Charter to the Nobility is well known for granting the nobility a number of rights and guarantees pertaining to their ownership of land.[70] Thus, for example, the Charter promised nobles the right not only to the surface of their land, but also to the minerals, waters, and agricultural products. In addition, Catherine reiterated the distinction between patrimonial land and acquired land, and gave landowners complete rights of disposal over their acquired land. Finally, the Charter to the Nobility pledged that no noble would be deprived of his property without due process. When confiscation was necessary, the guilty party's property would be handed over to his children.

It is important to note, however, that all of the rights and guarantees promised by the Charter had in fact appeared in some form in previous law. For example, as the Charter itself recognizes, the promise to nobles concerning the riches of their land had been set forth by a law three years earlier. Thus, the Charter stated,

> The right of well-born [nobles] to private property, granted by [Our] gracious decree of 28 June 1782, not only in [whatever is to be found on] the surface of the land belonging to each of them but also in all the hidden minerals and vegetation [found] both in the bowels of the land and in the waters belonging to him, and in all the metals produced therefrom, is confirmed in full strength and meaning, as explained in that decree.71

The distinction between family and acquired property had an even longer history in Russian legislation. The principle of distinguishing between the various origins of property had existed in Russian law at least as early as the seventeenth century, appearing in the Ulozhenie and subsequent legislation.[72] Both the Law of Single Inheritance and the law that repealed it in 1731 contained references to these distinctions as well. These distinctions had always held significant meaning for potential heirs; the law of November 1731, for example, specified that dowries of immovable property could not include family property, but could only be composed of acquired property.[73] Similarly, the laws of redemption stated that acquired property was not eligible for repurchase by relatives.

The distinction between family and acquired property appeared even more frequently in legislation in the second half of the eighteenth century, particularly in inheritance decisions. In 1764, for example, the Senate reviewed the case of the siblings Ivan and Praskovia Shakhovskii, both of whom died childless. The Senate decided that Ivan and Praskovia's family immovable property inherited from their father and grandfather should go to their cousin Nikolai Miloslavskii, as the closest blood relative to the original landowner, Andrei Shakhovskii. Ivan's acquired property, however, was to go to other male relatives in the clan.[74] Many other inheritance decisions in subsequent years adhered to this pattern of division, particularly in cases of childless landowners. Property was distinguished as family or acquired, the former being given to the closest clan member in a female line, the latter being given to a more distant relative in the male line.[75] Catherine's distinction in the Charter between these types of property, then, was hardly an innovation.

The concept that a landowner could freely dispose of his acquired property also had a history that predated Catherine's Charter. Indeed, landowners had long enjoyed this right over their acquired property.[76] Throughout the eighteenth century, the owner of acquired property had the right to bequeath that property to anyone of his, or her, choosing. Acquired property included the widow's, or widower's, portion whose occasionally ambiguous status had been more clearly defined in 1731, when Anna declared it to be the true and sole property of the recipient. The freedom of disposal over acquired property that the Charter supposedly granted, then, was a right the nobility had enjoyed for some time.[77]

The same was true of the Charter's stipulations about confiscation. The wording of the Charter acknowledges this, declaring, "We consider it proper once more to forbid and strictly to reaffirm the ancient prohibition [to the effect] that no one presume arbitrarily to confiscate the estate of a well-born [nobleman], or lay it waste without trial and verdict according to the laws of those judicial instances to which trials are assigned."[78] Thus the basic concept had existed prior to Catherine's Charter that a noble should not be deprived of his property without due process.

The Charter to the Nobility also addressed the issue of property confiscation and its effect on potential heirs. Catherine ordered that "In the event of his conviction of even the most serious crime, the inherited estate of a well-born [nobleman] shall be passed on to his legal heir or heirs."[79] This was also not entirely an innovation. In fact, prior to the Charter the ruler and the courts had occasionally returned confiscated property to the heirs of the guilty. In 1750, for example, Elizabeth ordered that Semen Iurlov be given the property that was confiscated from his father eleven years earlier.[80] Later, in 1763, Catherine responded to a Senate report about the petition of Sergei Chikin for his father's confiscated property with the following statement: "The remaining confiscated property of a father is to be given to his children."[81] In subsequent years, Catherine adhered to this policy. In 1765, for example, she made a similar decision, granting Alexei Putatin's request that the confiscated property of his relative Ivan be given to him and his five children as the closest heirs.[82] Moreover, the abundance of petitions from heirs requesting the return of confiscated property suggests that this was considered a real possibility.[83]

In short, the Charter embodied very little that was new, however prominently it may have served to reinforce and guarantee the privileges that it embodied. Nor were its articles as generous as they appeared. This is particularly true regarding its stipulations about the disposal and security of property. For example, although the Charter gave nobles freedom of disposal over their acquired land, patrimonial land was still governed by the laws of inheritance.[84] Thus patrimonial property could not be transferred to anyone other than the direct legal heirs except by sale. This exception of transference by sale was an important one, for it allowed the owner the possibility of transforming patrimonial into acquired property by selling it to, and then repurchasing it from, non-kin. This scheme, however, could be both expensive and risky. Even if there was no actual exchange of cash, both the sale and the repurchase price were taxable. Moreover, the alienated property was temporarily vulnerable to redemption by a relative. And if a relative redeemed such property, it once again became patrimonial.[85] These distinctions persisted into the nineteenth century so that as late as 1875, critics of the institution of patrimonial property argued at the First Congress of Russian Jurists, that the restrictions on property disposal stifled "individual initiative, discouraged investment and impeded trade."[86]

The Charter's guarantee regarding confiscation of property was also limited in nature. A close reading of the text of the law reveals that there were still possibilities for confiscation. Although the Charter promised the nobility security from arbitrary confiscation and corporal punishment, it also established that a noble's status, and thus his privileges, could be taken away if he committed a crime "irreconcilable with the principles of noble dignity." This rather vague condition included such crimes as "violation of an oath," "deceitful conduct," and "crimes that by law entail deprivation of honor and corporal punishment."[87] Moreover, once a landowner had lost his noble status he was no longer protected by the guarantees of the Charter. This exception is illustrated in a number of published legal decisions.[88] In 1790, for example, Catherine ordered that Alexander Radishchev was to be spared the death penalty, but was to be deprived of his rank and noble status and exiled to Siberia. His property was to be set aside for the use of his children.[89] In 1797 the Senate addressed this matter directly. In reviewing the case of Praporshchik Rozhnov, who was found guilty of slandering the crown, the Senate noted that the Emperor had responded to their report with the words, "As soon as the status of nobility is removed, then the privileges no longer apply." Taking this opinion into consideration, the Senate declared that Rozhnov was to be stripped of his noble status and privileges, beaten with the knout and condemned to hard labor. Paul agreed with their decision.[90]

Deprivation of noble status was not necessarily a prerequisite to confiscation, however. On more than one occasion, Russian rulers simply disregarded the promises of the Charter, making no mention of the loss of noble privilege. In 1792, for example, Catherine ordered that the property of Princess Shakhovskaia should be taken into guardianship by the Senate, granting the princess access only to the profits of the estates and forbidding her from carrying out any sales or mortgages. Shakhovskaia's crime was that, while living in Paris, she failed to obtain royal permission before marrying her daughter to Prince Aremberg, who had "participated in two rebellions against legal power." Thus Catherine all but confiscated Shakhovskaia's property and further threatened that if Princess Aremberg failed to return to

Russia upon her mother's death, she would be deprived of her inheritance. Furthermore, Aremberg's children would retain their rights of inheritance only if they returned to Russia prior to the age of five and were raised in the Russian Orthodox faith.[91] Such confiscation persisted under the reign of Paul as well.[92]

There is little question that the Charter to the Nobility was an important document that attempted to address some of the nobility's most serious complaints regarding noble status and privilege. However, the Charter was neither as innovative nor as generous as it has been portrayed. Most importantly, the Charter should not be viewed as an empowering and wholly advantageous document, wrested from Catherine in an effort to establish a strong foundation for noble privilege and independence. Such a view fails to take into account the many elements of the Charter that were not advantageous or the fact that the Charter's promises could be and were sidestepped in subsequent years. Moreover, the Charter to the Nobility fell short in one other important area—inheritance law. The noble nakazy had requested changes in a number of areas—maintenance allotments for surviving spouses, inheritance arrangements for children, dividing land "to one place," and allowing parents to inherit from their children. None of these questions were addressed in the Charter. This is a significant omission and deserves some consideration. Given Catherine's attention to detail in other areas of law, it must be assumed that this omission was intentional. It seems clear that Catherine designed the Charter to the Nobility, and the other charters, to concentrate on defining the various social strata in society. Inheritance was a separate issue, and one that Catherine had hoped to deal with in the new ulozhenie. When that new law code never transpired, inheritance issues were left to be dealt with on a piecemeal basis.

Conclusion

By the end of the eighteenth century, the Russian nobility had experienced a number of significant changes in its legal status, rights, and privileges. It had been freed from obligatory service, granted a monopoly on landholding, and promised a number of rights over the land it held. In addition, Catherine had addressed many of the more complex issues of inheritance that had been plaguing the nobility, Senate, and other deciding bodies for decades. Nonetheless, at the close of Catherine's reign many noble complaints remained unanswered. A number of important inheritance issues—such as the inheritance rights of parents and the division between aunts and nieces—would be settled in the early part of the nineteenth century. Other questions, however, such as complete freedom of disposal, the abolition of patrimonial property, and the male preference in inheritance, would continue to be subjects for debate and discussion until the upheaval of 1917. These questions were closely tied to the concepts that had for so long empowered and supported the monarchy—paternalism, kinship, and authority. Any change in the fundamental principles of inheritance law thus threatened the basic principles of the absolute monarchy. Such a link made it impossible for the crown to grant the nobility all of the freedoms it desired.

As Griffiths and Munro wisely point out, the Charter was written to define the nobility's relationship with the crown and with the rest of society. This relationship, however, was defined by the Empress herself and presented to the nobility as a fait accompli.[93] Thus, the privileges and promises the Charter granted to the nobility were limited by the realities of autocracy. Though Catherine fancied herself an enlightened monarch, she was, in the end, still a monarch, and one who had no intention of sharing power in any significant way. As she indicated in her Nakaz, "The Sovereign is absolute; for there is no other Authority but that which centers in his single Person."[94] Thus, even the heralded Charter to the Nobility was just a shadow of what it might have been, and its promises were easily manipulated or subverted by subsequent rulers.[95]

5

Women, Inheritance, and the Boundaries of Kinship

ANY DISCUSSION OF NOBLE LANDHOLDING AND INHERITANCE IN Imperial Russia must naturally include an examination of women and their rights regarding land. A woman—wife or daughter—was an important family member and yet her position was more complex and difficult to define than her male counterparts. A woman's status was strictly defined by the rank of her husband or father, and her position within the household was determined by the men in her life. Daughters were particularly vulnerable to the power politics of the family and the restrictions of society. Since ideally they were destined to leave their natal home and enter another clan through marriage, their place within their own clan was tenuous. As a result, they were the last to inherit and often last in line in other landownership disputes. At the same time, daughters held the potential for power. A well-matched daughter could bring status and prestige to her family, as well as opportunities for advancement through new patronage connections. Conversely, a wealthy daughter who settled for a less-than-wealthy husband might find herself in a position of relative power and authority within her new home.

Once a woman became a wife, there were new issues regarding land that she had to consider. In Imperial Russia, women were allowed to own certain types of land in their own name and had significant control over that property. They also served as guardians for their children's land in certain instances. Moreover, as we have seen, upon her husband's death, a woman was allowed to receive a portion of his estate as a maintenance allotment. The rights of women in landownership changed over time, often the result of noble complaints and legislative debate. Indeed, some of these debates over women's rights to land would last well over a half a century. Recently, some historians have suggested that the changing rights of women over land are a reflection of the development of greater property rights for the nobility as a whole.[1] Thus, the position of women in regards to landownership and inheritance is essential to any understanding of property rights of all nobles.

Generally speaking, women in Imperial Russia enjoyed greater property rights than their Western counterparts. While European women had to wait until well into the nineteenth century before they were deemed capable of managing property, Russian women saw significant change in their rights beginning in the early eighteenth century. In 1715, the Senate issued a decree that permitted women to carry out sales and mortgages in their own names. Three years later, women were promised that confiscation resulting from a husband's crime would not result in the wife's loss of her dowry. Finally, in 1753, a decree gave married women complete legal control over their own property.[2] So well known were Russian women's legal advantages in this realm, that an American illustrated weekly commented on it, somewhat sarcastically, in 1872: "In spite of all these privileges the Russian women are profoundly discontented with their condition . . . Mr. John Stuart Mill's work on the 'Subjection of Women' . . . enjoys immense popularity among them, few of its enthusiastic readers perceiving that they already possess many of the privileges it claims for them."[3]

There were, however, certain areas of property law where women faired less well. Though the decree of 1753 gave married women complete legal control over their own property, among some groups at least, there was still a preference for women to consult their husbands before making any major decisions concerning property. The nobility of Sudislavskii uezd complained in its nakaz that some women squandered all of their fortunes so that when they died there was nothing to leave their husbands; they requested that a wife be required to get her husband's permission to prevent such irresponsibility.[4] Similarly, even after 1753, the law still recognized a woman's probable, or possible, subjection to her husband. With this in mind, a law of 1763 outlawed sale transactions from wives to husbands based on the assumption that women were under the control of their husbands and therefore not in a position to refuse in such instances.[5] Thus, even with Russian women's extended property rights, they were far from equal to men in the eyes of the law. Moreover, like their male counterparts, they were constrained by the powers of the state and the clan.

Dowries

One of the first instances when a family might have to make decisions regarding the dispersal of property to female members was when a daughter got married. The determination of the dowry was one of the most important issues within a family. Usually a reflection of the family's status and wealth, the dowry could help secure a desirable match for the daughter and could offer her some security in her new home, since her dowry property was considered by law to be her own. Because dowries were central to marriage arrangements among Russian nobles, the rules dictating them were the subject of much complaint and debate. Consequently, the laws and customs pertaining to dowries changed over the course of the eighteenth century in some rather significant ways, in some cases resulting in a strengthening of women's rights in landholding.

The issue of daughters and dowries was very closely tied to the problem of inheritance. Daughters often received their share of the inheritance at the time of marriage in the form of a dowry. A dowry could include movable items, such as money, clothing, jewels, icons, and household items, but it also could be land of various types.[6] As in cases of inheritance, initially, the law tried to restrict gifts of dowry land to pomest'e. Thus, on occasion, daughters were granted dowries of pomest'e instead of movables. In 1703, for example, Lev and Iakov Khotiantsov petitioned that they gave their sister Katerina in marriage to Fedor Koliupanov with a dowry from their pomest'e in Epifanskii uezd. According to procedure, Fedor then petitioned and was granted the right to register the land to himself.[7] The Ulozhenie also permitted daughters to use their maintenance allotment of pomest'e as a dowry.

Despite the tendency to restrict the ownership and inheritance of votchina land to male clan members, daughters did receive dowries of votchina. The clan, however, retained an interest in this land. As with a dowry of pomest'e, this land would be registered to the groom. However, he did not have unlimited rights to it. At least as far back as the Sudebnik of 1589 the principle was established that upon a man's death, his widow received her own dowry, among other things. This practice was upheld in the Ulozhenie and subsequent legislation. Moreover, the law stated that if a husband sold his wife's votchina without her knowledge, then upon his death, she could petition and the votchina would be returned to her; the purchaser would be compensated by the heirs of the seller. A husband was not supposed to carry out transactions on his wife's votchina without her permission. In 1741, for example, the Votchina College nullified a mortgage made by Pavel Belolibskii on his wife's dowry property because "that immovable property was not Pavel's, but the dowry of his wife," and according to the law of 1716 he was not entitled to carry out transactions on it without her permission.[8] If in such a case a female died without reclaiming her votchina dowry from an unlawful sale or mortgage, her relatives would be given the right to redeem it according to the rules for redemption in the Ulozhenie.[9]

In the early eighteenth century, the rules pertaining to dowry determination changed rather drastically. On the one hand, Peter's Law of Single Inheritance in 1714 reaffirmed the principle that a woman's immovable dowry property was her own, specifying that the single heir chosen by the father would only receive the father's immovable estate; the mother's dowry land was to pass to her children under separate arrangement.[10] This reaffirmation, however, was only of limited benefit to women, since Peter's law also prohibited the granting of landed dowries to daughters. This new rule created particular hardship for nobles whose wealth was tied up primarily in land and serfs.[11] The dissatisfaction of many nobles on this count was expressed in the Senate report of 1730 that advised Anna to repeal Peter's law. The report argued that the Law of Single Inheritance's stipulation that all dowries be in cash tended to undermine the law's primary purpose of preserving noble estates by forcing fathers with insufficient cash to sell villages in order to establish a lawful dowry. Anna's law of 1731 ended this restriction and ordered that dowries were to be granted as before, according to the Ulozhenie. However, this new freedom was almost immediately curtailed by a law of November 1731, which specified that dowries of immovable property could not include family property, but could be composed only of acquired property.[12]

The case for widows was somewhat different, of course. Many widows remarried with rather substantial dowries. Since 1714 the law had permitted widows to use their *ukaznaia chast,* or widow's portion, as a dowry in a subsequent marriage; thus, a widow could combine that property with her original dowry, which would have returned to her upon her husband's death, to create a larger, more impressive dowry. In 1726, for example, Maria Divova petitioned the Votchina College to register her dowry to her new groom, Boris Shcherbatov. The dowry was composed of the immovable property that she had taken as dowry to her first marriage along with her one-fourth legal portion received after Divov's death.[13]

There was yet another important change regarding women's dowries that took place in the early eighteenth century. As discussed earlier, dowries in the pre-Petrine period were registered in the name of the groom, although the wife was still considered to have a genuine owner's stake in the land and could expect to reclaim the dowry upon her husband's death. Despite a woman's legal right to her dowry, the practice of registering the property to the groom instead of the bride persisted into the eighteenth century. In 1713, for example, Nikita Ivanovich Goriukin agree to marry Natalia Satsyporova, who was given a dowry from her brother's pomest'e. Both Goriukin and his brother-in-law requested that the property be registered to him.[14]

On occasion, this registration practice could lead to misunderstandings or outright fraud. In 1725, following his wife's death, Nikita Vepreskii appealed to the Votchina College for the right to all of the immovable property that she had brought to their marriage in 1708. Vepreskii had registered his wife's dowry to himself in accordance with the law and practice of that time. Now, after her death, he argued that this registration supported his claim to ownership. Vepreskii's claims were rejected by the Votchina College in 1725 and the Senate in 1727 on the basis of the supplemental inheritance law of 1725, which stated that immovable property that had been given to widows or unmarried women prior to the ukaz of 1714 was the sole property of the woman, and her husband had no control or right over it. This included situations where a woman had married before "the points" of 1714 and her land had been registered to her husband.[15]

The practice of registering dowry property to the husband began to fade after the publication of Anna's inheritance law of 1731. Although the exact year in which this change occurred is unclear, by the early 1740s it had become common practice for the dowry to be registered to the bride herself instead of her groom. In 1742, for example, Corporal Sergei Semenovich Cheglokov of the Preobrazhenskii Regiment, requested that the dowry property in Toropetskii and Rzhevskii uezds belonging to his wife, Aksinia Matveevna, be registered to her. In 1754, Iakov Semenovich Barantsov made the same request concerning his wife's dowry property in Livenskii uezd.[16] Of course, there are also examples of women petitioning on their own behalf. Thus in April 1774, Marfa Markova, who had married Egor Nikitivich Markov in 1768 with a dowry of immovable property in Zubtsovskii and Staritskii uezds, petitioned that the land be registered in her name.[17]

Whether the dowry had been registered to the bride or the groom, its return to the woman was, at least in legal terms, considered a guaranteed right. This is not to say that there were not challenges to this right by family or other interested parties. Despite her legal rights, occasionally a woman had to fight to obtain the return of her dowry. In May 1728, for example, Ekaterina Shinshina petitioned the Empress that her husband Alexei Danilovich had left her and taken up residence with his house servant (*dvorovaia devka*), Natalia Semenovna. When confronted with his sin, Alexei married the girl off to Ivan Merkulov with a dowry of 2,000 rubles, the very dowry that Ekaterina had brought to their marriage. Furthermore, she argued, once Natalia was married off, Alexei conspired with his mistress and her brother to kill Merkulov. Ekaterina went on to plead that she was currently unaware of her husband's whereabouts, but was herself in dire financial straits and requested that she be compensated for her loss from her husband's movable and immovable property. Although the record of this case contained no apparent conclusion, it is an interesting example of a woman recognizing and vocalizing claim to her dowry.[18]

The return of a woman's dowry did not always involve such contention and drama. Many examples demonstrate that a woman's dowry was given undisputed preferential treatment in the settlement of a deceased's property. In 1753, for example, the widow of Brigadir Fedor Kochenevskii, the childless Tatiana, and the deceased's brother Kiril petitioned Her Majesty, declaring that as the closest heirs remaining after Fedor, they had come to an amicable agreement to divide all of Fedor's movable and immovable property into two even portions. One portion was to be given to Tatiana with the understanding that she could not later ask for the return of her dowry. The other portion was to go in permanent and inheritable possession to his remaining brothers Kiril and Mikhail and the young children of their deceased brother, Ivan. They drew up their petition for this division of property and requested that the Empress sanction their agreement. Elizabeth, however, was savvy enough to question the amicable nature of this agreement and chose to settle the matter differently. In an ukaz to the Senate, she ordered that instead of the requested division, Tatiana's dowry, which consisted of 7,000 rubles and various other items, should be returned to her, and Fedor's movable and immovable property then divided between the widow and Fedor's legal heirs. Thus, even in a case where a woman was willing to forfeit her dowry, Elizabeth enforced the law on dowry return.[19]

The sanctity of a woman's dowry also extended to the arena of confiscation. According to a law of May 26, 1718, a woman's dowry was not to be confiscated for the crimes of her husband.[20] This did not prevent such confiscation from taking place, however, and it was thus common for women to invoke this law in an effort to retrieve wrongly confiscated property. In 1729, for example, Anna Mikhailovna Nikitina requested compensation for her lost dowry, which had been confiscated along with the property of her husband, the fiscal Alexei Nikitin. On January 22, 1724, an ukaz had ordered the confiscation of all of Alexei's movable and immovable property as punishment for taking bribes and "scorning his duties as fiscal." Anna's dowry was among the confiscated property, much of which was sold. In October 1730, the Senate decided to give Anna the money received from the sale of her husband's homes and possessions as compensation for her loss, basing its decision on the law of 1718.[21] Thus, it would seem that in the early eighteenth century, women were gaining greater rights in the realm of dowries and these rights were recognized and supported in the courts.

Widows and the Ukaznaia Chast

A similar evolution occured in the legal rights of widows. It will be recalled that by the close of the seventeenth century a widow was entitled to receive a maintenance allotment, or prozhitok, from her husband's service land together with the return of her dowry, to the degree to which that was possible. She also might receive some of her husband's purchased estates. Votchina was only granted when there was a shortage of pomest'e and in such cases, the widow was forbidden from alienating that land during her lifetime. In addition to her immovable allotment, a widow could expect to receive one-fourth of her husband's movable property.

The Law of Single Inheritance significantly altered the allotment for widows, giving a childless widow all of her husband's immovable property for her use until she died, remarried, or took religious vows, at which time the land returned to her husband's clan.[22] She was not permitted to alienate this land. This article, however, referred to only childless widows, so in a supplementary article Peter granted widows of both types the right to one-fourth of their husband's movable and immovable property as a life portion, which included the right to use that property as a dowry in a subsequent marriage. A woman's rights to this ukaznaia chast, or legal portion, ended with her death, when it returned to her husband's clan.[23]

A review of contemporary Senate documents demonstrates how this aspect of the law functioned in practice. Some nobles certainly viewed this new rule as a blessing. In 1716, for example, Stepan Buzheninov complained that when his brother Moisei died in 1714, all of his property had gone to his childless widow, Tatiana. Now, Stepan, pointed out, the law had been changed to allow widows only one-fourth of the property, and so he requested that the property be redivided according to this new rule.[24] Soon, the one-fourth portion became the understood norm. In 1728, for example, Avdotia Samarina petitioned the Senate for her one-fourth share, stating that, prior to his death, her husband Semen Mikhailovich had allotted one-fourth of his movable and immovable property to her in a written will in accordance with the law.[25] Even if the deceased had not specified such division in a will, however, the eligible parties still received their ukaznaia chast. Thus, when Savva Mavrin died on November 8, 1719, he left behind a widow, Tatiana Ivanovna, and a brother, Sisoi. Sisoi, as the only heir, petitioned and was granted three-fourths of his brother's movable and immovable property, having acknowledged in his petition his sister-in-law's right to the remaining quarter.[26]

Anna's repeal law of 1731, as we have seen, enacted significant changes in the rights of a widow to a portion of her husband's land. In a new inheritance statute, Anna reduced the widow's portion to one-seventh of her husband's immovable property, but gave real meaning to the phrase "possession in perpetuity" by giving a widow the right to sell or mortgage her portion and to appoint heirs.[27] Later legislation would underline this new right by emphasizing that the one-seventh allotment of a surviving spouse should go to that person's clan upon his or her death, so long as the widow or widower had requested the portion prior to death.[28]

The impact of this rule upon actual practice is demonstrated by an abundance of archival evidence. After 1731, we find numerous petitions from women asking for, and being granted, their allotted one-seventh portion of their husband's immovable property. On June 13, 1732, for example, the Votchina College decided to grant Sofia Mezintsova her one-seventh portion of her first husband's immovable property in Volnovskii and Kholmyshkii uezds; the remainder was allotted to her daughter, Maria. Although Sofia's husband, Grigorii, had died before Anna's law came into effect, the matter was not settled until after 1731, and therefore, had to be decided according to the new law.[29]

The definition of a woman's allotted portion was a very precise matter. When Nikita Vozzhinskii died, he left behind immovable property in Pereslavlskii, Kromskii, Bielozerskii, and Koporskii uezds totaling 520 chetverts and 234 souls, as well as a stone house in St. Petersburg and a wooden house in Moscow. He also left a childless wife, Elena Konstiantinovna, who according to the ukaz of 1731 was entitled to an allotted portion of one-seventh of the total immovable property, or seventy-eight chetverts and thirty-four souls. In ca. 1763, Vozzhinskii's brother, Ivan, filed a petition to Her Majesty for permission to divide the property with his sister-in-law. Catherine ordered that an inventory be made of all the property, a task that proved difficult since the two parties disagreed and accused each other of deception. The case was eventually settled by Catherine's ukaz to the Senate of October 11, 1766. This ukaz ordered that Elena be given sixteen servants with their spouses and children, where applicable, and the stone house in St. Petersburg. However, since these items were valued at 3,600 rubles, this put Elena above her one-seventh share, obliging her to pay a balance to Ivan of 2,305 rubles 85¾ kopecks. The rest of the property was to be given to Ivan.[30]

Upon the death of her husband, a widow had inheritance rights that went beyond her allotted one-seventh of her late husband's estate. She was also entitled to receive her dowry, any lands that she had purchased herself, and any acquired lands that her husband had elected to give her. The latter situation was addressed in a law of October 20, 1745. Natalia Ivanovna Baskakova, widow of Andrei von Vitten, petitioned about the decision of the Malorussian General Military Court and the General Military Chancellery in 1744, which had assigned the movable and immovable property of her husband to his nephew, General Mayor von Vitten. The military court decisions were based on a will that her husband had written in 1739, prior to their marriage. At its writing he was still a widower. The following year, however, von Vitten married Natalia. The first will was renounced by a petition, and in 1741 he wrote another will leaving all his property to her. The Senate took up this affair and found that Natalia was correct: although her husband had named his nephew Khristofor von Vitten as his heir in a will of July 26, 1739, that will had been canceled in 1740 when he married Natalia. Furthermore, since that land did not come from his father or grandfather, but had come to him after his first wife died childless, the law permitted him to give it all to his second wife.[31]

Inheritance and Daughters

Yet another instance when a family would likely have to disperse land to women was at the time of a father's death. Until Anna's repeal law of 1731, a daughter's right to inherit hinged on the absence of living brothers. Peter's Law of Single Inheritance reinforced this virtual exclusion of females by demanding that fathers leave their immovable property to one child—a son—or in the absence of sons, a daughter. With Anna's law, however, daughters were guaranteed a legal portion of one-fourteenth of their father's property and, significantly, their portions were carved out first, and only then were the brothers permitted to divide the remaining property. If, for some reason, a daughter failed to receive her legal portion before she died, her children could petition for it, as did the children of Avdotia (Tsyzyreva) Lonskaia who, in 1770, inquired about the inheritance of which their mother had petitioned in 1736.[32] Thus, as of 1731, an unmarried daughter's inheritance rights were relatively secure; as we will see, the rights of married daughters were more problematic.

There was, however, one circumstance in which a daughter's right to inherit continued to be called into question. The debate centered around the rights of aunts to inherit property in shares with their nieces; that is, the rights of the deceased's sister to split land with the deceased's daughter. This situation usually occurred when there were no male heirs in that particular branch of the family. As discussed earlier, a woman's right to inherit votchina from her father had been somewhat tenuous if she had nephews and nieces, children of a deceased brother. Although a law of 1676 had given daughters the right to inherit along with their nieces and nephews, in 1677 this decision was overturned and it was ordered that aunts were not to be included in inheritance with nephews, citing the Ulozhenie's rule that sisters could not receive votchina in the presence of brothers. The law thus provided that in this situation the property of the deceased should be given first to his grandsons (the deceased son's sons), excluding daughters and granddaughters (the deceased son's sisters and daughters). The aunt and her niece could inherit only if her brother and brother's son were dead.[33] This was reaffirmed in 1691, when it was ordered that in the case of a deceased son without male heirs, the property was to be given to the deceased son's daughter and his sister in shares (see figure 5.1).[34] Thus, the principle was reiterated that sisters in the presence of brothers could not be votchinnitsi, even upon the brothers' deaths, so long as there were male heirs. In the absence of male heirs, sisters shared the inheritance with their nieces, the female heirs of their brothers.[35]

Despite the establishment of this rule about aunts and nieces, the issue continued to elicit debate and confusion throughout the eighteenth century. Part of the confusion involved the question of when the male (the aunt's brother, the niece's father) had died. The law of 1691 had stipulated that if a son predeceased his father, then the father's property should be given to his daughter (the aunt) and his granddaughter (the niece) in shares. This was to occur only if the son had died before his father, however. Otherwise, the son's daughter would be the sole heir and his sister would have no claims on his property. The key question was whether or not the son had ever possessed the land. If he had, his daughter's right was secure; if he had died before ever assuming

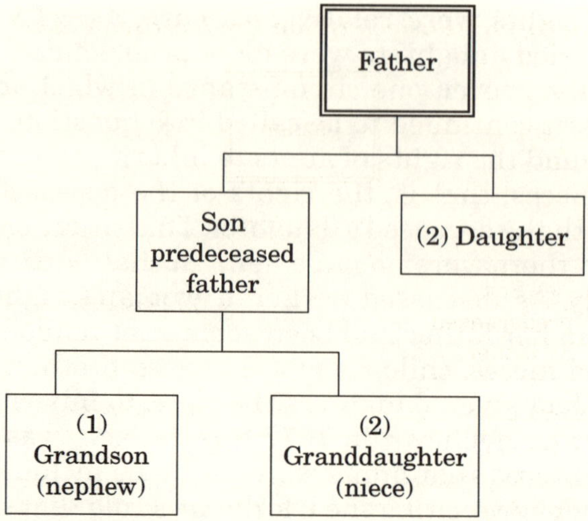

Order of inheritance:
(1) grandson (nephew)
(2) daughter and granddaughter (niece) in shares

Figure 5.1. ***The Law of 1691***

possession of the land, his daughter had to share the land with his sister, her aunt (see figure 5.2).

This stipulation of the law was repeatedly challenged and misunderstood by petitioners and the courts alike. Thus, in 1728, Avdotia Fedorovna Burdukova initiated a suit, claiming that she should be granted the property of her brother Danil in Kostromskii uezd in shares with her niece, Danil's daughter, Anna. Danil had received this property from their father, although Avdotia claimed that the property had never been registered to him, but instead had been in the possession of their mother. Thus, when Danil and their mother both died in 1724, Avdotia saw an opportunity to obtain this land. Anna and her mother disputed Avdotia's claims, however, and the suit dragged on for years. Finally, in 1750 the Senate declared that Avdotia was entitled only to a one-fourteenth share of her father's property which, according to the records of the Guberniia Chancellery, Danil had indeed possessed. The remainder was to go to Danil's daughter, Anna. The crucial fact in this case was that Danil had died *after* his father, and his possession of the land in question meant that his daugh-

Inheritance Pattern if Son Predeceased Father

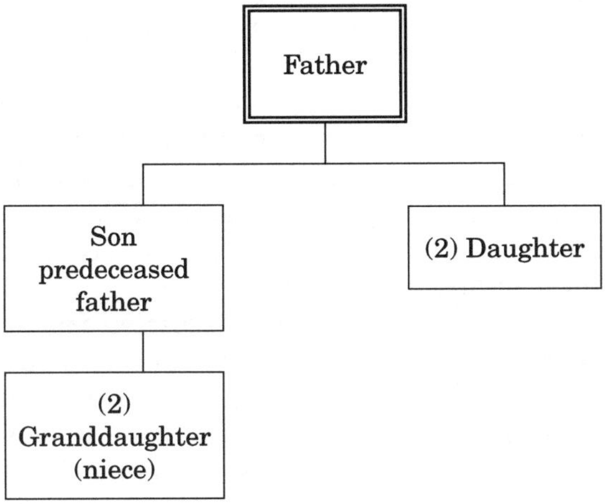

Granddaughter (niece) and daughter (aunt) would share inheritance.

Inheritance Pattern if Son Died after Father

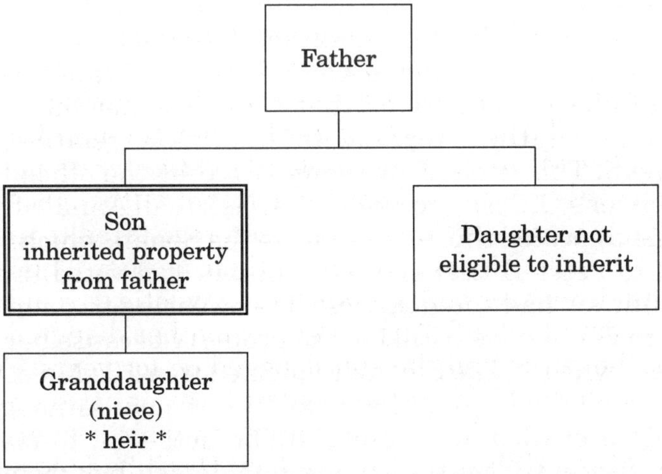

If the son died after his father, then when the son died, only his daughter would be eligible to inherit, according to the standard order of inheritance.

Figure 5.2.

ter's right to inherit superceded his sister's right. Had Danil predeceased his father, Avdotia's claims would have been valid.[36]

Despite the apparent clarity of this stipulation, this inheritance rule continued to cause confusion throughout the eighteenth century. In 1764, for example, the Senate concluded a case that had plagued the courts for some twelve years. The Senate decided that upon the death of Andrei Sontsev-Zasekin, his property was to be divided between his sisters, Maria and Irina, and his granddaughter, and their grandniece, Avdotia (see figure 5.3). In fact, the Senate had come to this decision in 1754, but then a later Senate decision of 1756 had overturned that division and ordered instead that the property be given solely to Andrei's sisters. Thus, even the Senate found this inheritance question to be a perplexing one. In its final decision of 1764, however, the Senate reaffirmed the law of 1691 and its decision of 1750 in the case discussed previously and the property was to be divided between the aunts and their neice. Once again, the significant fact in the 1764 decision was that Andrei's son had predeceased him, thus opening the way for Maria and Irina to inherit.[37]

The outcome was even more uncertain for a daughter whose mother predeceased her father. In such a case, the granddaughter might be denied the right to inherit the property of her grandfather precisely because her mother had died first and thus was never the legal heir. In 1726, Anna Iurlova petitioned the Senate about the property of her grandfather, Mikhail Shekhovskii. Because Anna's mother had predeceased her grandfather, the Votchina College had decided that Anna was not the legal heir and had given the property to her male relative, Alexei Shekhovskii. This decision was supported by the officials in the Reketmeister's Office, who went so far as to call Anna "of an alien rod." Anna appealed these decisions to the Senate which, in 1728, reported to Peter II that sixteen senators had voted in favor of Anna, while six had voted against her, declaring that she was "of an alien rod" and not entitled to the property because her mother had never owned it. The Senate requested that His Majesty issue an ukaz along the lines of the majority decision. Although Anna ultimately prevailed, it is important to note that to many officials, her descent from the female line denied her membership within her grandfather's clan.[38] Within two decades, however, a granddaughter's right to inherit directly from her grandfather was more secure. When in 1741 Ekaterina Vasilchikova peti-

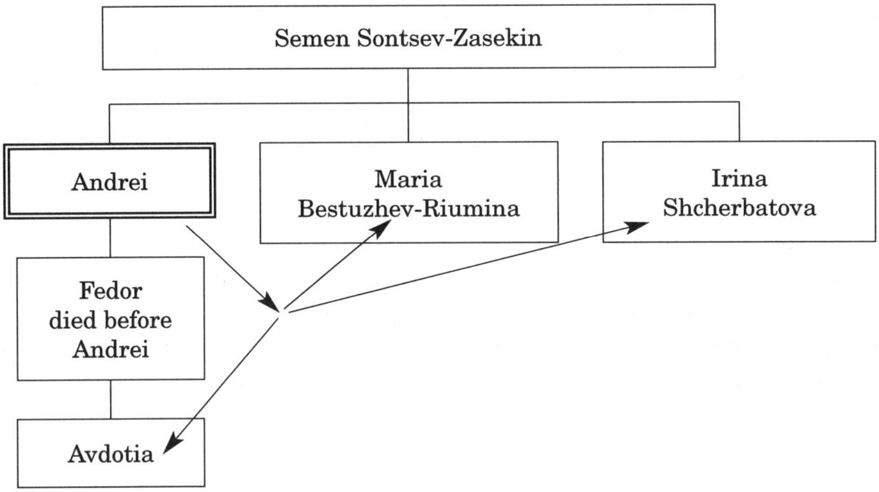

In this case, because Fedor predeceased his father, Andrei's property was divided between his granddaughter, Avdotia, and his sisters, Maria and Irina.

Figure 5.3. ***The Sontsev-Zasekin Family***

tioned for the property of her grandfather, Afonasii, the Votchina College granted her request. There was no mention of her being from an alien rod, though the circumstances of the case were identical to those of the earlier case.[39]

The debate over the inheritance rights of aunts versus nieces would continue to challenge the courts through the end of the century. In 1794, the Senate concluded a five-year-old case concerning the property of Pavel Glazunov, who died childless in 1788. Both Pavel's sister, Anna, and his niece, Olga, claimed to be the rightful heir. Initially, the uezd court had decided to give the property in its entirety to Olga, but this decision was overturned by the Orlov Upper Land Court and later by the Senate. The Senate ultimately decided that because Olga's father predeceased his brother, Pavel, he was never Pavel's heir and therefore Olga could not claim to be the sole heir. Instead, the Senate ordered that Olga and Anna were equally heirs to Pavel's property.[40]

The inheritance battle between aunts and nieces highlights a number of observations about property law in the eighteenth century. First, the continuing uncertainty concerning this question and the repeated misinterpretations of the law provides some indication of the confused state of Russia's legal system at this time. Even the Senate itself was unclear on how to decide this question and on more than one occasion overturned its own decisions. Second, despite the relatively advanced property rights of women in eighteenth-century Russia, this inheritance question shows that even at the end of the century, there was still a strong preference for males as heirs. The women in the cases discussed above were eligible to inherit only because there were no male heirs in the immediate family. As we will see in subsequent chapters, a woman was often the heir of last resort when a male family member died without children and their rights were sometimes called into question in cases of redemption. A woman's right to inherit was even more tenuous if she was married.

The Inheritance Rights of Married Daughters

The inheritance rights of married daughters was another important legal issue addressed in the eighteenth century and early nineteenth centuries, and one that had important implications about clan definition and a woman's place within her father's clan. Historically, a married daughter was considered an undesirable heir, but there were many different circumstances that could make this arrangement necessary. On occasion, a married daughter might be the only heir available within an extended family. In such cases, the law tried to ameliorate the problems associated with giving land to a daughter who had essentially already left her natal clan. Peter's Law of Single Inheritance, for example, required that when the last surviving member of a clan willed his family estate to a female member, her husband and his heirs were obliged in perpetuity to attach her family name to theirs. If they refused, subsequent legislation decreed, the property would go to the state.[41] In such a case, then, the married woman was seen as the last remnant of her clan and thus the perpetuation of her family name by her husband and heirs was deemed essential.

Not all circumstances were so extreme, of course. Often married daughters remained as the only heirs within their immediate families, as well. If there were no other children to inherit, then a married daughter received her father's property as the only surviving heir. In 1741, for example, the Votchina College ordered that Timofei Kuzmenkov's immovable property in Karachevskii uezd should be divided between his two married daughters, Alena and Agrafena, as the only surviving heirs.[42] Even a granddaughter could inherit under such circumstances if her mother, the sole heir, had predeceased her grandfather. In such a case, the granddaughter would step into the mother's shoes, so to speak, and her marital status was not given much attention.[43] So long as there were no rival male heirs, a married woman's claims were usually upheld. Under such dire circumstances, lawmakers tended to emphasize a married daughter's membership in her father's clan over her transfer into her husband's clan. If there were rival male heirs, particularly brothers, the situation became somewhat more complicated. The issue revolved around this dilemma: Was a married daughter always entitled to a share of her father's property when he died, or did it depend on the amount and composition of the dowry she had received when she married?

This issue was more complex than may immediately be apparent. Russian law had never specified the amount of property that a daughter was entitled to as a dowry.[44] Peter's law of 1714 had forbidden land dowries but had not defined the size of a movable dowry, leaving room for disagreement and debate between family members. In 1727, for example, in the dispute over Vasilii Zeremskii's property, one of the hopeful owners declared that Zeremskii's sisters were not eligible heirs to this land because they had all been married with dowries long before their brother's death.[45]

Nor was this omission corrected with the repeal of Peter's law. Although the inheritance law of 1731 permitted land dowries according to the rules of the Ulozhenie, it did not specify the preferred size of a dowry. At the same time, the law did establish a specific inheritance portion for daughters, one-fourteenth of their father's immovable property. The discrepancy between these two elements of the law created much confusion for courts and lawmakers in subsequent years. Essentially, these parties had to determine whether a woman's dowry was truly an advance on her inheritance, even to the extent of granting her a portion of her father's property at the time of his death if her dowry had been less than the specified one-fourteenth inheritance portion.[46]

This problem was recognized by the Votchina College almost immediately after the publication of Anna's law. In a report of June 1732, it recommended to the Senate that a married daughter should be given a share of her father's immovable property, even in the presence of brothers and unmarried sisters. The specific meaning of this vague recommendation is unclear; in any event, the suggestion went nowhere and the Senate failed to issue an ukaz about this problem.[47] Inheritance disputes also reflect the early recognition of this legal question. In the records of the Senate, for example, we find the 1733 petition of Natalia Korobova whose parents had recently died leaving behind one son and four daughters. Natalia asked to be granted her legal portion from her father's immovable property in Vladimirskii uezd, for although she was now married, she had not been given a dowry of any sort; this, she declared, entitled her to a share of her father's property.[48]

Although Korobova's case record contained no conclusion, there are other archival and published sources that indicate that for several decades after Anna's law, the courts tended to rule that a dowry of any sort was to be considered a renunciation of future claims on inheritance. In her work on women and property in Imperial Russia, Michelle Marrese cites the case of Avdotia, daughter of Prince Shakhovskii, who in 1731 claimed that as the eldest daughter she was entitled to three-fourths of her father's estate according to the Law of Single Inheritance. The Votchina College denied her request, and emphasized that Avdotia's acceptance of a dowry, even of movable property, was tantamount to a renunciation of her father's immovable property.[49]

This certainly seems to have been the assumption of many family members, eager to exclude rival heirs. In 1741, for example, Danil Tarkhov defended his wife's claim to her father's property by emphasizing that her sister had been married with a dowry before the death of her father.[50] This became a recurrent theme of petitions: litigants in inheritance disputes frequently argued that their female relative had been married with a sufficient dowry and was thus ineligible for further grants. In 1732, for example, Maria Maslova petitioned the Senate, stating that in 1725 her father-in-law died, leaving behind five children—her husband, the heir, and his four married sisters. Her husband, Ivan, petitioned to have the land registered to himself, but before this was accomplished he was called into service and died. In response to Maria's petition, the Votchina College decreed that she should receive her legal portion from her husband's share of the property, the other shares going to his sisters. Maria appealed this decision to the Senate, emphasizing that all of the sisters had been married with villages and substantial dowry grants, thereby making them ineligible to receive any further property.[51]

The married daughter did not have to be one of the disputants for this issue to be raised. In 1735, Ivan Tyrtov requested that the property of his deceased wife, Stefanida, be divided between him and his three unmarried daughters. In this and subsequent petitions, Ivan underlined the fact that his eldest daughter Sophia had been married with a dowry and was thus not a participant in the inheritance division. Although Ivan's dispute was with his sister-in-law, he thought it important to clarify why one of his daughters was not eligible to participate in their claim.[52] Similarly, in July 1749, Petr Sokovnin petitioned the Votchina College about assigning his immovable property in various uezds to his wife and children. In his listing of the specific division, he stated that his married daughter Natalia was to receive nothing since she had been given a dowry of movable property and money.[53] Even as late as 1764, Catherine decided that the eldest daughter of the merchant Fedor Volodimirov was not entitled to a share of her father's estate since she had been given a dowry when she married.[54]

The tide began to turn for married daughters, however, in the early years of Catherine's reign. Some of the noble nakazy expressed a desire to distribute land by inheritance to married daughters. Moreover, in the notes of the Votchina College of 1767, probably written in response to the calling of the Legislative Commission, it was recommended that married daughters who had received a sufficient dowry not be granted any further property. If a daughter was married without a dowry, however, or with a dowry that was smaller than the legal portion, then the Votchina College suggested that she be duly compensated.[55] These opinions are reflected in subsequent legislation. In 1770, for example, the Senate upheld the Votchina College's decision of 1768 that Anna Somova was entitled to her legal portion of inheritance since she had been married "in the points" of the Law of Single Inheritance, when daughters were not permitted to receive dowries of immovable property.[56] In 1772, this ruling was taken a step further. The Senate ordered that Daria Lavrova was to be given one-fourteenth of her father's estate since she had been given a dowry of only two female house serfs when she married in 1712. Whereas the former Senate decision seemed to be an attempt to right the injustice of Peter's prohibition of immovable dowries, the latter Senate decree compensated a daughter who had been married prior to Peter's law. Thus, although Daria's family had been permitted by law to give her a dowry of immovable property, the fact that they did not (or could not) did not diminish her claims later to a portion of her father's estate. In this way, even a family's conscious decision about the size and makeup of a dowry essentially could be overruled long after the deciding parties were dead.[57]

Over time, the validity of a daughter's claim to further inheritance became linked to the question of whether or not she had renounced her share in writing.[58] Thus, in 1787, the Votchina College ordered that Maria Zinovieva should receive her legal portion from the property of her father, Andrei Molchanov. Only then would her brothers Nikolai and Ivan be allowed to divide the remainder between themselves. Furthermore, their claims that Maria should receive only her mother's land, since she had received a dowry from her father's land when she was married, were overruled. The Votchina College's investigation determined that the brothers' claims were entirely false—not only had Maria received only movable property when she married in 1759, but there had never been any agreement on her part to renounce her legal portion of their father's immovable property.[59] Such disputes could be avoided if fathers stated in petitions of dowry registration that the dowry was to be given in lieu of further inheritance. Thus in 1776, Ivan Shatilov stated that he had agreed to give his daughter Natalia in marriage with a dowry of movable and immovable property with the understanding that this would be in place of her legal portion, emphasizing that she had no further claims on his property.[60]

Although the Senate rulings of the 1770s favored the rights of daughters in the question of dowry versus inheritance, the issue was far from settled and women did not have automatic preference in these cases. In 1789, for example, the Senate decided that Avdotia Vadbolskaia, the daughter of State Councillor Semen Molchanov, was not entitled to a share of her father's immovable property in Aleksinskii, Epifanskii, and Versiskii uezds. Although Avdotia claimed that she was married in 1751 with a small dowry of only movable property, the Senate was persuaded by the testimonies of her sister and stepmother who stated that Avdotia had received a substantial amount of money with which she purchased villages and 102 serfs. Overturning an earlier decision of the Votchina College, the Senate declared that Avdotia had received a dowry when she married and so was not entitled to any of her father's remaining estate. The Senate further elaborated that since the time of the Ulozhenie, a specified dowry amount had never been determined, but had always been left to the discretion of the parents and the prospective grooms. Thus, Avdotia should be content with the dowry that she had received.[61]

The previous case illustrates that even at this late date the question of a married daughter's inheritance rights was still not clearly resolved. This dilemma would only be settled in the Digest of Laws in the early nineteenth century, where it was established that daughters could be excluded from further inheritance only if they had agreed to renounce their legal portion in writing.[62]

Women and Redemption

One final example of how the property rules for women differed from those for men can be found in the laws of redemption, the legal right of family members to repurchase land that was sold or mortgaged outside the rod. The legal rules of redemption will be discussed in detail in a subsequent chapter, but it is useful to examine those pertaining to women here as well. As with other areas of property law, Russia's redemption laws had always favored males over females. This continued to be true in the eighteenth century. In 1744 Elizabeth defined the order of eligible redeemers in keeping with the laws of inheritance; if there were no sons, then daughters would be allowed to redeem, beginning with unmarried daughters and extending to married or widowed daughters in the absence of the former. The right of redemption in the female line would extend only to the daughters' sons and unmarried daughters; married or widowed granddaughters of daughters were not eligible for redemption.[63] Two decades later, the law of 1766 extended the right of redemption to more remote females. In the absence of sons, daughters and granddaughters (daughters of deceased sons) would equally be eligible for redemption; in the absence of these, then the redemption right passed to his daughter's children, first males, then females. Once all eligible heirs in the descending line had been exhausted, eligibility moved to the collateral line, to uncles and nephews; in the absence of these eligibility would be extended first to the seller's sisters and nieces (daughters of deceased brothers), and then to the sisters' sons and daughters.[64] Despite these restrictions, women did succeed in redeeming family property, both in cases where they were the only redeemers and in cases where the other eligible redeemers, male and/or female, renounced their right to redemption.

Married women, however, were less secure in their rights and were either ineligible or the least desirable redeemers. Again, this prejudice was linked to the uncertain place of a woman within her father's clan once she married and took another name. As we have already seen, neither lawmakers nor family members were consistent in their decisions on this question. As the law of 1744 illustrates, though married daughters were not the preferred redeemers, even their tenuous claim to rod membership was apparently deemed superior to leaving the property in completely alien hands. Thus, when there were no other eligible redeemers a married woman could redeem property of her father's clan. The law of 1766 omitted the distinction between unmarried and married daughters, perhaps an early indication of the changing attitudes toward married women. Yet the dilemma of married daughters and redemption continued into the nineteenth century. In 1815 the question again arose as to whether a married woman would be allowed to redeem property of her original clan. The law clearly indicated in its wording that a married woman had "transferred into another clan." Nonetheless, it was determined that she could enjoy the right of redemption. Furthermore, it was determined that property sold to a married woman, despite her new name, could not be redeemed by her original clan members, since the laws of redemption clearly stated that property sold or mortgaged to another family member was not eligible for redemption.[65]

Conclusion

All of the property issues discussed in this chapter point to the conclusion that a woman's place within the clan was tenuous and not always supported by law once she married and took another clan's name. Thus, in all cases of inheritance, males were preferred to females and unmarried daughters were preferred to married daughters. Although the debate about married daughters receiving a share of inheritance can also be interpreted as one over fairness and equality in property distribution, there is little doubt that at least part of the issue at hand concerned the undesirability of giving family land to a daughter. Many laws had, in fact, defined a generational cut-off point beyond which females were no longer eligible to inherit. It was only in 1823 that the State Council rejected this principle and ordered that males should not be automatically preferred over more distant females in a descending line.[66]

This discussion also indicates that in all matters concerning women and land, it would seem that the boundaries of kinship were flexible and depended upon the circumstances at hand. When the clan was in dire straits, perhaps on the brink of extinction, a married woman who had "transferred into another clan" might still be considered a viable, if undesirable, heir. She could also be considered an heir for purposes of preventing excessive acts of redemption. On the other hand, when family members quarreled over property, all bets were off and disgruntled claimants were quick to label their married sisters and cousins "of an alien rod." Lawmakers, in an attempt to address this problem, often contradicted themselves or overturned previous interpretations. Consequently, even by the early nineteenth century a married woman's clan status had yet to be determined with any clarity.[67]

6
The Best-Laid Plans: The Problem of the Childless Landowner

> The chief news of the day, which all Moscow is talking about, is the death of old Count Bezukhof and his will . . . it is Monsieur Pierre who has inherited everything . . . been declared legitimate, and is therefore Count Bezukhof, and the possessor of the finest fortune in Russia.
>
> —Tolstoi, *Voina i mir*

DESPITE THEIR BEST ATTEMPTS, RUSSIAN LAWMAKERS COULD NOT anticipate every possible circumstance that might arise with the death of a landowner. Throughout the Imperial period, then, the state was forced to respond to specific inheritance questions that fell outside of the general rules. One such question was that of the childless landowner. In dealing with this problem, Russian lawmakers established rules that were consistent with the other laws of inheritance. Specifically, the laws on childless landowners stressed the importance of the clan, sometimes over the rights of the individual and, much like the question of women and inheritance, raised interesting questions about definitions of kinship and its importance in the most fundamental elements of everyday life. Men were, as always, the preferred heir and a woman's right to inherit was determined by the absence of a male heir and by her proximity to the childless landowner. This seemingly narrow question, then, can be used as yet another window through which we can better understand the nature of noble landholding in Imperial Russia.

The determination of who should receive the property of a childless landowner was an important decision since many landowners died without heirs in Imperial Russia. Historians have estimated that for Western Europe approximately 17 percent of parents would die without any heirs. The percentage is even higher for the cases used in this study; approximately 27.6 percent mentioned a childless landowner, some describing as many as five childless landowners in one family.[1] The term "childless" could mean that the landowner had never had children, or that all his children had predeceased him without issue of their own.[2] Thus the discussion of the childless landowner pertains to situations where there were no heirs whatsoever in the descending line. A childless landowner, of course, could also be a woman, and this situation was more complex, because the fate of the property depended on its origins and on the vacillating opinion of lawmakers about the scope of clan membership. Given the frequency of this problem, it was essential that the inheritance laws take this dilemma into consideration.

The Childless Landowner

The earliest mention of the problem of the childless landowner appears in the 1550 Sudebnik, which decreed that when a male landowner died intestate, with no descendants, his property should be given to his next of kin. This arrangement, however, was too vague and required elaboration in later years. Subsequent legislation, in keeping with traditional inheritance patterns, favored collateral relatives in the male line of the clan. The Ulozhenie, for example, stated that if a childless landowner died intestate, his votchina should be given "into the clan of the deceased, to natural brothers and to cousins, and into the clan, to whomever is closest."[3] A female collateral relative in this situation was permitted to inherit votchina only if the deceased had named her as heir in a will. This article, however, was still not precise enough, for it failed to define who had the first right of inheritance, the deceased's brothers or his nephews, the sons of other deceased brothers. This question was addressed in a law of March 14, 1676, that ruled that when a man died without children, his brothers and nephews should share the inheritance, receiving the votchina in portions.[4] If he died leaving behind sisters on the one hand and nieces and nephews, children of his deceased brother, on the other, the land was to be given to his sisters and nephews in shares. In the absence of nephews it would go to his sisters and nieces. These arrangements were in accordance with the mandate of the Ulozhenie that sisters in the presence of brothers could not inherit votchina land.[5] This changed in 1677 when a new law specified that in such a case the votchina should be given to the nephews alone, thus preempting the inheritance rights of the deceased's sisters. If there were no nephews then it could be given to the sisters and nieces in portions.[6] In all of these laws, there was a persistent preference for devolution in the male line.

The laws about childless landowners were expanded further in the eighteenth century. Peter's Law of Single Inheritance permitted a childless landowner to give his property to anyone in his family whom he chose, and despite the law's ultimate repeal, this particular stipulation remained in force. This law, then, gave childless landowners considerable freedom of disposal, particularly since it lumped the various types of land into the category of "immovable." Thus in 1740, the Senate ruled on the validity of Lev Chelishchev's will by which he had left his immovable property to his wife and to his brother, Petr. Lev's uncle, Artem, citing his position as a close relative, argued that the will was invalid for a variety of reasons, including illegality and fraud, and that the decision of the Votchina College in 1734 to support the will was incorrect. The Senate, however, reviewed the case and upheld the Votchina College's decision, thereby underscoring the rights of disposal for childless landowners.[7] Similarly, in 1752, Anton Valuev, being childless, wrote a will leaving all of his movable and immovable property to his brother Fedor. This will was witnessed in the Justice College, and upon Anton's death, it was executed. Years later, in 1767, Fedor's widow, Praskovia, petitioned the Votchina College to receive her widow's portion and mentioned this will in describing her husband's various assets. The Votchina College reaffirmed the validity of Anton's will and Praskovia was granted her one-seventh portion from all of her husband's immovable property, including that which he had received from Anton.[8]

Not everyone appreciated the testamentary freedom of childless landowners, however. Disinherited relatives frequently protested the provisions of wills, usually arguing closer proximity to the deceased than the chosen heir. In 1749, for example, Ivan Chebyshev named his cousins Vasilii and Alexander as the heirs to all of his immovable property located in various uezds, minus the portion that his wife would receive. When Ivan died childless in 1757, his niece, Katerina, challenged this decision on the basis that she was the closest eligible relative.[9] Similarly, in 1791, several of Fedor Apraksin's relatives challenged his will, arguing that they were closer to the deceased than the designated heir. Their claim was dismissed.[10] Despite these periodic challenges, lawmakers were fairly consistent in upholding the rights of childless landowners. Consider, for example, the ukaz of February 23, 1804, which sanctioned the will of State Councillor Verderevskii by which he had bequeathed his property to his distant relative Rotmistr Verderevskii, bypassing closer relatives. The ukaz supported Verderevskii's freedom of disposal, citing the Law of Single Inheritance and specifying that the repeal law of 1731 did not abolish this right.[11] Nonetheless, as late as 1811, this question continued to pose a challenge for lawmakers. Thus, when Alexander Sheremetev disinherited his brothers and a nephew in favor of a younger sister, the Moscow Civil Court upheld his will based on the law of 1714. The Senate, however, disagreed and declared the will invalid.[12] Later, in 1818, the State Council supported the right of Supreme Privy Councillor Derzhavin to leave his property to his nephew, even though that individual did not share Derzhavin's family name.[13]

The situation was more complex if the childless landowner was a woman. In such a case, the outcome of the decision depended upon the origins of the property in question and the year in which the decision was being made. The laws pertaining to women's rights regarding property, including dowries and maintenance allotments, changed several times between 1714 and 1731. Peter's law of 1714 did not exclude women in his article on the freedom of disposal for childless landowners. However, there were circumstances that could strip a woman of these rights. Between 1714 and 1716, the law stipulated that a childless widow had usufruct of all of her husband's property until she took religious vows, remarried, or died, at which point the property returned to her husband's clan. During her lifetime, she was not permitted to alienate this land. In 1716, Peter revised this arrangement to grant all widows, with or without children, one-fourth of their husbands' immovable property as a maintenance allotment. Again, the law specified that upon the woman's death, the property was to return to the husband's clan. It was only with Anna's law of 1731 that the widow's portion became her real property, which she could sell, mortgage or bequeath. A woman's dowry, however, was a different matter; Russian tradition and law had long granted women freedom over any property they received as a dowry.

These changes regarding women and property rights determined the fate of a childless woman's property and her freedom of disposal. If the property had originated as a widow's portion, until 1731, it had to be returned to her husband's clan and she had no right to bequeath the land to anyone else. In 1716, for example, Fedor Everlakov petitioned for the immovable property of his deceased, childless aunt, Anna, who had died in 1715 in possession of property that had belonged to her husband, and Fedor's uncle, Iakov Everlakov. Fedor cited current law about the return of a husband's land to his clan, and claimed to be the closest family member. The Senate granted his request. Even had she wanted to, Anna could not have bequeathed this property to anyone else.[14] After 1731, however, a woman had the right to bequeath her widow's portion to whomever she chose. In 1736, for example, the Votchina College granted the request of Daria Frolova regarding the bequeathal of her immovable property. Daria had received the land in Pskovskii uezd as a maintenance allotment after the death of her first husband. She had then remarried, but had no children. Now, suffering from old age and illness, Daria chose to leave her husband Fedor his legal share of her property, and named her brother Vasilii as heir to the remainder. Both Daria and Vasilii petitioned the Votchina College about this arrangement, and in accordance with Anna's law of 1731, the division was approved.[15]

Women did have greater testamentary freedom over property acquired in other ways, however. When a husband chose to give his wife property, separate from the widow's portion, then that property became hers and if she approached death with no heirs, she could bequeath it to whomever she chose, including a new husband. This is precisely what happened in the case of Irina Mukhanova who, while gravely ill, declared before witnesses that she wanted her second husband, Ipat, to be the recipient of her property. These villages included those that had been given to her by her first husband and those that had comprised her dowry when she married the first time.[16] This case illustrates another important point: that if the property in question came to the woman as part of her dowry, she could bequeath it as well.

The abundance of inheritance disputes that came before the various state institutions would indicate, however, that most landowners—male or female—did not write a will or name an heir in advance. In these cases, the standard order of inheritance went into effect. When a childless woman failed to designate an heir, her husband, if she had one, would receive his allotted portion and the remaining property was returned to her clan, to the closest male relative. If there were brothers, they were first in line to inherit. In 1741, for example, Stepan Eremeev Bogdanov petitioned for the immovable property that had belonged to his two childless sisters. The Votchina College granted his request.[17] In the absence of brothers, males in the ascending or descending collateral line inherited. An example of this occurred when Daria Khripunova died childless in 1714. Since she had no descendants or close heirs, the Senate approved the request of her great uncle Grigorii for her property, which had originally belonged to his brother, Daria's grandfather.[18] In a slightly more complex case, when Elena Beketova died childless in circa 1753, the potential heirs to her property in Novgorodskii and Simbirskskii uezds were her aunt Irina, her father's sister, and her cousin Natalia, the daughter of her uncle Ivan, and Irina's niece (see figure 6.1). In that year, the Votchina College ordered that all of Elena's property was to go to her cousin, Natalia, and upon Natalia's death, to her son Ivan. Irina challenged this decision, asking that she be granted the property in halves with Natalia. In 1767, the Senate decided that the decision of the Votchina College had been correct and that the property should go to Natalia, and then to her son Ivan. Irina, although alive, was superseded by the descendants of her deceased brother Ivan, once again demonstrating the principle that male heirs or the descendants of males were almost always preferred to females.[19]

Despite this preference, females did indeed inherit in these circumstances. Thus, when Elena Annenkova died childless, the Senate decided in 1763 to give all of the property that she had inherited from her grandfather and father to her cousin Daria, as the closest member in the Beklemishev clan. Although Daria did not carry the Beklemishev name due to her descent from a female clan member, she was nonetheless an eligible heir by virtue of her descendance from Pakhon Beklemishev, her grandfather and Elena's great-grandfather. Once again, the presiding principle

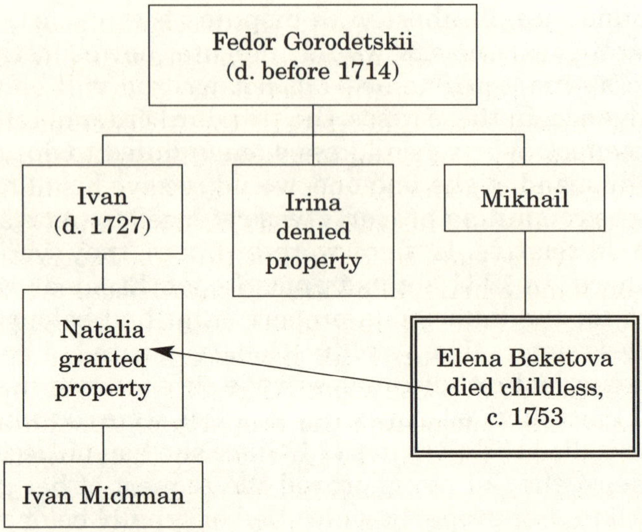

Figure 6.1. ***The Case of the Childless Landowner, Elena (Gorodetskaia) Beketova***

was that the property of a childless woman should be returned to the clan whence it came.[20]

A woman's dowry property, however, was not subject to the rules for a widower's portion. It returned intact to her family. In 1715, for example, when Stefanida Malygin died childless only one year after marrying, her uncle, Polikarp Velezh, claimed possession of the immovable property that she had been granted as a dowry. This property had belonged to the dead woman's father and so according to law had to be returned to the Velezh clan.[21]

The same rules applied for men who died intestate. In the simplest and most straightforward situations, the family property of a childless landowner would go to his brother. In 1741, for example, the Votchina College granted Ivan Spasitelev the immovable property in Moskovskii uezd that had belonged to his childless brother Grigorii, citing the inheritance law of 1731.[22] If there were no brothers, uncles or their descendants could inherit. In 1736, for example, the Votchina College decided that the immovable property of Ivan Sheremetev, who died without children, should be divided in the following way. His widow should receive her one-seventh portion and the remainder was to be divided in thirds. One third was to be given to Ivan's uncle; one third to his nephews and great-great-nephews, the descendants of his brother Boris; and one third to his nephews and great-nephews, the descendants of his brother Vasilii[23] (see figure 6.2). As we have seen, sisters and nieces only inherited in the absence of close male heirs.[24] In January 1741, the Votchina College granted the immovable property of Fedor Kozlov, who had died childless the previous year, in halves to his two sisters, Avdotia and Daria, as his only heirs.[25] It was only in 1805 that the Senate altered the restriction on female heirs, allowing Varvara Klochkova to inherit the land of her childless aunts along with her uncle Maior Lev Azancheev.[26] Sixteen years later, however, a decision of the Ministry of Justice and State Council reaffirmed the preference for the male line. Concerning the property of the childless Ivan Lutovinov, it was decided that his niece, the daughter of his brother, had the right to inherit before his sister, presumably because the niece was descended from a male relative.[27]

There were, however, exceptions to these standard inheritance rules. Even when the property in question was that of a childless male, the provenance of the property was relevant. If the deceased's property had come to him from his mother, it would return to her clan. Thus, in 1764, the Votchina College and Senate decided that the property of the childless Mikhail Kologrivov should be given to his uncle, his mother's brother, Petr Zasetskii, and his heirs. The property in question had belonged previously to Mikhail's mother, Afimia. Afimia had received some of this land as a dowry when she married, received some of it upon her husband's death in 1701, and purchased some of it herself. The Votchina College and Senate ordered that the property should go to the closest male heir in Afimia's family, her brother.[28]

The situation became more complicated when the childless man was the last in his clan, that is, the last male in his family to carry the clan name. On January 23, 1712, Peter the Great issued a law that prohibited the last surviving male of a clan from giving or selling his inherited immovable estate to people outside the clan, either during his lifetime or by means of a will. Instead, he was required to bequeath it to a female within the clan, but no further removed in degree than granddaughters. Beyond that point, the land was to be considered escheated and was to revert to the state. The law of 1712 reaffirmed the traditional tendency of Russian land legislation to protect the interests of the clan even at the expense of the individual. According to this law, indi-

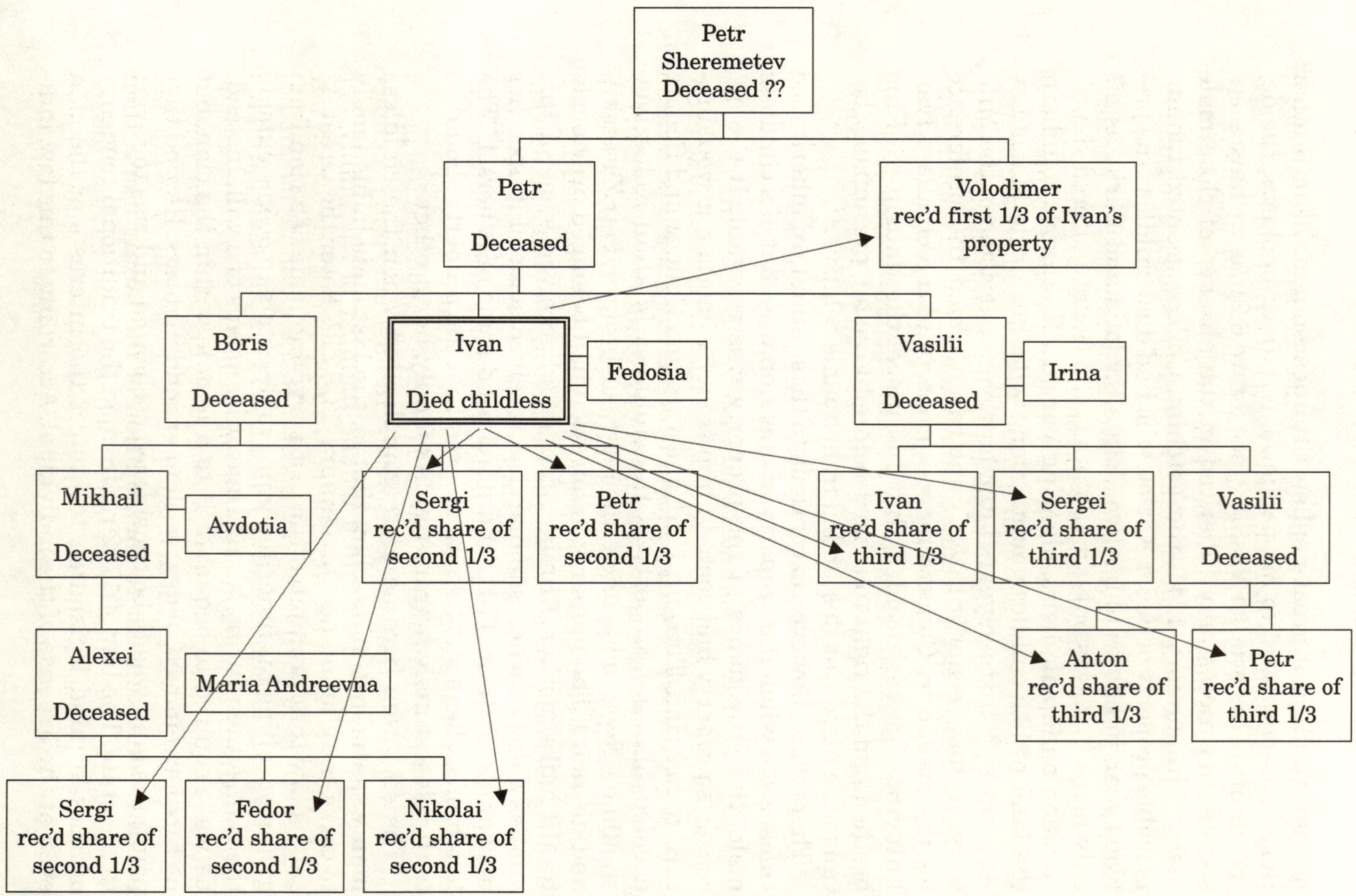

Figure 6.2. ***Inheritance of the Childless Landowner, Ivan Petrovich Sheremetev***

vidual landowners were forbidden from exercising the full rights of ownership over their land, being restricted instead to very specific channels of disposal, namely to female clan members. Although women may not have been the preferred recipients of clan lands, this law established that they were preferable to non-clan members.

There is ample archival evidence to demonstrate that confiscation under the terms of this law did occur. On September 1, 1729, for example, Peter II ordered that the immovable property of General Mayor Vasilii Korchmin be confiscated in accordance with the law of 1712. Three years later that order was carried out by the Chancellery of Confiscation when all of Korchmin's immovable property was "written" to Her Majesty. On occasion, the law was applied in error, when a viable heir was mistakenly, or intentionally, overlooked. In 1716, for example, Martyn Kharlamov requested that his childless uncle's property, which had been written to His Majesty, be given to him, explaining that he had been unable to petition earlier, due to his service in the army. The last in a clan, of course, could also be a woman. In 1728, for example, the Votchina College ordered that the immovable property of the deceased widow Maria Chasnikova should be written to His Majesty since there was no one remaining in her clan, the Kochanovskiis. Three decades later Naval Captain Nikita Pushkin was stripped of property that he had received by will from Fedosia Esipova because, as the last in her clan, she was not permitted to give the land to an outsider. Instead, the property was to be "written" to Her Majesty. Pushkin's repeated pleas to have this decision overturned were to no avail.[29]

In the single inheritance law of 1714, Peter modified the law of 1712 to provide that in cases when the last surviving member willed the family estate to a female member of the family, her husband and his heirs were obliged in perpetuity to attach her family name to theirs. Peter himself set the example for his nobles. When F. I. Romodanovsky died in 1717, Peter married off his two daughters to noblemen on the condition that they adopt their wives' family name.[30] Later, after Peter's death, the supplemental law of 1725 strengthened this point, adding that if no eligible parties would consent to the addition of the family name, then the property would be considered escheated and written to Her Majesty.[31] Thus, although women were considered clan members in many circumstances, their status was clearly different from male members in most matters of inheritance. Moreover, the fate of the clan name was clearly an important factor in determining eligibility.

When a man died childless and was the last to carry his family name, his property would go to the closest family member in the closest female line. For example, Ivan Zherebiatnikov died in 1754, with no children, brothers, or uncles. In 1770, the Senate confirmed the Votchina College decision to give all of Ivan's property to his cousin, Ivan Nagatkin. Nagatkin was the grandson of Zherebiatnikov's aunt, the sister of his father. Thus, although Nagatkin did not share the clan name, he was the preferable heir as the closest descendant of Zherebiatnikov's grandfather, even to the extent of excluding more distant relatives who carried the Zherebiatnikov name.[32] Females could also be the heir of the "last in the clan," according to the same rule that the property should go to the closest family member by a female line. Thus, upon the death of Nikolai Golitsyn, the Senate decided to give his property to his cousin, Irina Shcherbatova, the daughter of his grandfather's sister. In its decision, the Senate explained that the property should be returned to the closest member of the Golitsyn clan; thus, if Nikolai had had an uncle or aunt it would have gone to them. Without these, it should go to the closest relative of the "first votchinnik," Nikolai's great-grandfather Andrei. Thus, as the descendant of Andrei Golitsyn, Irina was eligible to inherit, despite the fact that she did not carry the family name.[33] In both of these cases, proximity by blood was deemed preferable to proximity by name.

Nothing, however, could be taken for granted in the complex world of inheritance law and the natural complications that arose from unique family situations were often made worse by the lack of coordination between the various bodies that made these crucial decisions. The case of the childless landowner Alexei Sobolev is a good example. Until Alexei died childless in 1704, he possessed family property that had originally belonged to his grandfather, David, and then had belonged to his own father, Ivan. Upon Alexei's death, this property was "written" to the state for some twenty years until his sister, Praskovia, and his cousin, Ivan, both petitioned for it. Ivan was the victor in this dispute and held the property for ten years until he too died childless. At that point, two claimants emerged: Andrei Surmin, great grandson of David Sobolev, and Maria, the granddaughter of

David Sobolev. Andrei claimed that his mother Praskovia, as the daughter of Ivan (and Alexei's sister), should have been the rightful heir to Alexei's property. Maria Surmin declared that she and her son Fedor should be the rightful heirs and requested that should she be granted the land that her grandson, Ilia, be named as her heir. In 1740, the Economic College decided to give the property to Maria, "as the closest in the line." Praskovia was already dead and the property had never been given to her, therefore, it was determined that it was not possible to give it to either her or her son. Andrei died several years later, leaving behind a wife and two sons, Ivan and Semen. In 1747, however, the previous decision was reversed and it was ordered that the property be given to Ivan and Semen. Again, the final decision favored a family member closer in blood to the deceased landowner[34] (see figure 6.3).

As these examples remind us, under normal inheritance circumstances the preferred heir was a male family member who carried the family name. But when a landowner died childless with no close male relatives, the end of his line necessitated that female family members and descendants of females should inherit. In such cases, the important principle became proximity to the "original landowner," that is, the father or grandfather of the deceased. In this way, those closest to the deceased, even those with a different family name, had the advantage over more distant relatives who carried the family name.[35]

The Inheritance Rights of Parents

All of the laws previously discussed concerning the property disposal of a childless landowner contain one significant omission: none of them raise the possibility of parents as eligible heirs. Traditionally, parents had no claims to the property of their deceased children. That property was to pass to the heirs of those children, either in the descending or collateral line. The only concern of pre-Petrine legislation with the rights of parents referred to the provision for a mother from her son's pomest'e and votchina. According to the Ulozhenie, if a mother had not already been granted a maintenance allotment of pomest'e, then upon her son's death she received a prozhitok from his land. If he died without any pomest'e or purchased votchina, then this prozhitok

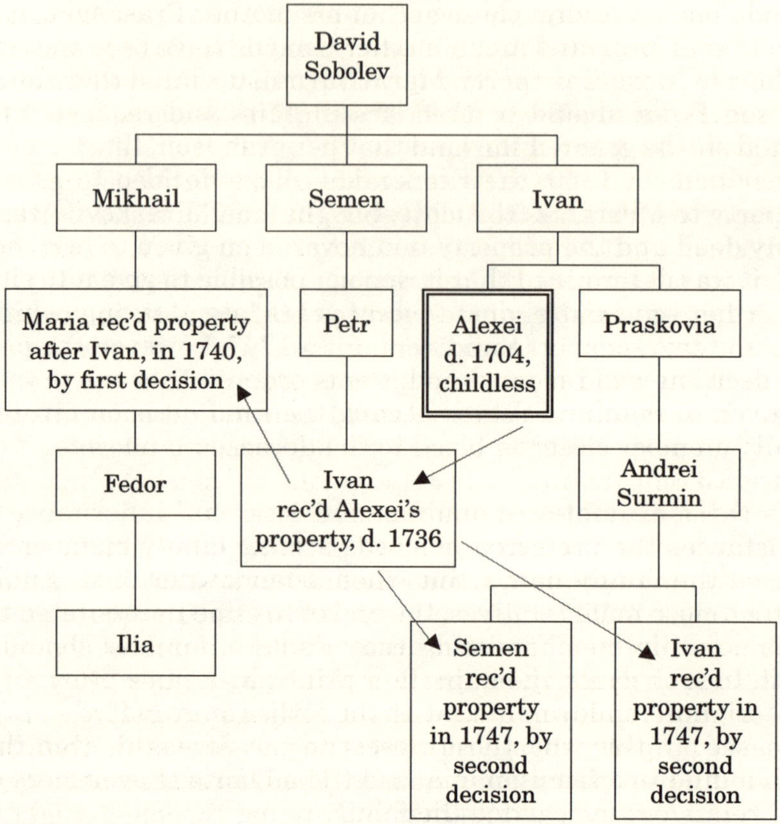

Figure 6.3. ***Devolution of the Property of the Childless Landowner, Alexei Sobolev***

could be granted to her from his service votchina.[36] Nowhere does pre-Petrine legislation raise the possibility of a father inheriting from his son.

Children, however, could and did die before their parents. In such a case, if an adult child had children of his own at the time of death, then the standard rules of inheritance applied and his wife and descendants received his property. When, however, an adult child died without issue, a complex situation arose. According to the standard laws of inheritance, the wife would receive her maintenance allotment and the remaining property would be distributed to collateral relatives. Russian law had no provision for inheritance in the ascending line, so parents were not considered viable heirs. There was one minor exception. The inheritance law of 1725 provided that a mother had the right to give her personal property and her one-fourth portion to her children, but then if she changed her mind, she could petition to take it back and give it to other children.

This omission of parents as legal heirs was problematic for several reasons. Parents frequently bought land for a child, either as a dowry or a gift, or sometimes purchased land in their children's names to circumvent the restrictions of inheritance laws. On occasion parents also granted land to children with the condition that the child support the parent until death.[37] In such cases, the death of the child meant the parents lost all rights to the property. Thus, collateral relatives could inherit and enjoy the benefits of property that the deceased's parents had purchased with very different intentions in mind, while the parents themselves suffered both emotional and material loss.

Noble parents, of course, wished to change these laws, and this was a frequent request among the nakazy of 1767. The nakaz of the Livensk nobility, for example, addressed the problem honestly and directly, admitting that parents purchased property with their own money, but in their children's names. They argued that if those children died without siblings or children of their own, the property should return to the parents rather than being distributed to other clan members. The Ostrovskoe nobility seconded this request, adding that such an arrangement might prevent property from going into an "alien rod." By returning it to the rod, they argued, families would not fall into impoverishment. Many of these requests acknowledged the right of the deceased's spouse to a maintenance allotment; it was the remainder with which they were concerned.[38]

The argument that parents should be able to inherit from their children was tested in the second half of the eighteenth century. In 1772, the Senate ruled on the inheritance dispute between Avdotia Pronchishchev, formerly Ovtsyn, and her niece, Elena (see figure 6.4). Avdotia's brother, Avram, had predeceased both his sister and his mother, Praskovia, sometime around 1740. At this time, Avram's widow had been given her portion and the Votchina College and Senate Kontor had decided to give the remainder to Praskovia, since it had been her property originally. Praskovia had then given the property to her daughter, Avdotia. In 1773, the Senate reversed the earlier decision and decided to give the

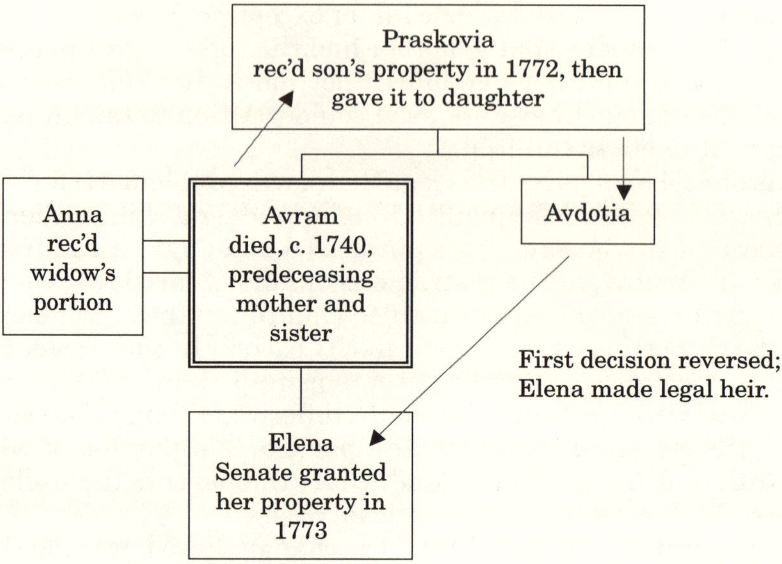

Figure 6.4. ***Ovtsyn Family Tree***

property to Avram's daughter, Elena. The Senate, referring to the law of 1725, noted that Praskovia had only petitioned about the return of this property after Avram's death, at which time she had no rights to it.[39]

It was only in 1823 that lawmakers lifted the prohibition on inheritance in the ascending line. In that year the State Council decided that clan property that is given to children by their living parents could be considered a gift. Therefore, if the children predecease the parents and leave no heirs of their own, the property should be returned to the parents from whom it came. The State Council also made a significant decision regarding the acquired property of a childless landowner that had important implication for the definition of the clan. Regarding this question, the Senate had earlier declared that every individual belonged to two clans, that of the mother and that of the father, and therefore concluded that acquired property could not be declared escheated as long as there were relatives on the mother's side. Therefore, the Senate decided that the acquired property of a childless landowner should be given to the parents jointly, with the condition that they not alienate the land in any way. The State Council supported these decisions with the exception of the opinion about escheated acquired property. On this issue, it proposed that acquired property should be considered escheated when there were no potential heirs in either the immediate descending or collateral line in the father's clan. This opinion clearly emphasized that clan membership was defined primarily through the male line. Nonetheless, the Senate's different interpretation illustrates that the scope of clan membership was a question still open to debate.

Conclusion

The case of the childless landowner underscores the complexity of Russian property law and highlights some of the underlying principles behind it. First and foremost was the assertion of clan rights. In most cases, the law stressed that the property of a childless landowner should remain within the clan from which it originated; a widow's portion after 1731 was the notable exception. Thus, there was a special concern for the provenance of the property. Within each clan, males were first in line for inheritance, and females inherited only in conjunction with males or in the absence of males, emphasizing the tenuous place of a woman in her clan. Finally, the problem of the childless landowner reminds us of the uncertainties of life and the role that unfortunate surprises could play in legal and family strategies. Surely, most of the childless landowners discussed in this chapter never planned to be childless, yet fate and biology dictated otherwise, leaving behind a complex and often unexpected set of problems for their extended families. Such circumstances could result in long, drawn-out disputes and wreak havoc within a clan, underscoring the fact that the clan network was, after all, a fragile structure, its perpetuation always at risk and susceptible to extinction if too many family members failed to produce heirs. This vulnerability no doubt helps to explain the flexible and constantly shifting definition of kinship. Just as European nobilities frequently have had to incorporate new members to sustain themselves, so the Russian noble clan had to keep its definition for membership flexible to accommodate problems such as the childless landowner.

7
The Long Arm of the Law: Redemption and Confiscation

Laws and decrees should be written clearly so that they cannot be reinterpreted. There is little justice in people, but much perfidy.
—Peter the Great

MANY HISTORIANS HAVE ARGUED THAT DURING THE EIGHTEENTH century the Russian nobility made significant progress in obtaining greater property rights. As we have seen, there is some validity to this claim, though the advances were substantially less clear or secure than some historians have asserted. Though Catherine's statute had reaffirmed some preexisting property rights and had clarified certain points of inheritance, there remained some aspects of property law that were less than favorable to noble interests. Redemption and confiscation were two such practices. The policies of redemption and confiscation contributed to noble feelings of insecurity regarding their property and encouraged mercenary behavior among landowners who came to view land as an impermanent investment. Moreover, both of these practices illustrate the degree to which noble property rights were defined and constrained by two overwhelming forces: the clan and the state.

REDEMPTION

One of the ways in which the clan exercised an overwhelming influence in the lives of Russian nobles was through the practice of redemption.[1] The term "redemption" was used to denote two different situations in the reclamation of land. First, it was used to describe the procedure by which the original landowner redeemed mortgaged property from forfeiture by discharging the obligation within a proscribed period. The second use of the term is the one that is of interest here. In this usage, redemption referred to the legal prerogative of certain family members to purchase, or redeem, family property that had been sold or mortgaged outside of their clan without their permission.[2] Family land was defined as land that had belonged to a family for more than one generation. Family property could also include human chattel. In 1769, Mayor Nikifor Sysoev petitioned about the redemption of two house servants and their families mortgaged by his brother, Fedor.[3] If, however, an individual acquired property by purchase or mortgage, it would be classified as acquired property until it passed on to his children. Acquired property was not eligible for redemption.[4]

The origins of this practice in Russia are uncertain. Initially, it would seem, redemption was a practice that attempted to give the original owner the right to reclaim land in case of later need; over time, this right was extended to the family as well. Thus, in the fifteenth century, there are some examples of an individual stipulating in a sale or gift of land that if he or his relatives needed that property in the future, they would have the right to repurchase it. In this common practice of redemption, all family members were eligible, even the original owner's children. In this first manifestation of redemption, landowners could choose to override this possibility by including the phrase "without redemption" in their sale documents.[5] Over time, the practice of redemption was incorporated into law, and here, the focus was preserving the prerogative of the clan while the emphasis on need was removed.

Redemption was first legally established by the Sudebnik of 1550, which ordered that if a man sold or mortgaged his ancestral lands, certain members of his family had the right to redeem, or repurchase, that land from the new holder. Specifically, any of the original owner's brothers or nephews who had not agreed to the transaction could redeem the alienated land, provided that the claim was made within the forty-year time limit set by the Sudebnik. Other family members were excluded from redemption by virtue of their relation to the owner or their participation in the transaction. Thus, direct offspring of the owner were denied the privilege of redemption since it was assumed that, being under their parents' control, they were not in a position to disagree. In addition, none of the owner's brothers who had witnessed and agreed to the transaction could claim the right of redemption, nor could their children, as subject to the will of their fathers. The Sudebnik, then, narrowed the pool of eligible redeemers by excluding direct descendants and also more narrowly defined which land was eligible, limiting it to inherited lands alienated by sale or mortgage. At the same time, it has been noted, the Sudebnik expressed for the first time the concept of "rod" immovable property by giving collateral relatives a legal interest in the land of other family members. This idea was reinforced by the Sudebnik's rule that anyone who redeemed family property was forbidden from alienating it to an alien rod in any way; the redeemer could only give, sell, or mortgage the land to other family members.[6]

Subsequent legislation further refined the rules for redemption. An ukaz of 1625 repeated the forty-year term limit, ordering that once the term had expired, even by a few weeks, hopeful redeemers should be turned away, the critical question being why they had not redeemed the property before the mortgage expired or at least before the forty-year term had expired.[7] In 1649 the Ulozhenie reaffirmed the basic rules of redemption regarding eligibility and the time limit of forty years.[8] It did however, make some alterations to current law and practice. The Ulozhenie established that the original owner had the first right of redemption; this rule was clarified in subsequent law.[9] It also redefined what land was eligible for redemption: it added service votchina as a type of land that could be redeemed and specified that property acquired within the lifetime of the owner, by purchase or mortgage, was not eligible for redemption.[10] Finally, the Ulozhenie failed to include the prohibition of the Sudebnik regarding the alienation of repurchased land by the redeemer. Thirty years later another law of redemption appeared and stipulated that land was to be redeemed according to the last transaction, whether it be sale or mortgage, and in 1698, it was ordered that land not be given in redemption if it had been mortgaged from brother to brother.[11] This latter rule is important since it demonstrates that the emphasis was on keeping land within the clan. In all cases, the original owner had the first right to reclaim his land, but if he could not or chose not to do so, family members had the right to step in. The exception was in cases of treason, where the clan as a whole lost the right of redemption.[12]

The next landmark of legislation that dealt with the matter of redemption was Peter's Law of Single Inheritance in 1714. Peter's law reaffirmed the forty-year term limit, but made some significant changes in other areas of redemption law. First, by combining the two land types into one general category, Peter made more land eligible for redemption, not to mention the other "immovable property," such as villages and shops. The end result was that more property fell under the influence of the clan. Moreover, the Law of Single Inheritance specified that noninheriting children were not eligible redeemers for any family land and that immovable property could only be redeemed by one person, the designated heir in any given family group. Moreover, it emphasized that land being redeemed should be assessed at its actual value, rather than the transaction price. Peter apparently anticipated the possibility of individuals writing land transactions with intentionally low prices, not at all reflective of the land's actual value, to permit an easier redemption for family members and low transaction fees. This particular statute of the law, then, was an attempt to prevent families from using redemption as a loophole around the single inheritance rule.[13] Similarly, after Peter's death, Catherine I ordered that a son could not redeem his father's property while he was alive, another attempt to prevent circumvention of the Law of Single Inheritance by selling land so that children could "inherit" it through redemption.

By the eighteenth century, the right of redemption was so firmly established that it could not be circumvented even if the seller tried to do so by including an exclusion clause in the sale document. In 1693, for example, Ivan Monastyr sold family land that he had received from his father to Vasilii Saltykov. In the sale document, Ivan stated that the land was being sold "without future redemption." Despite this, Ivan's brothers sought to redeem this property. Initially, the Pomestnyi Prikaz rejected their claim, but when the Senate reviewed the case in 1711, it overturned that earlier decision and ordered that the property in question be given to Andrei and Alexei in redemption.[14]

Russia's law of redemption was unique in early modern Europe. Though a similar system had existed in medieval Hungary, already by the end of the fourteenth century the rights of the clan were considerably weakened. Moreover, in the Hungarian case, clan rights pertained to the sale or exchange of property, but did not involve the right to demand repurchase.[15] In France, the custom of *retrait lignager* comes close to the Russian practice, however, it differs in several significant ways. First, it was a custom, not a law, and it was only practiced in certain regions, mostly in south-southwest France, and on a limited scale in the north, but in all cases with strong regional variations. Second, it was practiced across class lines and did not focus on the landowning nobility.[16] Elsewhere in Europe, the nearest comparison to the Russian practice of redemption was the seigneurial right of landlords to claim first right of refusal when tenures on their estates were being sold or to assume the right of inheritance when the holders of the tenure failed to produce a male heir. These rights, however, very specifically dealt with the rights of landlords vis-à-vis their tenants and (with the exception of France) did not apply to the property of nobles and their families.[17]

The procedure for redemption depended upon the kind of transaction that had taken place. In the event of a mortgage, the involved parties drew up a document that stated the amount of the loan and the date by which the borrower had to pay back the loan, and this agreement was deposited with the land office, the Pomestnyi Prikaz, and later, the Votchina College. The standard term for a loan was one year, but some terms were as short as a month while others could be several years.[18] During that term, the lender could not officially register that property to himself, nor could he sell or mortgage the property. This was true even if the borrower died during that period. On October 5, 1706, Iurii Dokhturov mortgaged his votchina to Grigorii Ovtsyn for 500 rubles with an expiration date of January 1, 1707. On October 12, 1706, Iurii died. Six days later, Grigorii petitioned to have the property registered to himself and then on December 4, still twenty-seven days before the expiration date, he sold that property to Iurii's widow for 1,000 rubles. Grigorii explained that Iurii's brothers had given him permission to register the land to himself since neither of them had any intention of redeeming it. The problem with their generous offer was that they failed to consider the redemption of other family members. Indeed, in late December 1706, a distant cousin, Vasilii, petitioned to redeem that property. The case dragged on for twelve years, during which the property changed hands at least once more. Finally, in 1718, Vasilii won the right to redeem Iurii's votchina and register it as his own.[19]

Things were much simpler, of course, if the borrower settled his debt before the term expired; in that case, the land remained his and the mortgage document would be returned to him, while the land office would be informed that the loan had been paid.[20] If the borrower failed to pay off the loan within the agreed time, all hope was not lost; borrowers usually were given a grace period of as much as two months, during which the debt could be paid or an extension could be requested.[21] What happened next depended on the year in which it occurred. Prior to 1737 and after 1744, such expired land was written over to the lender. The law of 1737, however, had ordered that mortgaged and expired land should be auctioned at a public sale and the proceeds, should the lender choose not to bid himself, would be given to him, even if the final sale price was less than the loan. This practice ceased in 1744 when it was once again decided that expired property should be immediately awarded to the lender. In either case—public sale or immediate award to the lender—once the transaction took place, the right of redemption was opened up to the borrower's family. If the property had been sold, rather than mortgaged in the initial transaction, the extended family could usually execute the right of redemption immediately.

When family property was sold or mortgaged into another clan, any eligible family member could petition the Votchina College to reclaim that land by redemption. When a person petitioned, however, he or she was expected to submit the redemption money and taxes at the same time and, in fact, the land office was not supposed to accept the petition without the money. Thus, in the complex redemption case of College Secretary Ivan Kamenev, the Senate traced the history of the property in question and found that a number of inappropriate transactions had taken place, not the least of which was a redemption carried out by a man who had never paid the redemption money.[22]

As we have seen, not all family members had the right of redemption. Children, for example, were excluded from this right. In the Ulozhenie 22: 6, it was established that children were under the full control of their parents. In 1746, the Votchina College used this article to reject the claims of Natalia Voeikova against her mother, Katerina Miloslavskaia, who had mortgaged and lost some of her deceased husband's lands.[23] Moreover, since redemption only applied to property sold or mortgaged into another clan, petitioners were sometimes turned away if the property transaction in question had occured between family members. Thus, in 1717, Vasilii Elagin's petition to redeem land alienated by his nephews was invalid, because that land had been mortgaged to Bogdan Elagin, a distant cousin.[24] Thus, the first order of business for the land office or court was to determine eligibility.

Once the courts had established a pool of potential redeemers, it was necessary to select those most eligible. First among these would be an immediate family member—a brother, for example—who had not been consulted before the property transaction had taken place. In 1715, for example, Fedor Voinov petitioned the Senate about redeeming family property that his brothers had sold without his permission, emphasizing that his signature was not on the sale document.[25] If the redemption case arose during the period of Peter's Law of Single Inheritance, then only the eldest among a group of heirs would be considered eligible. Thus, when Iakov Sytin petitioned in 1718 to redeem the family property that had been mortgaged and lost by his brother, a crucial element of his claim to primacy was his position as the eldest surviving brother in that family.[26] Before and after Peter's law, when the rules of partible inheritance were in effect, there could be more than one redeemer and sometimes there were as many as five. As with the rules of inheritance, the preferred redeemer was the male relative closest to the owner. Thus, petitioners often argued their proximity to the seller or mortgager.[27] For example, in 1720, Iakov Sytin explained that he was the most eligible redeemer to his brother's mortgaged property, since his older brother Fedor had died without children and his younger brother Ivan had died in state service.[28] The Votchina College investigated these claims, simultaneously seeking out testimony from any relatives who were closer in relationship than the petitioner that they had no objections to the redemption by their clansman.

Renunciation by other eligible redeemers was an essential part of this process. In 1777, for example, Natalia Sheremeteva stated that her brother Prince Alexander Golitsyn had mortgaged his property for 3,000 rubles to Artillery Captain Mikhail Turgenev but had failed to pay off the loan in time. Although Natalia was the closest person eligible for redemption, she had no interest in redeeming the land and asked that her nieces be allowed to redeem it.[29] In this way, distant relatives could sometimes exercise the right of redemption. When Osip Kudriavov petitioned in 1741 to redeem the land in Rzhevskii uezd, which had been sold by his distant cousin, Lavrentii Kudriavov, the Votchina College ordered that Lavrentii's first cousins be questioned to be certain that they did not want to redeem this property. Once this was ascertained, the property could be given to Osip in redemption.[30] Obtaining renunciations from other family members was not always as easy as it sounds. On occasion, family members were away in service or their whereabouts were unknown. In 1762, Alexei Rzhevskii petitioned to redeem some family land mortgaged by a female relative. In describing the other potential redeemers, he stated that his cousin, also named Alexei, was in the army abroad, taken prisoner by the Prussian army and no one knew if was he dead or alive.[31]

This was not the end of the process, however. Once a petition was accepted and approved, the Votchina College would order that the land in question be appraised, taking into account any improvements or structures that had been added to the property.[32] The redeemer would then pay the "redemption money," the assessed value of the land, along with a required fee to the Votchina College, which would in turn give the assessed value to the deprived owner. In May 1741, for example, Dmitrii Kushnikov sold his immovable property in Rostovskii uezd to Ivan Bykov. Less than two months later, Dmitrii's uncle, Andrei Kushnikov, petitioned the Votchina College, asking that the land be given to him in redemption. His request was granted, and he paid the "redemption money" of 48 rubles and the fee of 4 rubles, 82½ kopecks. In December 1742, the Votchina College ordered that the "redemption money" be given to Bykov.[33] If the new owner of the land had died, the redemption money would be given to that person's heirs. In 1751, Grigorii Bredikhin purchased immovable family property from Nastasia Sykhotin. Two years later, Nastasia's sister petitioned to redeem the property and presented the redemption money and fees to the Votchina College. Before Grigorii could receive the money, however, he died with neither a wife nor children. His brother, Andrei, petitioned for and was granted the right to receive that redemption money in his brother's place.[34]

The problems that the legal principle of redemption presented for noble landowners are easily imagined. For a period of four decades, the new owner could never be sure that the property was truly his to develop, since he was always threatened by the possibility of clan redemption. Furthermore, he could not be sure that at the time of redemption he would be adequately compensated for the money and materials he had invested in the property. In this way, for as long as forty years, a noble landowner could live with the legitimate fear that at any moment he might be forced to resell his land to the family from which he had bought it. In 1727, for example, Ustinia Zubatova petitioned to redeem the family property that her brother, Dmitrii, had mortgaged and lost to Agafon Pavlovich and his unmarried sister Pelagia Miakinina in 1715, twelve years earlier. While her request was granted in 1731, she did not manage to pay the necessary redemption fee until February 1736. Thus, some twenty years after acquiring this property, the Miakininy were forced to give it up.[35] In a similar case, in 1740, Iakov Dashkov was granted the right of redemption to property sold by his distant cousin fifteen years earlier. Indeed, complex redemption cases often lasted many years and spanned several generations.[36]

Lenders were susceptible to various scams as well. Unscrupulous landowners sometimes mortgaged the same piece of land to more than one person, then failed to pay the mortgages, leaving the duped lenders to fight it out. In other cases, borrowers lied about the condition and profitability of the villages being mortgaged; the lender, trusting the borrower's assessment, would lend the requested amount of money only to find at the expiration date that his newly acquired property was inaccurately described and essentially worthless.[37] Finally, there was a great deal of waiting and uncertainty for lenders before they could consider the land to be theirs. For most of the eighteenth century, borrowers were given a two-month grace period in which to pay the debt on an expired mortgage; this time limit was extended to a generous six months in 1800 and to a year in 1849. Thus, even after a borrower failed to meet his obligations, a lender had to wait for many months before he could even attempt to claim the land as his own.[38]

The practice of redemption posed certain threats to the redeemer as well. The wheels of the bureaucracy could often turn very slowly; as the nobles of Kashinskii uezd complained in 1767, "in the Votchina College, for many cases, it is impossible to receive a quick decision."[39] As a result cases often dragged on for years. Larion Safonov petitioned in 1743 to redeem property sold by his uncle and presented the property amount of money to the Votchina College. In 1756, however, he was still fighting to receive that land, declaring that the property was still in the buyer's possession. Similarly, in 1745, Alexei Makarov complained that four years earlier he had been given permission by the Votchina College to redeem his relative's property, and yet the proper documents had somehow never appeared in the Velikolutskii Provincial Chancellery; he asked that the Votchina College send that local body yet another ukaz about his right of redemption.[40]

While this legal process of redemption was in motion, the new owner of a piece of property might decide to thwart the redeemer's intended goal of repurchase, and there was a variety of ways in which this might be done. One very easy way to circumvent the redemption laws was to simply make oneself unavailable for payment by the redeemer. In 1757, for example, Irina Trusova asked the Votchina College to receive her redemption money since the man to whom she had mortgaged her property was nowhere to be found. In 1777, Artillery Captain Mikhail Evreinov made the same complaint about the man whom he owed 2,600 rubles.[41]

On occasion, landowners might try to quickly resell land, forcing the redeemer to pay a higher price. In 1717, for example, Vasilii Elagin hoped to redeem some property in Pskovskii uezd that his nephews had mortgaged and failed to retrieve before the expiration date. Vasilii feared that, having heard about his petition, the new owner would resell the property for a higher price, leaving him to pay this higher price in order to redeem it. He asked the courts to get a statement from that current owner that he had not resold the property.[42] According to a law of February 26, 1679, any person wanting to redeem property was obliged to pay the price of the most recent sale or mortgage; this principle was reiterated in a law of March 23, 1744.[43] This rule was frequently invoked in redemption cases. In 1767, in the redemption case of Marfa Tolmachev, the Votchina College ordered that Marfa must redeem her cousin's property according to the last transaction.[44]

Some landowners, in an attempt to extract compensation before the property changed hands, or to prevent redemption entirely, stripped the land of its most valuable assets, including serfs. In 1741, for example, Riga Garrison Primier Mayor Alexei Sverchkov, while attempting to redeem property that had been sold by a relative, alleged that the new owner, Leontia Shishkov, having heard about Sverchkov's petition, removed grain and livestock from the land in question and transferred it to some of his other property. Sverchkov thus requested that the land be placed in Her Majesty's care until the redemption matter could be settled, in the hope that the land could be saved from ruin.[45]

Finally, in 1737, a new law on redemption attempted to prevent abuses of the system and shortened the time limit for redemption to three years. The law enumerated many of the problems that arose in the process of mortgage and redemption and set punishments for certain transgressions; mortgaging the same piece of property to more than one person would warrant a beating with the knout, for example. Lying about the number of souls or villages on a piece of mortgaged property would result in a beating with the knout and confiscation of souls from other properties to compensate the lender. The same punishment was ordered for borrowers who intentionally ruined land before mortgaging it or relocated serfs by sending them to other estates or as recruits for the military. Finally, the law of 1737 stated that the forty-year term was problematic in that new owners invested in their property, only to have it severely undervalued at the time of redemption, receiving only half or less its real value. This created a situation in which nobles not only refrained from improving their newly acquired property, but even intentionally ruined it, so that the seller's relatives would have no desire to redeem it. In an attempt to prevent such destructive practices, the law of 1737 determined that the new term for redemption of family and service votchina should be shortened to three years. After that term had expired, no redemptions were to be approved. For this reason, when Vera Ogareva complained about her uncle's redemption of family property, Catherine sent an ukaz to the Senate denying Vera's requests because the three-year window for such claims had closed. In 1752, Ivan Kamenev's petition was rejected because over twenty years had passed since the land in question had been sold. Subsequent legislation upheld this shorter term.[46]

The new three-year term was an improvement in many ways, but it created more problems for individuals who were serving in the military far from home. These men frequently complained that their military service had interfered with their ability to exercise their rights of redemption. For example, in April 1743, Larion Safonov petitioned about redeeming family land that his uncle had sold three years earlier. With the expiration date for redemption only two days away, Larion explained that he had been unable to initiate the process sooner because he was away in service. He now asked that the redemption money and taxes be accepted from him and the land be registered in his name. This problem was only addressed in 1805, when a new law ordered that soldiers abroad would be given an extra year for redemption.[47]

Only seven years after the new redemption time was put in place, Elizabeth found it necessary to augment and elucidate the existing laws on redemption. In an ukaz of May 11, 1744, she reaffirmed the three-year term and emphasized the standing rule that redemption applied to land that was alienated to another clan, not to another family member.[48] Elizabeth also defined the order of eligible redeemers more clearly, basing this succession on the order of heirs in inheritance. The exception continued to be direct heirs. Once again it was established that children of the seller or mortgager did not possess the right of redemption during their father's lifetime. It was now added, in a significant departure from the Ulozhenie, that if their father died before the three-year term had expired they could claim the right of redemption; similarly, grandsons who lived with their grandfathers after their fathers died could claim the right of redemption if their grandfather died prior to the three-year term. Grandsons, whose fathers, living separately from their grandfathers, died, could claim the right of redemption even while their grandfather was still alive. If there were no sons, then daughters would be allowed to redeem under the same restrictions, beginning with unmarried daughters and extending to married or widowed daughters in the absence of the former. Overall, however, male relatives of the closest degree were still the preferred redeemers. The right of redemption in the female line would extend only to the daughters' sons and unmarried daughters; married or widowed granddaughters of daughters were not eligible for redemption. At that time, the next eligible redeemer would be any of the seller's brothers or nephews who had not witnessed the transaction, then his sisters and their children, always preferencing sons over daughters and unmarried daughters over married daughters. In all cases, it was necessary for eligible redeemers who declined their right of redemption to put their renunciation in writing.[49]

Finally, the new redemption law of 1744 made one significant change designed to simplify the process of redemption. It ordered that the recipient of expired mortgaged property had to wait one year before selling, mortgaging, or including that newly acquired property in a dowry. At the end of a year, he was free to alienate it in any manner he chose, and anyone desiring to redeem it would have to do so according to the most recent transaction price. This portion of the law was designed to give redeemers a chance to petition before the land changed hands again. The new one-year waiting period became an important factor in redemption cases. In 1773, for example, Ivan Shatilov argued that Nikolai Maslov's petition to redeem property from him was invalid. Shatilov explained that in 1765, Nikolai's relative, Alexei Makhov, had borrowed 1,800 rubles from him with an expiration date of exactly one year. Makhov failed to pay off that debt and several years passed with no petitions for redemption from any of Alexei's relatives. Though Shatilov was within his rights to register that land to himself immediately, he waited four years. Having done this, he waited yet another year as required by law and then mortgaged the property to someone else; Maslov would have to redeem the property from that new owner.[50]

The redemption law of 1744 was certainly an improvement, but it did not entirely eliminate redemption as a source of insecurity for noble landowners. In 1755, the state enacted another redemption law, which posed even greater problems. The new law ordered that redemption transactions were not to be carried out until the completion of a new law code, although petitions would still be received. In the meantime, the mortgaged or sold property was to remain in the hands of the new owner.[51] Thus, when Katerina Nilova petitioned the Votchina College in 1765 about redeeming her niece's mortgaged and expired property, her request was put on hold. Although the Iaroslavl Provincial Chancellery would attempt to prevent the new owner from ruining the property, the law of 1755 prevented Nilova from redeeming the property at that time.[52]

This new law unwittingly encouraged exploitation and abuse, a fact that was soon recognized and resulted in the law's repeal in 1766. The redemption law of 1766 reported that the new owners, knowing that petitions for redemption had been filed, but also aware that these would not soon be carried out, began to ruin their properties, overtaxing and otherwise extorting money from their peasants. As a result, it was decided to resume the execution of redemption transactions.

Though the new redemption law mainly reiterated previously established rules, it also made some significant changes in the list of eligible redeemers. First, the law of 1766 extended the right of redemption to more remote females. If a parent died before the three-year term had expired, in the absence of sons, daughters and granddaughters (daughters of deceased sons) would equally be eligible for redemption. If the original owner had no living daughters or granddaughters, then the redemption right passed to his daughter's children, first males, then females. Only in the absence of grandchildren through the female line (through a daughter) would the right move collaterally to the owner's brother and nephews. Moreover, the distinction between unmarried and married daughters that had been included in the laws of 1744 and 1755 was omitted in the law of 1766, perhaps an early indication of the changing attitudes toward married women.[53]

Despite these attempts by the crown to clarify and reform the laws of redemption, the nobility continued to be troubled by abuses of the system. The complaints about redemption that arose during the Legislative Commission of 1767 give some indication of the problems the nobility faced. Many of the nakazy complained about abuses in the system. The nobles of Orel province, for example, described how wealthier nobles lent money to poorer nobles at usurious rates, being certain to take a mortgage on the borrower's property and foreclosing as soon as the mortgage expired. Often, those foreclosing thoroughly ruined the property, so that if the borrower's family managed to scrape together the money to redeem it, they would find it ravaged and serfless.[54] A similar concern was expressed by the Chuklomskie nobles who lamented the exploitative behavior of some landowners who, "having forgotten the fear of God," obtained land through a small loan, then quickly mortgaged it themselves for a larger sum, making it impossible for the original owner or his relatives to repurchase it. When the three-year limit had passed, the mortgage would be paid off and the ruthless landowner would regain the land and keep it for himself.[55] Finally, some nobles also requested that serfs who were sold or mortgaged separate from the land not be eligible for redemption.[56]

Other nakazy focused on questions of eligibility. The nobility of Maloiaroslavetskii uezd asked that close family members be given the right of first refusal before family land could be sold.[57] Still another nakaz asked that sales or mortgages between spouses not be eligible for redemption, just as if they were in the same family.[58] Nobles were also concerned about the rule against children not being able to redeem their father's land while he was still alive; several nakazy asked that this rule be changed, citing the hypothetical case of a father who did not love his children and so intentionally sold off and deprived them of their inheritance.[59]

Despite these varied complaints, the laws of redemption did not change in any significant way in the remainder of the Imperial period. In 1786, the Senate stressed the importance of separating acquired from family property during the process of redemption if both types of land had been included in the sale or mortgage transaction. Fourteen years later, a Senate ukaz reiterated the standing rule that acquired property was not eligible for redemption. The most important amendment to the current rules came in 1815 when a new law more directly addressed the question as to whether a married woman would be allowed to redeem property of her original clan. The law determined that although a married woman had "transferred into another clan," she could enjoy the right of redemption. Moreover, the new law ordered that property sold to a married woman, despite her new name, could not be redeemed by her original clan members, since the laws of redemption clearly stated that property sold or mortgaged to another family member was not eligible for redemption.[60] These minor alterations, however, did little or nothing to alleviate the overall problems associated with the system of redemption. In fact, the policy of redemption continued to threaten the security of landholding well into the next century. As late as 1875, critics of the institution of patrimonial property argued at the First Congress of Russian Jurists that redemption prevented new owners from trying to improve their property.[61]

It is clear that the policy of redemption was inherently flawed in that it contributed to the nobility's insecurity about its property, thereby discouraging investment and encouraging what under other circumstances would have been considered self-destructive behavior. Its persistence through the Imperial period, then, raises interesting questions about its purpose. Recalling the earliest incarnation of redemption, one might be tempted to argue that the entire redemption process was created as a primitive credit system. It was certainly true that many nobles used sales and mortgages as a way to obtain quick cash. In 1755, for example, Mikhail Lanskoi purchased some property in Zubtsovskii uezd from Vasilisa Ravinskaia for fifty rubles, then only four days later, because of his "desperate need," he mortgaged that property for 4,000 rubles—a tidy profit, indeed. Perhaps, one could argue, the possibility of redemption made such emergency transactions less onerous; but the risks of such ventures were high. In the above case, for example, Ravinskaia's cousins petitioned to redeem that land and had to fight to redeem it according to the sale, not the significantly higher mortgage price.[62] Moreover, all transactions were taxed and even filing a petition could cost a pretty penny; in addition to the cost of special stamped papers, petitioners had to pay a filing fee which, ca. 1767, was three rubles for an original petition and two rubles for a petition of appeal. That nobles found these fees burdensome is clear from their complaints in the nakazy.[63]

There were other risks as well. Though a landowner might mortgage land with some hope of reclaiming it before the end of the term, a sale was more final and opened the door to other family members to redeem that property. But even mortgages carried some potential for loss. In 1764, Nikolai Lodyzhenskii mortgaged immovable property for 4,000 rubles, from June 6, 1764, to January 1, 1765, to Andrei Buturlin. On February 28, 1765, that mortgage document appeared in the Votchina College with Buturlin's petition to register the land and the required taxes. Almost a year later, on February 8, 1766, there was a petition from Nikolai's sister, Nastasia, asking to redeem that land. In May, the Penzensk Provincial Chancellery informed the Votchina College that it had granted that land in redemption to Nastasia. In the meantime, apparently unbeknownst to Nastasia, Nikolai had repaid Buturlin in February 1766 and had reclaimed the land as his own. In May 1768, the Senate ordered a compromise: Nastasia received half of the land in question and paid the redemption money of 2,200 rubles to her brother, since he had already paid the entire amount to Buturlin, and Nikolai was able to keep the other half of the land for himself. Presumably, Nastasia's claim was honored, in part at least, because her petition predated Nikolai's repayment of the debt. As this story illustrates, once a landowner mortgaged his land, there was no way of knowing who might redeem it or when that might occur. In this case, Nikolai lost half his land to his sister who was quicker than he at assembling the necessary cash.[64]

If redemption was not created as a primitive credit system, then what was its purpose? Konstantin Nevolin suggests in his history of Russian law written in 1851 that redemption laws persisted because they played a practical financial role. Since all alienation of property was taxed at a percentage of the land's assessed value—the rate at that time was 4 percent—landowners might be tempted to list a lower price than the real one in order to pay lower fees. Redemption prevented this, since listing an artificially low price would have the unpleasant side effect of making it easier for relatives to redeem the property in question.[65]

Money may explain why the government favored redemption policies, but it does not explain why members of the nobility helped to perpetuate these rules. The answer to this question can be found in considering all of Russia's property laws as a whole. Russia's inheritance laws had always favored the interests of the clan, often at the expense of individuals' desires. The same is true of Russia's redemption laws. The redemption system was created and perpetuated to ensure the survival of the clan. Even as Russian noble families may have made the slow drift to individualism and more tight-knit families, they still held on to a traditional view of the clan, particularly in regards to landholding; Nevolin acknowledges this interest in the clan as well.[66] The result was a hybrid form of landholding most accurately described as "restricted ownership"—not exactly ownership by the entire clan, but not exactly private ownership either. This overwhelming clan influence was a significant hindrance to the development of modern conceptions of private property in Imperial Russia and helps to explain why nobles complained about specific problems associated with redemption without demanding its abolition.

Confiscation

The ultimate sanction in landholding that could be visited upon a member of the nobility was confiscation, a practice through which a noble might lose not only his land, but his personal property, including clothing, household items, and religious heirlooms. Confiscation served a multitude of purposes. It was a punishment for a variety of crimes, including bribe-taking, service evasion, filing a dishonest petition, and the most serious crime, treason. Members of the various state organizations, such as the Senate and Votchina College, were also occasionally penalized with confiscation for making an incorrect decision. Finally, confiscation also occurred as a result of excessive debt. Confiscation, then, was one very significant factor in the overall insecurity of the nobility in eighteenth-century Russia. It was also a useful tool for the monarch, to punish wayward subjects and to keep others in their places. Though confiscation decreased in frequency during the Imperial period, it remained a source of anxiety for property owners well into the early nineteenth century.

The practice of confiscation in Russia has a long history. It can be dated back to the late fourteenth century when, in an attempt to curb the growing independence of the landowning boyars, the principle was established during the reign of Vasilii I that the prince could confiscate the property of a departing servitor if the prince decided that the boyar had committed treason. During the civil wars of the early fifteenth century, Vasilii II put this principle into practice, confiscating the lands of some boyars who had departed, and forcing others to renounce their right of free departure in order to keep their land.[67] In the late fifteenth century, Ivan III seized some million hectares of land from the wealthier citizens of Novgorod, redistributing it as service land.[68] Perhaps most notoriously, Ivan IV utilized this practice during his oprichnina when he confiscated estates from his enemies and then redistributed the confiscated votchina as pomest'e.

By the seventeenth century, confiscation was regularly threatened as punishment for a variety of crimes. Both the Ulozhenie in 1649 and subsequent legislation contain such threats. Thus the Ulozhenie threatened confiscation for treason, for evading or fleeing military service, for illegally registering pomest'e as votchina, for failing to register purchased land properly, and for illegally transferring votchina to a monastery. Moreover, the state reserved the right to confiscate a man's votchina in the absence of legal heirs.[69] Legislation that appeared in the years after the Ulozhenie also promised confiscation for various crimes; for example, either improperly surveying land or falsely accusing a surveyor of such a crime would result in the loss of half of one's pomest'e and votchina. Failure to appear in court could also lead to confiscation of property. Finally, those who committed the sin of *raskolnikism,* that is, adhering to the Old Belief, would also lose their property.[70]

Confiscation as a method of punishment continued into the eighteenth century under Peter and subsequent rulers. Dozens of Peter's laws threatened or enacted the punishment of confiscation for crimes ranging from illegal woodcutting to service evasion to treason. An ukaz of 1710, for example, promised that service evaders would be punished with confiscation and those who had informed on them would be the beneficiaries of the confiscated property. In 1711, Peter threatened members of the newly created Senate with loss of honor and property for making unjust decisions. In 1713, Peter ordered that those committing crimes "against the government interest" would suffer loss of property and life. Other laws listed confiscation as a penalty for bribe-taking, for failure to properly publicize government decrees, for failure to appear for military inspection and for improper procedure in a law suit or complaint. An ukaz of 1719 threatened confiscation and exile, and even execution, for individuals who failed to answer requests or ukazes from the Senate or colleges. Similarly, in 1724, Peter stated that government agents had a responsibility to keep abreast of the law and anyone who failed to do so would suffer confiscation of movable and immovable property.[71] Finally, the General Reglament of 1720 threatened loss of property for several crimes, including improper use of the government seal or dishonest activity by a College member.[72]

Nor did the rate of confiscation slow considerably with Peter's death. Between 1725 and 1762, the government continued to use confiscation as an incentive for good behavior. Thus, deprivation of property continued to be a punishment for service evasion and other service-related crimes. To this was added debt, an increasingly common problem in the wake of Peter's reign. Loss of property could also be a punishment for religious transgressions and illegal trade. Finally, crimes against the state or the monarch, of course, continued to be punishable by deprivation of property.[73]

The threat of confiscation embodied in these various laws was not an idle one, a fact that is well demonstrated by the establishment in 1730 of the Chancellery of Confiscation. First proposed in 1729, the Chancellery of Confiscation was created in St. Petersburg by an ukaz of June 27, 1730.[74] Shortly after, in 1733, a branch office was opened in Moscow. In subsequent years, the Chancellery of Confiscation gradually assumed the responsibilities of the government's other debt-collecting agencies, uniting with the Arrears Chancellery in 1736 and by 1741 becoming the most important debt-collecting agency in the realm.[75]

According to the instructions issued to the Chancellery of Confiscation in the summer of 1730, this institution was created to eradicate treasury losses and to facilitate the orderly confiscation and sale of movable and immovable property. Such order would benefit not only the government, but also the general public, which had suffered under the previous disorderly system. Thus the Chancellery's primary function was the confiscation of movable and immovable property for arrears and political crimes and the appropriation and management of escheated property. Having acquired movable and immovable property by these means, the Chancellery was to manage the property in question until it was either reclaimed or sold.[76]

Although the Chancellery of Confiscation suffered from significant shortcomings and was ultimately abolished in 1782, it did exert considerable influence during its fifty-three years of existence. An examination of the voluminous journals and records of the Chancellery reveals a pattern of daily meetings that dealt with a variety of matters, from the extraction of debts and the location of a delinquent debtor's heirs to the establishment of time periods for debts to be paid. In March of 1729, for example, the widow Avdot'ia Zybina paid twenty-four rubles on her standing debts and was given one month by the Chancellery of Confiscation to pay the balance.[77] The Chancellery of Confiscation was also responsible for levying fines against dishonest petitioners and incompetent state officials. An example of the latter occurred in 1770–72, when the Chancellery fined a member of the Votchina College for incorrectly handling a land dispute.[78] Finally, the Chancellery was charged with the sale of confiscated property, including such items as pants, stockings, belts, and boots.[79]

Confiscation occurred under a variety of circumstances. One of the most serious crimes that warranted confiscation was treason. Thus, in 1718, the famous "Alexei affair" provided the impetus for widespread confiscation of both movable and immovable property.[80] Treason, of course, could be broadly interpreted, and throughout the eighteenth century, large-scale confiscations regularly followed transitions of power as old favorites were swept out and new favorites came in. Thus, Alexander Menshikov, along with many of his supporters, was stripped of his property in 1727, after his benefactor was no longer there to support him. In 1737, Prince Dmitrii Golitsyn's movable and immovable property was "written to Her Majesty" for a variety of sins, including service evasion and concealment of important documents.[81] In 1742, Elizabeth commuted the sentences of the conspirators Andrei Osterman, Count Minikh, Mikhail Golovkin, Count Levenvol'd, President of the Commerce College Baron Mengden, and Ivan Temiriazev from death to exile, while all of their movable and immovable property was to be written to her.[82] Later, in 1743, Elizabeth ordered the confiscation of the property of a number of persons, among them Stepan Lopukhin and Prince Ivan Putiatin, who were accused of questioning her right to the throne.[83]

Indeed, such a broad and arbitrary definition frequently resulted in rapid and repeated reversals of fortune. The case of Alexander Ivanovich Rumiantsev effectively illustrates this point. During the reign of Peter the Great, Rumiantsev had been granted some of the villages that had been confiscated from the Lopukhins. Later, when Peter II came to power, these villages were returned to their previous owners. During Anna's reign, Rumiantsev experienced yet another series of reversals. In an attempt to secure his support, Anna made him a senator, promoted him, and awarded him 20,000 rubles as compensation for the villages seized during Peter II's reign. When Rumiantsev failed to meet the Empress's expectations, criticizing the excessive spending of the court and arguing with the brother of her favorite, Count Ernst Johann von Biron, Anna had him expelled, arrested, and tried by the Senate. The Senate sentenced him to be executed. Anna commuted the sentence to exile at his estate near Kazan, and among his other losses, Rumiantsev was ordered to return the 20,000 rubles that Anna had earlier granted him.[84] The fate of the Dolgorukiis and of Artemi Volynskii in the reigns of Anna and Elizabeth demonstrates the same point about the whims of the monarch and noble insecurity regarding property. Under Anna, several members of the Dolgorukii family were stripped of their ranks and movable property and were exiled. Volynskii was deprived of his estates and beheaded. A decade later, Elizabeth permitted the Dolgorukiis to return from exile and returned Volynskii's confiscated estates to his children.[85]

A number of less serious crimes could also result in confiscation. As previously mentioned, beginning in the seventeenth century and intensifying under Peter, evasion of service or the protection of service evaders was a crime punishable by confiscation. In 1715, for example, twenty-seven men were punished with confiscation of their pomest'e and votchina for failing to appear for military inspection the previous year.[86] One also occasionally finds documentation of confiscation for insubordination, as in the case of Captain Mikhail Dukhnovskii whose pomest′e and peasants in Smolensk uezd were confiscated in 1705 for his "cheekiness."[87] State officials were frequently subject to such punishment for bribe-taking and otherwise abusing their positions. The Ober-Fiscal Alexei Nesterov and his fellow fiscal Savva Popstov were both convicted in 1722 of a list of crimes, not the least of which was abuse of power and bribe-taking. As punishment for their misdeeds, all of their movable and immovable property was taken, along with their heads.[88] Similarly, government officials could be penalized for failing to execute their duties correctly.

The most common reason for confiscation, however, seems to have been debt. As historians from Soloviev to Arcadius Kahan have shown, the price for "Westernization" and an acceptable noble lifestyle was a high one, and consequently many nobles quickly found themselves unable to make ends meet.[89] As we have already seen, many nobles mortgaged property to keep themselves afloat. As a result, nobles frequently suffered confiscation for debts owed either to fellow subjects or to various state agencies. This reality is well documented in records of the Senate and the Chancellery of Confiscation. If these documents tell us regrettably little about the nature of the debt, they do testify to the extensive confiscation of both movable and immovable property. Thus, in 1723, Rodion Khodyrev's movable and immovable property was confiscated to settle his debts. In May 1729, the Chancellery of Confiscation recorded in its journal that the immovable property of the widow Aksinia Kolycheva in Volodimerskii and Koshirkii uezds had been confiscated and sold for her failure to pay money owed to the Arrears Chancellery. Similarly, in 1740, Nikolai Norman, a customs inspector in Vyborg, suffered confiscation for his tax arrears. Many others would suffer the same unfortunate fate.[90]

Although in theory, a noble could avoid confiscation by managing his finances properly, in reality, we know that most eighteenth-century nobles were overwhelmed by debt in an effort to meet the demands of the noble lifestyle as it had been defined by Peter the Great's reforms. Thus nobles were caught in a hopeless quandary, which only the wealthiest might hope to avoid. Wealthier nobles, however, also tended to be more politically connected and therefore were threatened by confiscations of a different sort.

Thus, we are left with the picture of a nobility whose overall insecurity often led to the cannibalistic exploitation of its own members and the further undermining of a corporate identity.

In the second half of the eighteenth century, confiscation as a punishment for crime did appear less frequently in legislation and, on the whole, confiscation seems to have been executed less frequently than under Peter I and Elizabeth. Nonetheless, confiscation was so firmly embedded in the state's vocabulary that even Peter III's Manifesto on the Freedom of the Nobility in 1762 warned of this possibility. The Manifesto freed the nobleman from mandatory state service and permitted him to travel abroad, but only with the explicit condition that he was to return home "when necessity demands . . . with all possible speed under pain of sequestration of his estate."[91] Moreover, some common crimes still warranted seizure of property. A law of 1778, for example, threatened confiscation for frivolous lawsuits regarding the surveying of land.[92] Later, Catherine's Charter to the Nobility pledged that no noble would be deprived of his property without due process. When confiscation was necessary, the guilty party's property would be handed over to his children.[93] As we have seen, however, this dimension of the Charter was less promising than it seemed. Although the Charter promised members of the nobility security from arbitrary confiscation and corporal punishment, it also established that a noble's status could be taken away if he committed a crime "irreconcilable with the principles of noble dignity," including such crimes as "violation of an oath," "deceitful conduct," and "crimes that by law entail deprivation of honor and corporal punishment."[94] Moreover, once a landowner had lost his noble status he was no longer protected by the guarantees of the Charter. This interpretation was confirmed by a law of 1797, which stated that once a noble lost his noble status, then the other rules regarding noble exemption from certain punishments no longer applied.[95]

This exception is illustrated in a number of published legal decisions.[96] In 1790, for example, following his publication of *A Journey from St. Petersburg to Moscow,* Catherine punished Alexander Radishchev with the deprivation of his rank and noble status, exile to Siberia, and confiscation of his property; that property was given to his children.[97] Two years later, Catherine threatened confiscation for Princess Varvara Shakovskaia, nee Strogonova, and her daughter who were then living in Paris.

Princess Shakovskaia, without the Empress's knowledge, and "against the will of God," had married her daughter to Prince Aremberg, who had participated in two uprisings against legal power. Catherine ordered that Shakovskaia's property was to be placed under restriction, and if Princess Aremberg failed to return to Russia upon her mother's death, she would be deprived of her inheritance. Aremberg's children would retain their rights of inheritance only if they returned to Russia prior to the age of five and were raised in the Russian Orthodox faith.[98] Such confiscation persisted under the reign of Paul as well.[99] In 1801, Count Vorontsov's property was confiscated for his failure to pay off his debts in London.[100]

Later in the nineteenth century, several intellectuals suffered a fate similar to that of Radishchev; having dared to challenge the government, they became outcasts, deprived of noble privilege. The historian Prince Petr Dolgorukov, for example, had strongly supported the emancipation of the serfs, but in 1859, disgusted with the slow pace of reform, he went abroad, declaring, "I was born and lived . . . in a country of general slavery; . . . I decided to end my days in a free country." In 1860, he published a collection of essays entitled, "The Truth about Russia," in which he predicted catastrophe for the Russian government if it did not introduce a constitution, abolish serfdom, and enact administrative and legal reforms. When he refused to withdraw his book from sale and return to Russia, he was deprived of all of his titles and honor, and in 1861, the Senate declared him permanently banished. Though his family still had rights to his property, Dolgorukov himself had no legal claims once his noble status was removed.[101] In a slightly different case, Vladimir Pecherin, a classics professor at Moscow University, left Russia in 1836, disillusioned by Russia's oppressive atmosphere. In 1845, while in England, he became a preacher at the Falmouth monastery. Hearing about this, the government of Nicholas I demanded his return. When Pecherin refused, the Senate deprived him of his rights and status and declared him banished from Russia.[102]

On occasion, confiscation could have unforeseen political consequences. During the reign of Peter the Great, the state had confiscated the property of Fedor Mirovich and his family as punishment for his participation in the Mazepa affair. Years later, in 1744, Mirovich's mother returned from exile and asked for some of that family land back, however, a final decision was never reached on the matter. Ultimately, though the Senate supported the old woman's claims, Catherine rejected them in 1764. This refusal had fateful consequences, for that very year, Vasilii Mirovich led an attempt to free and place on the throne Prince Ivan VI. At least one of the possible reasons for Mirovich's treasonous behavior was his anger over Catherine's refusal to return his family's confiscated lands.[103]

Although it is difficult to draw any statistical conclusions about the frequency of confiscation, the combination of evidence from secondary and primary sources suggests that it loomed as a persistent threat in the lives of eighteenth-century noblemen and women. In her study of the 179 men who held positions in the top four military and civil ranks in the year 1730, for example, Brenda Meehan-Waters determined that more than one-fifth (forty) of her study group were either victims or beneficiaries of confiscation. Twenty-three had suffered confiscation of their property, while a number of others had received confiscated properties.[104]

This portrait of a nobility continually faced with the possibility of confiscation is further enhanced by the data compiled by E. I. Indova. In her study of the Russian state's role in land redistribution, Indova has compiled a list of landowners whose land was taken away by the state in the first half of the eighteenth century (1701–55). The list includes the names of 124 different people of various positions and ranks, ranging from those described as princes, boyars, and other nobles, to clerks, stol'niks, colonels, captains, and admirals. Among those on Indova's list are Menshikov, along with Peter the Great's first wife and some of her relatives. The reasons given for the confiscations in Indova's list vary, covering the range of possibilities mentioned earlier—theft, embezzlement, debt, failure to appear for service, or political reasons, such as participation in the "Alexei affair" or the "Menshikov affair." Occasionally, the record cites no specific reason but simply indicates that the person's land had been confiscated "for political opposition" or "for disobedience."[105] Moreover, a close reading of P. N. Baranov's descriptions of Senate ukazy between 1725 and 1762 reveal over 200 references to confiscated property.[106]

The impression conveyed by these secondary studies is confirmed by an abundance of archival evidence. References to, and records of, confiscation of both movable and immovable property for all of the reasons cited above can be found in a number of collections, including documents from the Votchina College, the Senate, and the Chancellery of Confiscation. Thus, although it would be premature to draw firm statistical conclusions about the frequency of confiscation, the combination of evidence from secondary and primary sources makes a strong case for the argument that confiscation was a clear and ever-present danger in the lives of eighteenth-century noblemen and women, particularly given the prevalence of noble indebtedness.

The nobility's own complaints about confiscation support this impression. On more than one occasion in the eighteenth century, members of the nobility proposed exemption from confiscation. In 1763, for example, during the proceedings of Catherine's committee to discuss the matter of noble independence, Count Alexei Bestuzhev-Riumin requested due process before the confiscation of a nobleman's property.[107] Moreover, the noble nakazy expressed concerns about confiscation as well. Some nobles, for example, asked that confiscation of noble property be eliminated as a punishment, except in cases of excessive debt.[108]

There were efforts to protect women and children from the sins of their husbands and fathers. In 1718, Peter the Great had specified that a wife's dowry property should never be taken as punishment for her husband's crimes. The courts upheld this right in subsequent years. Thus in 1729, Anna Nikitina petitioned for the return of her dowry, valued at 1,200 rubles, that was confiscated along with her husband's property as punishment for taking bribes. In accordance with the law of 1718, the Senate ordered that the money received from the sale of her husband's property should be used to compensate her. Similarly, in 1741, Fedosia Putiatina petitioned for the return of her dowry property, which was confiscated along with her husband's property for his alleged misappropriation of funds. Putiatina underscored her "desperate propertylessness" and her need for subsistence for herself and her son. Anna granted her request. Even children could invoke this right if their mothers were no longer alive to do so. In 1721, Petr Rimskii-Korsakov petitioned for the return of his mother's dowry villages, which had been confiscated along with his father's property and then granted to someone else. The Senate considered the law of 1718; however, there was some question as to whether the law should apply since Rimskii-Korsakov's property had been seized for debts, not a crime. Despite this initial concern, the Senate ultimately decided that Petr should be compensated.[109]

In the second half of the eighteenth century, it became more common for confiscated property to be set aside for the heirs of the perpetrator. Such was the case with Vasilii Nesterov whose property was confiscated in 1762 for his brutal murder of a servant. Nesterov was exiled and the Senate ordered that his property should be distributed to his heirs as if he had died.[110] With Catherine's Charter to the Nobility, this increasingly common practice became law. Catherine ordered that "In the event of his conviction of even the most serious crime, the inherited estate of a well-born [nobleman] shall be passed on to his legal heir or heirs."[111]

Despite these attempts to shield innocent family members, confiscation was still an onerous threat. The ever-present threat of confiscation affected Russian nobles on a number of levels. First, it contributed to the sense of insecurity that Russian nobles had about their land. Already concerned about the possibility of redemption and the encroachment and intrigues of neighbors and enemies, nobles also had to fear punishment by the state. Although most nobles could expect to avoid confiscation for crimes such as treason, debt always loomed as a possible cause for confiscation.

There is yet another, more sinister, way in which confiscation affected the outlook of the Russian nobility. It is important to remember that if confiscation was devastating for some, it was nonetheless beneficial for others. The records from the Senate and Votchina College provide many examples of nobles directly petitioning for the immovable property, such as land and houses, of their fallen peers. Lev Selivanov was such an opportunist. In September 1730, he submitted a long petition recounting his faithful service record and requesting villages that had been confiscated from Alexei and Ivan Dolgorukov.[112] Likewise, there are many examples in the Senate and Votchina College records and the *Polnoe sobranie zakonov* of nobles being granted the confiscated properties of other nobles. Menshikov's properties, for example, were distributed to a number of people.[113] In other cases, property was put up for sale and available to the highest bidder.

Such opportunistic gain, however, was not limited to immovable property. Nobles also frequently saw the occasion of a fellow noble's misfortune as a chance to scoop up valuable household and personal items. Thus the records of the Chancellery of Confiscation provide lists of such items, sometimes along with the name of the purchaser and the price paid. It is interesting to note the extent to which confiscation often involved the removal of items of the most personal nature. In 1731, for example, the Chancellery records list such confiscated items as belts, trousers, silk stockings, ties, scarves, ladies' gloves, shirts, hats, winter boots, and a "board for writing numerals."[114] This was not an isolated case; there are many examples of the confiscation of personal property. In 1718, for example, during the "Alexei affair," a number of nobles suffered the confiscation of their silverware.[115] All of these cases lend some credence to the report of the otherwise notoriously unreliable Rulhiere who, in his account of Russia in 1762, described nobles returning from exile, hoping to regain some of their possessions. In Rulhiere's words:

> All these exiles, having been plundered at the period of their disgrace, demanded the restoration of their fortunes: they were conducted into the immense magazines, in which, according to the custom of the country, were preserved all the confiscations, the sad deposits of the ruins of favorites, where all the spoils of these famous wrecks were arranged in the order of time. They sought in the dust for their valuable moveables, their diamond insignia, presents which kings themselves had formerly made them to purchase their influence; and too often they discovered them, after fruitless researches, in the possession of the favourites of the last reign.[116]

The numerous lists of personal property found in the Chancellery records suggest that this was more than a product of Rulhiere's imagination.

This constant possibility for intrigue and opportunism certainly had an impact upon the mentality of members of the nobility. Denis Fonvizin, in an essay written in 1783, described this impact as follows:

> When justice has been turned into a mart, when one may fear to lose one's own property unfairly and hope to take another's unjustly, then everyone hastens to enjoy unreservedly that which he has in his possession, pandering to his own corrupt passions.[117]

Thus Russian nobles, confronted with the reality of confiscation, frequently saw the misfortune of one of their own as an opportunity for gain. This attitude, combined with the unscrupulous behavior frequently found in the provinces, helped to create a mood of mistrust and mutual exploitation among members of the nobility, so that instead of working together as a corporate unit, they frequently worked against one another.

Russia's rulers undoubtedly recognized the close connection between property rights and political freedom and sought to use this link to their own advantage. Indova has argued that the Russian state used its power in matters of land to manipulate the nobility, using the redistribution of property, through grants and confiscation, to strengthen those branches that were supportive and weaken those branches that were not. There is no shortage of examples of nobles falling from favor, particularly during power transitions, and being stripped of their property and sent into exile. Even the director of the Chancellery of Confiscation, Platon Ivanovich Musin-Pushkin, was not exempt; in 1740 he fell from favor and his estates were confiscated.[118] Moreover, one finds substantial archival evidence that confiscated property was frequently reissued to other nobles waiting in the wings. This circulation of property undermined noble solidarity and instead encouraged nobles to prey upon one another. The resulting insecurity was only heightened by the Russian system of service, with regular rotations and long periods away from home. Whether or not we should view these policies as consciously serving an agenda of the Russian state to keep the nobility in a state of relative weakness and subjugation is, of course, open to debate. It is clear, however, that the state's policies of confiscation contributed not only to the nobility's sense of insecurity about its land, but also to the weakness of its corporate identity.

8
The Many Dimensions of Noble Insecurity

Friends and relations advised Nicholas to decline the inheritance. But he regarded such a refusal as a slur on his father's memory, which he held sacred, and therefore would not hear of refusing and accepted the inheritance together with the obligation to pay the debts.

—Tolstoi, *Voina i mir*

ALTHOUGH THE OBSERVATION THAT RUSSIAN NOBLES SUFFERED from insecurity in landholding in itself is not new, it is useful to examine the diverse ways in which individual nobles experienced this insecurity. For the purposes of this discussion, we can highlight six major factors that contributed to the nobility's insecurity in landholding—the laws of inheritance and the nature of noble landholding, the land survey, the peripatetic nature of state service, the government's confiscation policies, noble debt, and the policy of redemption. Some of these factors originated prior to Peter's reign, but all of them grew in importance during the remainder of the century.

Russia's rulers had long taken an active role in the regulation and enforcement of laws pertaining to the inheritance of estates, a fact of which the nobility was most forcefully reminded by Peter's Law of Single Inheritance in 1714. Its repeal in 1731, changed, but by no means eliminated, state control in matters of inheritance. As we have seen, the state continued to tinker with the laws of inheritance throughout the century, addressing such issues as distribution in collateral lines and the inheritance rights of married daughters. None of these laws proved as controversial as Peter's Law of Single Inheritance, but various members of the nobility remained dissatisfied with the rules of inheritance, periodically seeking to have them altered in one way or another. The most vivid evidence of the nobility's interest in matters of property disposal occurred in the noble nakazy of 1767 which, although often in conflict with one another, clearly reflect the nobility's desire for full property rights, including the right to sell and bequeath land as they wished. While Catherine the Great's Charter to the Nobility in 1785 was a major step in creating greater property rights, it did not grant the nobility the security of property it desired; while it offered landowners the right to freely dispose of their acquired land by will, patrimonial land was still governed by the laws of inheritance under all circumstances. Although the Charter offered some new rights to the nobility, it did not grant complete freedom of disposal.

The practice of partible inheritance, which the nobility had fought to retain during Peter's reign, ironically produced insecurities of a different sort. When a father's land was parceled out at his death, specified portions were given to the widow and eligible heirs from *each* village and *each* holding. The results of this extreme method of division were twofold. First, the constant division of land from generation to generation quickly resulted in fragmentation and the ownership of smaller plots. These small plots were often barely large enough to support the heir, and thus the result was growing financial hardship and insecurity. The extent of this fragmentation could often be quite significant, and many nobles complained about this problem. Sergei Aksakov, in his family history, described the frustration of his grandfather, Stepan Mikhailovich, who felt crowded on his own estate because it was surrounded by rival claimants, the result of years of fragmentation. Aksakov explained:

> the trouble was, that the estate which his great-grandfather had held in absolute possession, had ceased to belong to one owner. This happened quite simply: for three successive generations the family consisted of one son and several daughters; and, when some of these daughters were married, their portions took the shape of a certain number of serfs and a certain amount of land. Though their shares were not large, yet, as the land had never been properly surveyed, at the time four intruders asserted their right to share in the management of it.[1]

This reality was particularly true in large families. Once a man's widow and daughters received their legal portions, there might be little remaining to divide among his sons. Let us consider the example of Stepan Opukhtin's immovable property, divided after his death in 1746. Leaving behind a widow, five sons, and three daughters, his property in Galich and Vladimir uezds was to be divided between them all.[2] Even when a landowner left no children of his own, his property would be similarly parceled between relatives if he had left no will. Thus when Nikolai Mikulin died in 1738, the Votchina College decided to divide his eighty-three chetverts of land in Simbirsk province in the following way: half of the property, approximately 41½ chetverts, was to be divided between Nikolai's cousin Semen and his nephew Vasilii; the other half was to be divided between Nikolai's four cousins, Gleb, Akim, Alexander, and Kondrat.[3] Bolotov's answer to the questionnaire of the Free Economic Society is testimony to the severity of this problem:

> there are not many villages belonging to only one landlord: most are divided among several landlords. These landlords usually come from one family . . . There are often quarrels between them . . . Even if there is little disagreement, there are many disadvantages which result from the distribution of land in pieces and the number of landlords. It is impossible to fertilize or plow the land properly. No one can do his sowing at the correct time.[4]

There were ways in which noble families could mitigate the effects of such division. As discussed in chapter 3, inherited property could be divided between heirs "to one place," that is, in consolidated parcels. Although there is substantial evidence that over the course of the eighteenth century many families elected to use such methods, it nonetheless remains true that, even with such options, the fragmentation of estates persisted. In fact, contemporary sources indicate that nobles themselves were aware of the hazards of partible inheritance. In 1764, for example, Elizaveta Lobkova petitioned the Senate about the division of her deceased husband Dmitrii's property between his heirs, arguing that if it were divided by the Votchina College according to the standard procedure—that is, each property divided between all heirs—then it would result in great ruin and make it impossible to settle his debts. For this reason, she asked that Dmitrii's property be divided "to one place."[5]

There were, however, nobles who acknowledged the possible benefits of some form of single inheritance. Already by 1767 this sentiment could be found in the noble nakazy of Moscow uezd. The first real entail was established by an ukaz of Catherine II in February 1774 at the request of Zakhar Chernyshev. Chernyshev requested that his land remain forever intact, to be handed down from generation to generation to the eldest son of the owner if possible. Should it become necessary for the land to go to a female family member, then her heirs were to assume the Chernyshev name and coat of arms. Most importantly, the land should never be fragmented between siblings nor given to members of another clan.[6] Chernyshev's lead was followed by several other nobles in the late eighteenth and early nineteenth centuries as well, but the establishment of entails was only made widely possible by an ukaz of Nicholas I in 1845. This law stipulated that estates must contain more than 10,000 *desiatiny* or land yielding at least 12,000 rubles in annual income.[7] In 1899 this minimum was lowered to 5,000 desiatiny. Nonetheless, the minimum requirements were too high for most nobles and thus between 1845 and 1905 only sixty entails were established.[8]

Despite the initiative of some nobles themselves and the support of the government, single inheritance never caught on as the predominant method of land transference. For many, it simply was not a financially feasible option. Thus even in the wake of these attempts partible inheritance continued to be the preferred practice for the majority of Russia's noble class. The result, of course, was the continued fragmentation of landholdings. Indeed, the problem of splintered landowning was still so severe by the reign of Alexander I that in 1804 the Free Economic Society organized an essay contest calling for a solution to the dilemma.[9] Nonetheless, until the end of the Imperial period, partible inheritance and fragmented estates continued to be the norm. At the end of the nineteenth century it was reported that in many gubernii there were entire villages of hereditary nobles with the same surname who inhabited what had once been a large estate but had since been repeatedly divided over many generations.[10]

The fragmentation of estates, combined with the selling and mortgaging of plots, also resulted in a growing interspersal of landholdings between owners. In the 1840s the German traveler August von Haxthausen reported having heard of one village that was split between eighty-three owners.[11] The complaints of nobles themselves support this claim. One noble, for example, reported that despite his substantial holdings,

> there was not more than five desiatiny in succession in a single place; the rest of our arable land was irregularly splintered to such an extent

> that would have been impossible to believe without seeing it. In one place there was less then half a desiatina of a strip, then, after a larger area, there was again a scrap less than a quarter of a desiatina.[12]

In 1734, Daria Golovkina made a similar complaint in a petition concerning her widow's portion. She argued that the villages that she received after the death of her husband and father-in-law, contrary to the dishonest presentation of her brother-in-law, were scattered, in some places as far as 170 versts apart, with many other landowners in between.[13]

Such interspersal of landholdings resulted not only in confusion, but opened the door to exploitation by the strong and unscrupulous. There is much evidence in both secondary and primary sources that theft and violence were a major source of insecurity for nobles outside of the capital. The noble nakazy, for example, contained many complaints about richer nobles exploiting poorer nobles by outright theft of their land.[14] At times, nobles simply used their peasants as private armies to seize the land in question.[15] At others, to judge from Pushkin's *Dubrovsky,* wealthy and powerful nobles used the bureaucracy itself to seize their neighbors' land.

As though the fragmentation and interspersal of landholdings due to partible inheritance were not troublesome enough, the noble pattern of landownership was further complicated by the fact that most landowners possessed land in more than one uezd, province, or guberniia. This pattern emerged as nobles were granted land in various parts of the empire and was exacerbated by their own acquisitions. In the second half of the eighteenth century this pattern of scattered ownership was further facilitated by the opening up of eastern and southern frontier areas.[16] Aksakov's father, for example, went to great lengths to acquire property from the Bashkirs.[17] Thus most inheritance disputes found in the records of the Votchina College and the Senate concern the division of land in more than one uezd. In many cases, such documents describe landownership by one person in five or more uezds. Alexei Khovanskii, for example, died around 1722 leaving behind property in six uezds—Suzdalskii, Donkovskii, Karsunuvskii, Volotskii, Novotorzhskii, and Moskovskii.[18] Similarly, when Iakov Pokhvisnev died in 1758, he left behind a childless widow and immovable property in five uezds in two guberniia—Venevskii, Kolomenskii, Epifanskii, Riazhskii, and

Efremovskii.[19] These scattered distributions are representative of the typical pattern of noble landholding in eighteenth-century Russia and contributed significantly to the problems of confusion and disorder in the countryside.[20]

Russia's rulers had attempted to eliminate confusion in the countryside several times over the course of the century. There had been a number of attempts at a general land survey, none of them particularly successful. A general survey had been initiated in 1676 in an effort to update land registers, which had last been updated in the 1630s. Like many subsequent attempts, this survey saw little success, though Sophia persisted in this endeavor throughout her regency.[21] In 1682 surveyors were sent out by the Pomestnyi Prikaz to all parts of Russia, armed with a list of penalties for anyone caught tampering with boundary markers.[22] These surveyors encountered such resistance that in May 1683 the government was forced to issue another decree on the matter, threatening fines, imprisonment, or the knout for those who interfered with the process of surveying or for those surveyors who were tempted by the offer of bribes.[23] Still, the problems continued. In June 1686 the government ordered that any landowner who harassed a surveyor or stole his measuring tape should be publicly flogged.[24] The survey itself was never completed.

In 1754, Elizabeth endeavored to succeed where her predecessors had failed, ordering a general land survey. Reaffirming Peter's consolidation of votchina and pomest'e, Elizabeth's decree also introduced new technology, replacing the rope previously used in measuring with a chain and also ordering that all surveyors be equipped with astrolabes.[25] In conjunction with this, all non-nobles were forced to sell their settled land within six months, even if they had acquired it legally. Despite these efforts, the land survey of 1754 also failed. The obstacles that the surveyors encountered were so formidable that by 1762 not even the Moscow district had been fully measured.[26]

Catherine's surveying efforts a decade later met with greater success. In 1765, she ordered a general land survey, specifying that surveyors would be expected only to measure and describe land; disputes over boundaries or titles would be referred to special land courts or the Votchina College.[27] Furthermore, the Commission on the State Survey recognized de facto possession of land, ordering all claimants to leave boundaries as they currently stood. In resolving disputes, the entire burden of proof lay with the claimant, who had to produce valid documentation.[28] Moreover, by claiming 10 percent of all disputed properties for the state, Catherine encouraged people to settle disputes out of court.[29] By 1796, about 144 millions desiatiny of land had been surveyed, and by the 1840s most of European Russia had been surveyed as well.

In many ways, however, the survey created as many problems as it solved.[30] First, the survey process itself had many shortcomings; for example, by resolving disputes over entire estates but failing to address the problem of quarrels over *portions* of estates, the survey left many disputes unsettled. In addition, the success of the land survey was both hindered and thwarted by the actions of nobles themselves. The entire process was rife with bribery and corruption, and the falsification of documents was common.[31] Bolotov, for example, admitted in his memoirs to having attempted to bribe steppe land surveyors and Moscow state officials to confirm his ownership of land in Tambov province.[32] Bribery was used not simply to assert effective claims over disputed lands, but also to protect one's own lands from outright seizure through reclassification. In general, the Survey Act of 1765 caused landowners, particularly absentee landlords, to worry about their properties and fear the machinations of both surveying officials and rapacious neighbors.[33] Thus even the state's efforts to eradicate confusion in the countryside only resulted, for the most part, in a heightened degree of noble insecurity.

The fears of absentee landlords arose, in part, from the nature of state service. The extreme centralization of the Russian state meant that personnel decisions were made on an empirewide basis, ignoring the nobleman's wishes, circumstances, or regional ties. The nobleman was a small cog in a big machine, his service assignment based on the needs of the empire. Thus the noble serviceman was frequently rotated through little or no choice of his own, continuously uprooted and prevented from developing strong ties either to his home estate or to his current region of administration.[34]

The results of this mobile service pattern were several. For most nobles, the peripatetic nature of state service meant long stretches of time away from home, family, and property. Countess Golovina recalls her husband's absences in her memoirs: "My husband's absence was of several months' duration, and he returned only to leave me again. He hoped to come back to me soon;

but the circumstances of the war had in the meantime changed, and he found it impossible to join me . . ."[35] From a practical perspective, this could be problematic as noble landowners were forced to entrust the management of their estates either to family members or to bailiffs. Absentee landlords were particularly vulnerable to the machinations of greedy and powerful neighbors, particularly during the resolution of boundary or ownership disputes. They feared, with good reason, that during such times their neighbors might take advantage of their absence to manipulate land boundaries and make false claims on their land. The memoirist Aksakov describes his father's concerns about this possibility. The senior Aksakov, who was no longer even in service, recognized the importance of being actively involved in his lawsuit. Thus, when family demands took the senior Aksakov back to his estate in the midst of a lawsuit in Simbirsk guberniia, he reportedly complained, "if I am not present to watch over my case, I lose it; that's all."[36]

The constant and peripatetic nature of state service posed other threats to absentee landlords as well. When conflicts over property arose, nobles frequently complained in their petitions either that they had been taken advantage of or had been unable to participate in some land transaction because they were away in service. In 1717, for example, Vasilii Elagin stated in his petition to redeem family property that his nephews had mortgaged this property in 1701–02 when he was away in the Ladoga Regiment in His Majesty's service.[37] In 1740, Egor Rozderishin made a similar claim in his redemption petition. He stated that while he was away in Her Majesty's service, his cousin had sold some family property. Well aware that the law stipulated a three-year term for redemption claims, Rozderishin emphasized that he had only recently been granted leave, and had been unable to petition earlier because of his lengthy service.[38]

Absence in service could also interfere with a man's ability to assume ownership of land that he obtained by inheritance or marriage. As we have seen, potential heirs and future husbands often found it impossible to complete the necessary steps of petitioning and registration if they were far away in the tsar's service. Many contemporary disputes cite this problem. During the inheritance dispute over the property of Semen Korobov, for example, one of the hopeful heirs, Demian, declared that although his cousin Ivan had been bequeathed Semen's immovable property by will, he had failed to register the property to himself due to his continuous absence in service. Demian emphasized that eventually Ivan died in a military campaign and thus never officially gained ownership of the land. Similarly, in 1712, Mikhail Engalychev asked for permission to register his wife's dowry in his name after their marriage, since his service obligation had prevented him from doing it before.[39]

In addition to the legal problems posed by extensive time away from home, the constant mobility of noble landowners also resulted in a sense of rootlessness. This rootlessness was a central theme of Marc Raeff's work on the eighteenth-century Russian nobility. Constantly on the move, noble servicemen were never permitted to develop geographic roots or local solidarities. This mobility and rootlessness further led to a fragmentation of the nobility as a class and hindered the development of a corporate identity. Finally, always away from home, noble servicemen had a weak sense of attachment to any individual estate. As a result, although the end of compulsory service in 1762 made it possible for nobles to retire to their estates, and while some did, there never developed the strong sentimental and familial attachments to land and locality that can be found in Western Europe. The long years of absence and detachment, for the most part, had done irrevocable damage to the nobility's sentimental ties to the land.[40]

The nobility's weak attachment to the land also can be attributed to the government policy of confiscation as well. As we have seen, though nobles had some control over the likelihood of their property being confiscated, there was still an insecurity that went along with the knowledge that the government could, and did, seize property. Moreover, confiscation often led to unseemly behavior from fellow nobles, eager to take advantage of another's bad fortune. Although confiscation occurred less frequently by the end of the eighteenth century, the damage to noble security and noble property rights had been done.

One of the major causes for the confiscation of immovable property—debt—was a serious problem in its own right.[41] All European nobilities were characterized to some extent by severe debt and in all countries the degree of that indebtedness depended on the circumstances of the individual noble. Nobles at court and in the cities were under great pressure to display their wealth in their homes, their personal appearance, and their leisure pursuits. Provincial nobles, though perhaps removed from the social pressures of metropolitan life, still often emulated their city brethren, spending much of their time engaged in visiting and other forms of entertainment.[42]

The Russian nobility shared this characteristic with Western elites. Like the aristocracies of Europe, there were vast discrepancies of wealth among members of the Russian nobility. Nobles at court or in the capitals, for example, became increasingly encumbered by the demands of a Western lifestyle over the course of the eighteenth century. They were expected to dress and entertain in keeping with their position in society, and were under pressure to provide for their families in the same manner. Life at court was expensive and wrecked the pocketbook of many a noble. Mikhail Vorontsov, for example, despite, or indeed because of, his close ties to Elizabeth's court, found himself pleading to the Empress for financial assistance in 1751. "We are all your faithful slaves," he wrote. "Without the grace and rewards from your Imperial Highness we cannot live. I do not know the family of a single house in the realm which on its own, without the rewards of the monarch's generosity, could sustain itself."[43] Nobles like Vorontsov and their wealthy counterparts in the provinces shared many of the same concerns, spending vast quantities of money on lavish estates and gardens, equipped with immense libraries, peasant orchestras and acting troupes.[44]

The concerns of petty nobles, on the other hand, revolved more around issues of survival. Many nobles lived in extreme poverty; not owning a single serf, they tilled the land themselves and became virtually indistinguishable from the peasantry.[45] Indeed, the poverty among provincial nobles was so great that in 1771 Stepan Tiutchev reported to the Senate that as many as 200 young nobles wanted to enter imperial service, but lacked the necessary clothes to report for duty.[46]

Whether rich or poor, virtually all Russian nobles, it seems, borrowed to make ends meet. The largest landowners borrowed the largest sums, of course. Prince I. B. Iusupov, for example, owed government lending institutions 100,000 rubles by 1798; this amount increased to 693,630 rubles by 1818, and to over 2 million rubles by the time of his death in 1831.[47] Iusupov was far from alone. Many other wealthy nobles, among them such men as N. P. Sheremetev and B. A. Kurakin, were in excessive debt as well.[48] The memoirs of Princess Dashkova testify to this pervasive problem. When Dashkova's husband died, he left behind significant debts that she and the other guardians had to settle; later, Dashkova had to bail her daughter out of debt as well.[49]

While Russian nobles were not unique in their problem with debt and continual borrowing, they seem to differ from some of their European counterparts in the degree and consequences of that indebtedness. Whereas in England, for example, the courts were reluctant to seize mortgaged estates so long as the owner paid the interest regularly, it is not clear that this arrangement existed in Russia.[50] Records from the Chancellery of Confiscation show that, on occasion, the Chancellery would make arrangements with a debtor, specifying a term for repayment. When that term was up, however, the property was ordered confiscated. As previously discussed, the Chancellery records indicate that this was no empty threat.

The indebtedness of the Russian nobility was so legendary that more than one visitor to Russia deemed it worthy of note. William Tooke, for example, visiting Russia in the 1790s, described the impressive ability of bankrupt nobles to live far beyond their means. He described how some nobles, "entirely run out their estates, and plunged their families in distress by unthriftiness . . . extravagant expenses, and idle speculations." Despite this, Tooke observed, "some noblemen whose estates by this means are put into sequestration and carefully managed, find them insufficient to satisfy the creditors, yet afterwards live in a sort of affluence and at a greater expence than would be reasonably imagined."[51] John Quincy Adams noted the profligacy of noble spending as well:

> The tone of society among us is almost universally marked by an excess of expenses over income. The public officers all live far beyond their salaries, many of them are notorious for never paying their debts, and still more for preserving the balance by means which in our country would be deemed dishonorable . . .[52]

The desperate financial plight of the nobility is reflected by numerous examples of nobles pleading for assistance, asking permission to sell land or petitioning for land grants. In 1751, for example, Stepan Bariatinskii explained in his petition that in 1747 his father, Andrei, died, followed by his mother, Lukeria, in 1750. Stepan was left behind with three underaged siblings. His parents left behind immovable property in various uezds, totaling some 1,600 souls; they also left behind, however, significant debts. Thus, Stepan asked for permission to mortgage some of his parents' property in order to settle these debts. The Senate granted his request.[53] Occasionally, a petitioner might request greater assistance. In the early 1760s, for example, General Mayor Vasilii Naryshkin petitioned Catherine that his immovable property was mortgaged into various hands, and because he was unable to pay off his debts, he was in danger of losing these properties. Catherine commanded that Naryshkin be given a loan of 35,000 rubles for ten years without interest, to be paid in yearly installments of 3,500 rubles. In return, a specified portion of his immovable property would be taken into mortgage.[54] In fact, debt became such a problem for Russian nobles during the eighteenth century that occasionally legal heirs would refuse their inheritance because of the heavy debt attached to it. On February 9, 1775, for example, the Saltykov children, Ivan, Natalia, and Alexandra, renounced their inheritance rights to the immovable property of their aunt, Natalia Likhoreva, because it was too heavily encumbered with debts and creditors.[55]

The state recognized the problem of noble indebtedness early in the century and made a number of attempts to address it. The first law that confronted the problem of noble indebtedness was enacted in August 1729. It considered the debts of the noble Captain Lieutenant Vasilii Sheremetev who died leaving behind a wife, Irina, and several small children. In the interest of the children's well-being, it was ordered to place the children in the guardianship of several trusted persons, among them Vasilii's father, Ivan Sheremetev, and Irina's brother, Prince Romodanovskii. The guardians were ordered to preserve the movable and immovable property for the children, but were given permission to sell some of his Nizhegorodskii votchina for the payment of debts.[56]

In subsequent years, this permission would be granted to the widow herself. In 1731, the widows Princess Maria Dolgorukaia and Fekla Protaseva petitioned for permission to sell some of their husbands' holdings for the payment of debts and the redemption of mortgaged property. The practical difficulty arose from the fact that their children, the heirs, were still minors. In such cases, women were not allowed to sell any of the property without royal permission. After reviewing the case, the Senate recommended permitting the women to sell the amount of property necessary to redeem property and pay debts. This scenario was played out several more times in the following years, and was not restricted to poor widows. In 1733, Prince Ivan Masalskii found himself in the same predicament. His wife, Princess Natalia Petrovna had died in 1732, leaving him five children and extensive mortgages on her immovable property. Thus the Senate decided to grant Masalskii permission to sell the amount of property necessary to settle his wife's debts.[57]

The recognition by the government that noblemen and women were becoming overwhelmed by debt can be found in other legislation of this period as well. A decree of 1733, for example, voiced concern that those in need of money were forced to borrow from foreigners or other Russians at high interest rates and with excessive collateral. Interest rates often soared to 12, 15, or 20 percent, and on occasion the interest was subtracted in advance from the sum being loaned. Also, unscrupulous lenders sometimes refused to return the collateral if the borrower was even a few days late in paying. Therefore, the decree ordered that henceforth the Bureau of Money (*Monetnaia Kontora*) was to loan money to people of all ranks at an interest rate of 8 percent.[58]

All of these early attempts were disorganized and insufficient, and it was only after midcentury that the state began to offer significant opportunities for noble borrowing, namely with the founding, in May 1754 of a Noble Bank, with branches in Moscow and St. Petersburg. Based upon a state-funded capital of 750,000 rubles, the bank was designed to enable landowners to borrow money at 6 percent, using immovable property as collateral. The bank was authorized to loan up to 10,000 rubles, assessing the value of the collateral at ten rubles per male serf. The borrowed sum was to be repaid within three years from the loan date.[59] It is worth noting that all conditions could be overridden if the Russian ruler chose to intervene on someone's behalf. For example, on January 14, 1763, Catherine declared that Prince Nikolai Davydov was to be granted an interest-free loan from the noble bank in the amount of 6,000 rubles for ten years, to be paid in yearly installments of 600 rubles, taking from him in mortgage 500 souls.[60]

The problem of noble indebtedness continued to grow in subsequent years, if the expanding system of loan banks and services is any indication. In the second half of the eighteenth century, the government created a number of means through which nobles could borrow money. In 1769, for example, the Assignat Bank was established to issue the new paper money. It was given permission as well to make loans to important nobles under special arrangements. In 1772, the government ordered state foundling homes in the two major cities to loan money to nobles, and three years later authorized the charity boards of the provincial governments to do the same. The Charter to the Nobility of 1785 also addressed the issue of noble debt. It gave permission to the noble assemblies of each guberniia to set up provincial noble banks. In 1786, the government set up a new bank called the Government Loan Bank with which the Noble Bank was merged. This bank was in turn merged with the newly created Auxiliary Bank in 1802.[61]

The amount of money available for loans also increased in the second half of the century. The Noble Bank, which started with capital of 750,000 rubles, boasted capital of 6 million rubles by the 1780s. The Government Loan Bank with which the Noble Bank merged in 1786 had some 11 million rubles in resources by the close of the century. These resources were in great demand by members of the nobility. Between 1798 and 1802, the Auxiliary Bank of the Nobility had provided a total of 50 million assignat rubles to needy nobles. Indeed, it has been calculated that by the end of the eighteenth century, the total of the government's loans to noble landowners exceeded its expenditures in all other areas.[62]

Other changes in loan assessment and repayment in the second half of the eighteenth century facilitated the borrowing of money by the nobility as well. When the Noble Bank was established in 1754, the value of land was assessed at ten rubles per male serf. This assessment rose in subsequent years, to twenty rubles in 1766, forty rubles in 1786, and sixty rubles by 1804. Moreover, whereas in 1754 the repayment period had been set at three years, by the beginning of the nineteenth century, borrowers had up to thirty-seven years to repay their debt.[63]

This system of lending institutions did not eliminate the problem of noble indebtedness, however. Nobles rarely used their loan money to reinvest in their property or to repair their financial situation. The money was primarily used for consumption, for the maintenance of an acceptable noble lifestyle. Arcadias Kahan has estimated that the eighteenth-century Russian nobility spent over 18 million rubles per year on Western-style luxuries, education, and travel.[64] Conspicuous consumption, however, was not the only factor contributing to the nobility's growing indebtedness. The salaries of government officials were usually very low and therefore inevitably led to debt and borrowing. Moreover, the low return on landed property and the practice of partible inheritance also contributed to the financial hardship of the nobility.[65] Thus, despite the state's efforts to lift the nobility out of indebtedness, there were inescapable realities about the nature of landholding and land management in eighteenth-century Russia that foiled these attempts. The creation of these lending institutions did, however, further develop the nobility's dependence on the state and the monarch and underscores the complexity of this relationship.

One way for an overextended noble to raise cash was to mortgage immovable property. Archival records indicate that this practice was all too common. Inheritance disputes, redemption petitions, and other types of documents complain of property mortgaged by relatives and the troubles that ensued. There was, of course, a serious danger in mortgaging property. If for some reason the debtor did not, or could not, repay the borrowed amount, the property would be lost. Prince Ivan Lvov, for example, mortgaged immovable property in Galitskii uezd for 700 rubles to Nastasia Svintina in 1734. Failing to pay the debt, Lvov allowed the mortgage to expire. According to law, Lvov was given several opportunities to reclaim this property himself, but when he did not, the property was legally granted to Svintina.[66]

Mortgaged property was also susceptible to loss by other means. Once mortgaged property was transferred into the hands of a new owner, it was vulnerable to that new owner's sins. Nastasia Naryshkina, for example, claimed that property in Viazemskii uezd, which should have been granted to her husband Ivan, was granted to one of his relatives, Alexei, who mortgaged this land to Menshikov. When Menshikov fell from favor, this property was confiscated with all of Menshikov's other property.[67]

The mortgaging of property by a family member did not necessarily mean that the property was lost forever. Family members could reclaim family property through the right of redemption. This policy of redemption, however, could cause a great deal of anxiety for both potential buyers and sellers and thus contributed to noble insecurity regarding land in several ways. As discussed earlier, the new owner could never feel that the property was truly his to develop, since he was always threatened by the possibility of clan redemption and the likelihood of inadequate compensation at the time of repurchase. Even after the redemption time was shortened to three years in 1737, redemption remained a source of insecurity for noble landowners. Moneylenders still worried that their new property might be undervalued at the time of redemption and so were often hesitant to improve on the land. Family members who hoped to reacquire family land frequently complained about the "ruin" of the property in question or faced a higher redemption price if the land had changed hands more than once.[68] Thus the policy of redemption was severely flawed in that it contributed to the nobility's insecurity about its property, thereby discouraging investment and encouraging abuse.

For all of the reasons cited above, the nobility of eighteenth-century Russia suffered from a profound sense of insecurity regarding its land. It should come as no surprise, then, that the Russian nobility viewed its land differently than its Western counterparts. Burdened by the peripatetic nature of state service, Russian nobles were less likely to develop strong sentimental attachments to individual estates. Centuries of partible inheritance reinforced this idea. As each generation attempted to provide for all of its offspring, the notion was perpetuated that land was to be *used,* both for personal maintenance and for the support of wives and children. For most nobles this meant that any hopes of large-scale landowning would only be attained by individual effort through purchases and other acquisitions. The abundance of sales recorded in documents of the Senate and Votchina College testify to the existence of an active land market in eighteenth-century Russia, and the frequent petitions for land indicate the nobility's consistent eagerness to obtain more land. Russian nobles also faced other threats to the security of their land. Both confiscation by the state and the practice of redemption discouraged nobles from viewing their land as a permanent possession and the pervasive problem of debt and repeated mortgaging only reinforced this attitude. Unlike their Western counterparts, Russian nobles rarely succeeded in maintaining family estates for more than a generation or two. All of these factors led Russian nobles to view their land as a commodity, a function of the here and now. From this vantage point, practices such as partible inheritance and frequent mortgaging were not irrational at all, but simply techniques of survival.

Conclusion: Nobility, Property, and the Nature of the Russian State

> Property! Sacred right! Soul of Society! Source of laws! Mother of plenty and pleasure! Only where you are respected, where you are inviolable is the country blessed, is the citizen secure and happy.
>
> —Ivan Pnin

DEFINING THE RUSSIAN STATE IS NO EASY MATTER AND WHEREever one falls on the spectrum, one is sure to encounter opposition. The previous examination of inheritance and property law should indicate that this study falls squarely within the traditional paradigm of Russian history that emphasizes the role of a dynamic autocracy. Russia's inheritance and redemption laws, policies restricting landownership, and the practice of confiscation all point to this conclusion. Russia was a society in which the monarch wielded a great deal of power and had the potential to exert a great deal of influence over his subjects. To the degree that there was such a thing as "absolutism," Russian rulers were absolute.

This is not to say that nobles had no power at all. The extent of noble assertiveness on issues of inheritance, particularly in reaction to Peter's Law of Single Inheritance, is indicative of this reality. Despite its place as first authority of the realm, there were real limits to the autocracy's power to enact change. Paul Bushkovitch's recent book on Peter demonstrates the possibility, and reality, of noble opposition to the monarch.[1] In this respect, LeDonne is correct to emphasize the strength of the nobility and its ability to resist change. Thus, throughout the eighteenth century, there are numerous examples of nobles defying the state's authority through outright opposition, subversive behavior, and circumvention.

These strengths, however, should not be exaggerated. LeDonne's placement of the nobility within the power structure of Russian politics is justified, for there is no doubt that members of the nobility often profited from their close ties to the Russian ruler and benefited from their privileged status in Russian society. The crown and the nobility had many interests in common, not the least of which was the power and wealth derived from their shared exploitation of Russia's peasant population. Thus, to some degree, the Russian ruler and the Russian nobility did enjoy a collaborative relationship.

This collaboration, however, had its limitations. There were many instances when the ruler and the nobility did not see eye to eye and came into direct conflict. Many of the decisions of the ruler and of governmental bodies such as the Senate and the Votchina College threatened the financial and social well-being of the nobility. Laws about inheritance and landownership, for example, were frequently the subject of debate and disagreement between ruler and ruled, and government policies such as confiscation can hardly be interpreted as beneficial to all parties involved. The fact that members of the nobility staffed the very institutions that determined and carried out these policies does not invalidate the suggestion that Russia's nobility was often in conflict and disagreement with the goals of the Russian ruler and interests of the "Russian state." Indeed, in any bureaucratic system, even an immature one such as existed in eighteenth-century Russia, there is the expectation that those persons staffing the bureaucracy will be called upon to make decisions and carry out orders that are unfavorable to their social peers. Perhaps in Imperial Russia, we can assume that nobles who staffed institutions such as the Senate, the Votchina College, and the Chancellery of Confiscation had a vested interest in deciding land and inheritance cases in a certain manner, knowing as they did that they themselves could profit from the fall from power and loss of property of others. Undoubtedly, there are examples of such duplicitous and selfish behavior. This self-interest, however, does not explain all.

Thus, the nobility may have been a ruling class, but it was a peculiar one. Clearly, it was not, as some historians have suggested, an equal partner in the power structure of eighteenth-century Russia. It certainly benefited at times from its shared interests with the Russian ruler and the Russian state; as such it should be viewed as a collaborative, but nonetheless subservient group. Although the nobility had the ability to defy the ruler or circumvent laws, it was sufficiently insecure and weak to prevent it from amassing any real strength or solidarity independent of and in contradiction to the ruler. The development of a strong corporate identity was undermined by the nature of the tsarist system and the state's practices of service rotation and confiscation, practices that kept nobles fragmented, insecure, and suspicious of one another. The nobility's severe financial indebtedness only intensified its weak position in relation to the state.[2]

The nobility's participation in and staffing of the various governmental bodies, particularly those that oversaw matters involving land, is further testimony to its subservient character and to the existence of an abstract state. The fact that nobles decided inheritance disputes according to established inheritance laws indicates that they perceived that there was a higher purpose behind these decisions, since we can assume that in the majority of cases the deciding parties could not hope to gain by settling a case in one manner or another. This higher purpose probably involved some sense of morality, a sense that family members should receive the inheritance that they were due. It also, however, indicates some understanding and acceptance of a state, one that determined the laws and benefited from their effectiveness and one to which the nobility was obliged to serve.

This is more apparent when we consider the nobility's participation in state policies of confiscation. Here it might be argued more convincingly that nobles who served in bodies that oversaw and carried out the confiscation of property acted against their fellow noblemen out of pure self-interest and a desire for personal gain. It is undoubtedly true that there were many instances when nobles hoped to and indeed did profit from the misfortune of their comrades. It is difficult to imagine, however, that in all cases of confiscation the men behind the decisions stood personally to gain from the decision that they rendered.[3] In fact, since throughout the eighteenth century Russian nobles called for greater security in their land possession, one might rightfully question why nobles who did not stand to gain from their punitive decisions would vote in favor of confiscation. Such decisions could, in fact, only further their sense of insecurity of property and person. Their behavior, then, must be explained as a subservience to the Russian state and the Russian ruler.

The nobility's subservient position vis-à-vis the state and the ruler also contributed to the incomplete development of private property in Imperial Russia. Some progress was made, of course. Regarding inheritance, it is important to remember that the nobility succeeded in having Peter's Law of Single Inheritance overturned, thereby returning to the practice of partible inheritance that they favored. Later, the Charter to the Nobility offered them more freedom of disposal by removing some of the restrictions on acquired property. The rules for redemption were also changed during the eighteenth century, shortening the time limit from forty to three years, thereby offering greater security to new owners. Moreover, the land survey, after many attempts, actually did succeed in settling some disputes and drawing some boundaries. Finally, Catherine's Charter to the Nobility promised nobles protection from confiscation without due process.

None of these developments, however, were as promising as they may sound. The state continued to be actively involved in matters of inheritance, and the distinction between patrimonial and acquired property meant that nobles still lacked complete freedom of disposal. The policy of redemption also continued to threaten the security of landholding well into the next century. As late as 1875, critics of the institution of patrimonial property argued at the First Congress of Russian Jurists, that the policy of redemption prevented new owners from trying to improve their property.[4] Finally, even the Charter to the Nobility was less effective than it might appear in guaranteeing property rights. Although the Charter promised the nobility a number of securities, it also established that a noble's status, and thus his privileges, could be taken away if he committed a crime that was "irreconcilable with the principles of noble dignity." This somewhat vague condition included such crimes as "violation of an oath," "deceitful conduct," and, "crimes that by law entail deprivation of honor and corporal punishment."[5] In this way, once a noble was stripped of his status he became vulnerable to confiscation again. Moreover, the Charter could be revoked, as the rule of Paul I illustrates.[6]

Even at the end of the eighteenth century the Russian nobility still suffered from a great deal of insecurity regarding its land. Can we say then that private property did not exist? The determination is not so simple. The mere presence of restrictions on property ownership and transference does not necessarily negate the existence of private property; if it did, then we could not claim to enjoy the benefits of private property today. Even modern societies have many restrictions regarding property relations, such as forced heirship and servitudes of use. Private property, then, does not mean a complete absence of restrictions. Private property does, however imply a certain set of expectations regarding one's property rights.

In his rebuttal of Wieckhardt's article regarding private property in Muscovite Russia, Pipes analyzed landholding in Russia by using the two criteria that he views as central to the Roman definition of ownership of property: 1) that the property is "absolute," meaning that the owner may dispose of his property as he wishes, and 2) that the property is "permanent," meaning that it cannot be taken from him without his consent. Thus, it is through an examination of inheritance and confiscation practices that Pipes built his case against the existence of private property in Muscovite Russia.[7]

Pipes's criteria are useful, but need revision. Although his point about the freedom to dispose of one's property as one wishes is well taken, his use of it as a determinant of private property is too extreme. As previously noted, even in modern societies landowners are restricted by laws of inheritance and ownership and are not entirely free to dispose of their property as they might choose. The question is whether the restrictions are perceived as excessive and unfair by the majority of those owning land. In eighteenth-century Russia, nobles were restricted by many laws about inheritance, ownership, and disposal, and chafed under these laws, calling repeatedly for greater property rights. Even with their strong sense of kinship and familial responsibility, Russian nobles felt that their property rights were incomplete and insecure.

If freedom of disposal is not sufficiently convincing as criteria for the existence of private property then freedom from confiscation certainly is. In this respect, Pipes's test for private property is very useful. In speaking of the expectations about property rights that accompany the existence of private property, one of these is the reasonable expectation that one's property will not be confiscated by the government without just cause, due process, and, depending on the circumstances, possible compensation. Thus, although there are circumstances in modern societies that allow the government to confiscate property, in those that have a strong sense of private property, confiscation occurs only under extreme and clearly defined conditions, requires due process in the legal system, and occasionally includes compensation. This was not the case in eighteenth-century Russia. As we have seen, although nobles could choose to avoid certain behaviors that promised confiscation, such as treason or failure to pay debts, there was a great deal of arbitrariness and corruption in the bodies that made such decisions. In addition, the ruler, at the center of the government apparatus, could order confiscation with little regard for legality. Moreover, crimes like treason could be broadly defined to include any action that displeased the ruler, thus leaving the monarch in a very powerful position. The frequency and regularity of confiscation threatened any growth of private property and contributed to the nobility's profound sense of insecurity. Even when nobles asked that the confiscated property of others be granted to them in "perpetual possession," the phrase had no real meaning. As Meehan-Waters has noted, "the confiscation of property was devastatingly thorough and ignored distinctions between privately acquired and officially acquired property."[8] Given the reality of confiscation, it cannot be said that the eighteenth-century nobility enjoyed any real security of private property. In the words of Jeremy Bentham, "Property is only a foundation of expectation—the expectation of deriving certain advantages from the thing said to be possessed."[9] That is, property rights involve a relationship to the future; the owner needs to expect that what he does today will have use to him in the future. Russian nobles had no such expectation.

Once we say that the eighteenth-century nobility did not have private property in our modern conception, then it is necessary to consider whether the nobility itself understood the concept of private property as we do and if they desired it. The answer to this query is probably in the negative. The nobility's understanding and the understanding of the state regarding property were based on traditional ideas of kinship. Thus property was possessed or owned, but the individualistic sense that we have today was not fully present. Instead, there was a strong sense of clan or family property, supported and reinforced by the laws of inheritance and redemption. These laws limited a landowner's actions, but did not restrict them completely. Thus landowners still had the right to buy, sell, mortgage, and bequeath land, albeit within certain guidelines. The nobility's aggressive pursuit of these activities and their desire to acquire more land indicates that nobles had some sense of ownership about their property. Their expectations about their rights, however, fall within the understanding of kinship and clan property. Furthermore, though eighteenth-century nobles enjoyed certain rights over their land, they suffered from feelings of profound insecurity, particularly regarding the confiscation and appropriation of property by the state or fellow nobles.

Even within the nobility's own conceptions and expectations about property ownership and rights, however, their desires for security were not met. In this regard, the persistence of noble complaints is indicative of the continuing desire for greater property rights. Thus, in the "Project for a Charter to the Russian People," drafted in 1801, the composers found it necessary to once again request the security of certain property rights. They asserted that nobles should be able to live anywhere, even abroad, "not in the least afraid that by leaving the confines of Russia their estates or rights might be jeopardized or violated." Moreover, they asked that all arbitrariness be eliminated from the execution of inheritance rules, specifying that the order of succession established by law should be adhered to and "all special regulations which undermine this order (as, for example, a confined testament, a petition confirmed by his Imperial majesty, or any other change in the legally established rule) shall have no [legal] force . . ." The composers also felt the need to underscore the rule established by Catherine's Charter to the Nobility that property taken from someone punished with "civil death" should pass to the convicted person's heirs, not the state. Finally, the proposal also addressed the state's traditional claim to the property of the last member of a family, declaring that such individuals should have complete rights of disposal so that the property would not end up in the hands of the Treasury.[10] The fact that nobles had to regularly reiterate these requests is indicative that despite the advances of the previous century, Russian landowners still felt that their control over their property was incomplete. To some degree, then, Russian nobles were still limited to "restricted ownership."

The Russian state in the eighteenth century was not, as some have argued, a more or less equal coalition between the ruler and the nobility, or ruling class. Already at the beginning of the century we can find evidence of a developing concept of an abstract state. This state, of course, was still dominated and largely controlled by the tsar. Despite a general sense of distinct state interests such as those expressed in much eighteenth-century legislation, the whims and favors of the ruler still largely determined the course of events in Russia, as well as the fate of many individuals. This is not to say that the tsar or the state had the power to control every aspect of life down to the local level. Such control was impossible given the size of the empire and the weakness and insufficient staffing of the young bureaucracy. There were, thus, limits to the powers of the autocrat and his bureaucracy. Nonetheless, on the whole, the Russian ruler possessed a great deal of power as the center of the Russian state and the broker of wealth and status for the nobility. The nobility, despite its collaboration with the ruler, was nonetheless a weaker partner, one who was more often than not a victim of its stronger counterpart.

This power struggle is most evident in the realm of property rights, where Russia's nobles, even within the parameters of their eighteenth-century views of kinship and property, were dissatisfied with their insecure position and struggled, with limited success, to wrest greater rights and security from the Russian ruler and the state. As Wagner has demonstrated, in the wake of emancipation, Russian jurists were still grappling with questions of freedom of disposal over patrimonial property and the rights of the individual over the clan. In fact, the lack of real private property persisted through 1917; after all, had there been a firmly entrenched, widespread tradition of private property in Russia, the Bolsheviks could not have done away with it so quickly and easily.[11]

Notes

INTRODUCTION

1. Denis Fonvizin, "Rassuzhdenie o nepremennykh gosudarstvennykh zakonakh," in *Sobranie sochinenii,* 2 vols., ed. G. P. Makogonenko (Moscow, 1959), 254–67.

2. See, for example, Paul Dukes, *Catherine the Great and the Russian Nobility* (Cambridge: Cambridge University Press, 1967).

3. Marc Raeff, *Origins of the Russian Intelligentsia* (New York: Harcourt Brace Jovanovich, 1966), 110.

4. LeDonne presents this argument in his two important studies, *Ruling Russia* (Princeton: Princeton University Press, 1984), and *Absolutism and Ruling Class* (New York: Oxford University Press, 1991).

5. LeDonne, *Absolutism,* ix. A number of other historians make the same argument for the Muscovite period; see, Nancy Shields Kollmann, *Kinship and Politics: The Making of the Muscovite Political System, 1345–1547* (Stanford: Stanford University Press, 1987), Valerie A. Kivelson, *Autocracy in the Provinces* (Stanford: Stanford University Press, 1996), Donald Ostrowski, *Muscovy and the Mongols: Cross-Cultural Influences on the Steppe Frontier, 1304–1589* (Cambridge and New York: Cambridge University Press, 1998), and Richard S. Wortman, *Scenarios of Power: Myth and Ceremony in Russian Monarchy,* 2 vols. (Princeton: Princeton University Press, 1995).

6. LeDonne, *Absolutism,* x.

7. Pipes's argument has been laid out in his overview of Russian history, *Russia under the Old Regime* (New York: Collier Books, 1974).

8. Pipes, *The Russian Revolution* (New York: Vintage Books, 1991), 54.

9. George Weickhardt, "Due Process and Equal Justice in Muscovite Codes," *Russian Review* 51, 4 (October 1992): 463–80, and "Pre-Petrine Property Law," *Slavic Review* 52, 4 (Winter 1993): 663–79; Richard Pipes, "Was There Private Property in Muscovite Russia?" *Slavic Review* 53, 2 (Summer 1994): 524–38.

10. Alexis de Tocqueville, *Democracy in America,* ed. J. P. Mayer, trans. George Lawrence (Garden City, NY: Doubleday and Co., 1969), 51.

11. See for example, Ann Kleimola, "'In accordance with the canons of the Holy Apostles': Muscovite Dowries and Women's Property Rights," *Russian Review* 51 (April 1992): 204–29; Valerie Kivelson, "The Effects of Partible Inheritance: Gentry Families and the State in Muscovy," *Russian Review* 53 (April 1994): 197–212; William Wagner, *Marriage, Property and Law in Late Imperial Russia* (Oxford: Oxford University Press, 1994); Michelle Marrese, *A Woman's*

Kingdom: Noblewomen and the Control of Property in Russia, 1700–1861 (Ithaca: Cornell University Press, 2002); Richard Pipes, *Property and Freedom* (New York: Alfred A. Knopf, 1999).

12. "Property," *Black's Law Dictionary,* 5th ed. (St. Paul, MN: West, 1979), 1096.

13. Louisiana Civil Code (St. Paul, MN: West, 2003), art. 477.

14. "Possession," *Black's,* 1047.

15. "Property," *Black's,* 1095–96.

16. Richard Hellie, "Sudebniki," *Modern Encyclopedia of Russian and Soviet History* (MERSH) (Gulf Breeze, FL: Academic International Press, 1976–2000), 38: 15–21.

17. *Polnoe sobranie zakonov* (Moscow, 1830), 6: 4084; hereafter referred to as *PSZ* followed by volume and *ukaz* (or law, or statute) number.

18. *PSZ* 9: 6849 and 6880.

19. The previous overview of the Russian legal system was drawn from first-hand experience with primary sources of the period, along with assistance from the following sources: Marrese, *A Woman's Kingdom,* 13–15, 243; Richard Wortman, *The Development of a Russian Legal Consciousness* (Chicago: University of Chicago Press, 1976), 9–14; N. F. Demidova, "Pomestnyi Prikaz," *Modern Encyclopedia of Russian and Soviet History,* 29: 33–34; I. A. Bulygin, "Votchina College," *MERSH* 43: 79–80.

20. N. Kalachov and N. Dubrovin, eds., *Doklady i prigovory, sostoiavshiesia v Pravitel'stvuiushchem Senatie v tsarstvovanie Petra Velikogo* (St. Petersburg, 1880–1901), vol. 6, kn. 1, no. 295.

21. Rossiikii gosudarstvennyi arkhiv drevnikh aktov (RGADA) [Russian State Archive of Ancient Acts], f. 1209, op. 83, d. 298; op. 84, ch. 14, dd. 56, 591, 1181, 1571; hereafter referred to as RGADA with appropriate document citation.

22. *PSZ* 21:15364, *PSZ* 21: 15971, RGADA, f. 1209, op. 84, ch. 14, d. 1091; see also, RGADA, f. 1209, op. 84, ch. 14, dd. 296, 375, 451, 627, 737, 1254.

23. *PSZ* 5: 3455; *PSZ* 6: 3521; *PSZ* 11: 8502.

24. RGADA, f. 1209, op. 83, d. 142.

25. *Zakonodatel'nye akty russkago gosudarstva vtoroi polviny XVI–pervoi poloviny XVIII veka,* ed. N. E. Nosov, (Leningrad: Nauka, 1986), 162, 390–94.

26. RGADA, f. 22, op. 1, d. 139; see also, *PSZ* 15: 11264.

27. RGADA, f. 1209, op. 84, ch. 14, d. 187; see also, f. 1209, op. 80, dd. 409, 448, no. 128, 131, 142, 412; *PSZ* 15: 11435; *Senatskii arkhiv* (St. Petersburg, 1888–1913),14: 341–42.

28. RGADA, f. 1209, op. 80, d. 904

29. RGADA, f. 22, op. 1, dd. 133, 149; f. 1209, op. 80, d. 713, f. 1209, op. 83, dd. 148, 366, no. 10; f. 1209, op. 84, ch. 14, dd. 293, 677, 871, 1034; f. 248, op. 13, kn. 749, d. 27, l. 433 and kn. 752, d. 34, ll. 329–53.

30. RGADA, f. 1209, op. 84, ch. 14, d. 1337. For examples of minors being taken advantage of, see, *Doklady i prigovory,* t. 5, kn. 1, no. 182; t. 5, kn. 2, no. 1303; RGADA, f. 22, op. 1, dd. 30, 134; *Senatskii arkhiv,* 14: 480–81.

31. RGADA, f. 1209, op. 84, ch. 14, d. 529.

32. RGADA, f. 1209, op. 84, ch. 14, d. 1151.

33. *Senatskii arkhiv,* 14: no. 34. See also, RGADA, f. 1209, op. 83, d. 253; op. 84, ch. 14, d. 180.

34. RGADA, f. 1209, op. 83, d. 150. See also, f. 1209, op. 84, ch. 14, dd. 276, 393.
35. RGADA, f. 1209, op. 84, ch. 14, d. 1519.
36. Failure to petition: RGADA, f. 1209, op. 84, ch. 14, d. 1345; *PSZ* 21: 15364; 22: 15971.
37. Problems due to illness: *Doklady i prigovory,* t. 6, kn. 1, no. 601. Problems due to absence in service: *Doklady i progovory,* t. 2, kn. 2, no. 716, 823; t. 6, kn. 1, no. 527; RGADA, f. 1209, op. 83, d. 232; op. 84, ch. 14, d. 2073.
38. RGADA, f. 1209, op. 84, ch. 14, dd. 163, 850.
39. Ibid., d. 325; f. 1209, kn. 14649, d. 34, ll. 162–294.
40. *Doklady i prigovory,* t. 2, kn. 1, no. 312, t. 5, kn. 2, no. 1303; f. 1209, op. 84, ch. 14, d. 1264.
41. *Senatskii arkhiv,* 14: 431–32; *Doklady i prigovory,* t. 5, kn. 2, no. 1104; RGADA, f. 22, op. 1, d. 140.
42. RGADA, f. 1209, op. 84, ch. 14, d. 260; see also, f. 1209, op. 83, d. 142.
43. See, for example, *PSZ* 15: 11563 and *PSZ* 17: 12447, both which ordered that requests should be dealt with on the local level before being sent to the Senate. See also, *PSZ* 15: 11392, *PSZ* 17: 12316, and *PSZ* 19: 13537, all pertaining to the proper form and submission of petitions.
44. Cynthia Herrup, *A House in Gross Disorder: Sex, Law and the 2nd Earl of Castlehaven* (Oxford: Oxford University Press, 1999), 153.
45. Steven Ozment, *The Bürgermeister's Daughter: Scandal in a Sixteenth-Century German Town* (New York: St. Martin's Press, 1996).

Chapter 1. Property and Inheritance Laws

1. This summary of the historical debates on Muscovy is necessarily oversimplified. A more thorough review can be found in Marshall Poe, "The Truth about Muscovy," *Kritika* 3, 3 (Summer 2002): 473–86, and the responses to his essay by Valerie A. Kivelson, "On Words, Sources, and Historical Method: Which Truth about Muscovy?" *Kritika* 3, 3 (Summer 2002): 487–99, and Charles J. Halperin, "Muscovy as a Hypertrophic State: A Critique," *Kritika* 3, 3 (Summer 2002): 501–7. See also, Donald Ostrowski, "The Facade of Legitimacy: Exchange of Power and Authority in Early Modern Russia," *Comparative Studies in Society and History* 44 (2002): 534–63, and Richard S. Wortman, *Scenarios of Power.*
2. Halperin, "Muscovy as a Hypertrophic State," 501.
3. Robert O. Crummey, *The Formation of Muscovy, 1304–1613* (London and New York: Longman, 1987), 8–10; Jerome Blum, *Lord and Peasant in Russia from the Ninth to the Nineteenth Century* (Princeton: Princeton University Press, 1961), 70–92; Raeff, *Origins,* 14–17.
4. A. E. Presniakov, *The Formation of the Great Russian State,* trans. A. E. Moorhouse, with an introduction by Alfred J. Rieber (Gulf Breeze, FL: Academic International Press, 1993), 388–91.
5. Janet Martin, *Medieval Russia, 980–1584* (Cambridge: Cambridge University Press, 1995), 280–83.

6. V. O. Kliuchevskii, *Boiarskaia duma drevnei Rusi* (Moscow, 1909; repr., The Hague: European Printing, 1965), 207–11; Crummey, *Aristocrats and Servitors* (Princeton: Princeton University Press, 1983), 13.

7. Martin, 365.

8. S. F. Platonov, *Ivan Groznyi* (Leningrad, 1923), 130; Similarly, R. G. Skrynnikov noted that the oprichnina resulted in the destruction of the old system of princely landholding; Ruslan Skrynnikov, *Ivan Groznyi* (Moscow, 1975), 113–14.

9. S. B. Veselovskii, *Issledovaniia po istorii oprichniny* (Moscow, 1963), 30–33; Richard Hellie, "In Search of Ivan Terrible," in *Ivan the Terrible* by S. F. Platonov, ed. and trans. by Joseph L. Wieczynski (Gulf Breeze, FL: Academic International Press, 1974), xxii.

10. Raeff, *Origins,* 19; Iurii M. Eskin, "Mestnichestvo v sotsial'noi strukture feodal'nogo obshchestva," *Otechestvennaia Istoriia* 5 (1993): 39–53, and S. O. Schmidt, "Mestnichestvo i absoliutizm (postanovka voprosa)," in *Absoliutizm v Rossii,* ed. N. M. Druzhinin (Moscow, 1964): 168–205.

11. Ann M. Kleimola, "Up Through Servitude: The Changing Condition of the Muscovite Elite in the Sixteenth and Seventeenth Centuries," *Russian History* 6, 2 (1979): 213–15.

12. Kollmann, *Kinship,* 69.

13. Ibid., 58, 90, 119, 121–24.

14. Kliuchevskii, *Kurs russkoi istorii: Sochineniia v deviati tomakh* (Moscow, 1989), 4: 78–80; Nikolai P. Pavlov-Silvanskii, *Feodalizm v Rossii* (Moscow, 1988), 109–16, 450–71; Blum, 84–85, 168–88; Crummey, *Formation,* 108–9.

15. Blum, 29–41, 71; George Vernadsky, *Kievan Russia* (New Haven and London: Yale University Press, 1976), 139–40; Pavlov-Silvanskii, 98–99; Crummey, *Formation,* 8–9.

16. Blum, 80–81; Crummey, *Formation,* 9; Pipes, *Russia,* 87–89.

17. Blum, 142.

18. Crummey, *Aristocrats,* 108.

19. Blum, 170–71; Pavlov-Silvanskii, 110; Raeff, *Origins,* 15; Crummey, *Formation,* 9; Pipes, *Russia,* 92–93.

20. *PSZ* 1: 400, 493, 1291.

21. Crummey, *Aristocrats,* 112.

22. Ulozhenie 16: 47, in L. I. Ivinoi, ed., *Sobornoe Ulozhenie 1649 goda* (Leningrad: Nauka, 1987). For a translation and commentary on this law code, see Richard Hellie, trans. and ed., *The Muscovite Law Code (Ulozhenie) of 1649, Part I: Text and Translation* (Irvine, CA: Charles Schlacks, Jr., 1988).

23. Ulozhenie 16: 8, 37, 40.

24. Ibid., 16: 13; *PSZ* 2: 643; *PSZ* 2: 754.

25. Crummey, *Aristocrats,* 108; Raeff, *Origins,* 16; Kliuchevskii, *Kurs russkoi istorii,* 4: 78–80.

26. Nikolai Rozhdestvenskii, *Istoricheskoe izlozhenie russkago zakonodatel'stva o nasledstve* (St. Petersburg, 1839), 42.

27. Kliuchevskii, *Kurs russkoi istorii,* 4: 78–80.

28. Ulozhenie 16: 5.

29. Ibid., 16: 13.

30. Ibid., 16: 33.

31. *PSZ* 2: 1070. For examples of sons and nephews receiving the pomest'e of older relatives in the seventeenth century, see, RGADA, f. 1209, op. 78, ch. 1, d. 805, 807, 809, and 1068.

32. For examples of this in the early eighteenth century, see, *Doklady i prigovory,* t. 5, kn. 2, no. 1339; t. 6, kn.1, 41, 132 148.
33. *PSZ* 1: 404, 450, 631, 1291, 1317.
34. Ibid., 1: 695, 1253.
35. Ibid., 1: 365.
36. Ibid., 2: 1175.
37. Ibid., 2: 724, 1165; ibid., 4: 1761.
38. Ibid., 1: 489.
39. Ibid., 4: 1960, 2385; ibid., 5: 2625, 2652, 2663.
40. Blum, 81.
41. Ulozhenie 17: 1.
42. *PSZ* 2: 765.
43. Ibid., 2: 765.
44. Ibid., 1: 34.
45. Ibid., 2: 764.
46. The law also prohibited the transfer of hereditary estates to monasteries or monastic persons. Furthermore, once a votchinnik took monastic vows, he or she was no longer permitted to own hereditary estates and was required to take the necessary steps to transfer his or her estate to an eligible person; Ulozhenie 17: 41–44.
47. *PSZ* 2: 634, art. 6.
48. Russkaia Pravda, art. 95, in Vernadsky, *Medieval Russian Laws* (New York: Octagon Books, 1965); Rozhdestvenskii, 34.
49. *PSZ* 1: 32.
50. Ulozhenie 17: 15. Sons could also receive their father's votchina jointly, in which case neither of them could carry out transactions on the land without the knowledge and consent of the others; Ulozhenie 17: 13.
51. Art 42, in Vernadsky, *Medieval Russian Laws;* Levin, 11.
52. Russkaia Pravda, art. 92; Rozhdestvenskii, 35.
53. *PSZ* 2: 634, art. 4; RGADA, f. 22, op. 1, d. 156. The 1731 statute repealing Peter's law says that land would henceforth be divided equally among children "according to the Ulozhenie."
54. RGADA, f. 1209, op. 83, d. 108, l. 4 ob. This phrase, "before the points," and its variant "in the points," occur frequently in primary sources and refer to Peter's Law of Single Inheritance.
55. Rozhdestvenskii, 39, 43; Ulozhenie 17: 2, 4.
56. Ulozhenie 17: 4; *PSZ* 2: 860, sec. 2, art. 1.
57. Ulozhenie 17: 4.
58. *PSZ* 2: 655. Rozhdestvenskii supports this conclusion, citing the laws of 1628, 1629, and Ulozhenie 27: 2, 4; Rozhdestvenskii, 48.
59. *PSZ* 2: 700, sec. 2, art. 9.
60. *PSZ* 3: 1428.
61. Rozhdestvenskii, 53.
62. Ibid., 17: 1.
63. Eve Levin, "The Role and Status of Women in Medieval Novgorod" (Ph.D. diss., Indiana University, 1983), 10.
64. So long as the land was purchased, and not redeemed, back into the clan, it was considered purchased; *PSZ* 2: 814.
65. Ulozhenie 17: 1, 2, 6.
66. Ibid., 17: 7.

67. *PSZ* 2: 634, art. 1.
68. Ibid., 1: 46.
69. Ulozhenie 17: 5.
70. Ibid., 17: 5.
71. *PSZ* 2: 764.
72. Ulozhenie 16: 13. If there were no clan members who fit this description, then the pomest'e was to be given to members of other clans; Ulozhenie 16: 13. Subsequent legislation, however, would mandate that escheated pomest'e be given to clan members only; *PSZ* 2: 949.
73. Ulozhenie 16: 34; this is one of the few places in the Ulozhenie where equal division of land is clearly mandated.
74. Ibid., 16: 29.
75. Ibid., 16: 33.
76. *PSZ* 2: 1070.
77. Ulozhenie, 16: 31, 32, 33.
78. Ibid., 16: 17.
79. Ulozhenie 16: 20.
80. RGADA, f. 1209, op. 84, ch. 14, d. 22; f. 22, op. 1, d. 186, l. 1; see also, RGADA, f. 1209, op. 84, ch. 14, d. 58, d. 1129.
81. *PSZ* 2: 633, art. 3.
82. Ulozhenie 16: 56; *PSZ* 2: 633, art. 11.
83. A similar situation occurred if a husband transformed some of his wife's allotment of pomest'e into votchina, either by purchase or as a reward for service. Upon his death, she was to receive half of that votchina land in possession, and half in lifetime usufruct, to be returned to his clan upon her death. If, however, the husband had then sold or mortgaged her converted land as votchina, then it was to remain in the hands of those who had acquired it. As of August 1677, however, husbands were ordered that, having transformed their wives' prozhitok pomest'e into votchina, they were not to sell or mortgage it while their wives were still alive; *PSZ* 2: 633, art. 18, *PSZ* 2: 700, art. 22.
84. Daniel Kaiser, "Women, Property and the Law in Early Modern Russia," unpublished paper (Grinell, Iowa, 1988), 9–10.
85. Pskov Charter, art. 89, *Pamiatniki russkogo prava,* ed., S. V. Iushkov (Moscow, 1953), 297; Levin, 26–28.
86. *Zakonodatel'nye akty,* ed. N. E. Nosov, no. 161; Kaiser, "Women, Property and the Law," 9–10.
87. Ulozhenie 16: 16.
88. *PSZ* 2: 781. For a full discussion of the treatment of childless widows in the law see George Vernadsky, "Studies in the History of Muscovite Private Law of the Sixteenth and Seventeenth Centuries: The Case of the Childless Wife," in *Studi in Memoria de Aldo Albertoni,* vol. 3 (Padova, 1938), 435–54.
89. *PSZ* 2: 788.
90. Ibid., 2: 1214.
91. Ibid., 4: 1832.
92. Russkaia Pravda, art. 106.
93. Ibid., art. 103.
94. Levin, 22.
95. *PSZ* 2: 674.
96. *PSZ* 2: 674.

97. Russkaia Pravda, art. 92.
98. Kivelson, "The Effects of Partible Inheritance," 199.

CHAPTER 2. THE PETRINE REVOLUTION

1. *PSZ* 4: 2015.
2. Iurii Lotman, "The Poetics of Everyday Behavior in Eighteenth-Century Russian Culture," in *The Semiotics of Russian Cultural History,* ed. Alexander D. Nakhimovsky and Alice Stone Nakhimovsky (Ithaca and New York: Cornell University Press, 1985), 69–70.
3. Priscilla Roosevelt, *Life on the Russian Country Estate* (New Haven and London: Yale University Press, 1995), 34–73.
4. Alexander Griboedov, "Woe from Wit," in *The Government Inspector and Other Russian Plays,* trans. with an introduction by Joshua Cooper (London: Penguin Books, 1972; repr., 1990), 47–124.
5. For a discussion of the effectiveness of Peter's Table of Ranks see, Brenda Meehan-Waters, *Autocracy and Aristocracy: The Russian Service Elite of 1730* (New Brunswick: Rutgers University Press, 1982), and J. Hassel, "Implementation of the Russian Table of Ranks During the Eighteenth Century," *Slavic Review* 29 (1970): 273–95.
6. Valerie Kivelson, "The Devil Stole His Mind: The Tsar and the 1648 Moscow Uprising," *American Historical Review* 98 (June 1993): 733–56. In the same vein, Marc Raeff has argued that the overthrow of Peter III in 1762 was in part a response to his reversal of Elizabeth's administrative system, which had attempted to rely on regulations and law, in favor of a new regime of favorites. Peter's new system "threatened to undercut the regular institutions and to transform orderly administration into the dictatorship of a coterie," while at the same time "appeared to undermine the personalism of autocracy by interposing an effective barrier of favorites between ruler and subjects"; Raeff, "The Domestic Policies of Peter III and His Overthrow," *American Historical Review* 75, 5 (June 1970): 1309.
7. For a discussion of the significance of family and clan in the pre-Petrine period see Kollman, *Kinship and Politics.*
8. Kivelson, "The Devil Stole His Mind," 755; Ulozhenie 10: 20.
9. Raeff, *Origins,* 21.
10. David M. Griffiths, "Catherine II: The Republican Empress," *Jahrbucher fur Geschichte osteuropas* 21, 3 (1973): 330.
11. Griboedov, 152; Meehan-Waters's research confirms this impression, revealing that the large majority of those in the top four military and civil ranks in 1730 were related to someone else in the top ranks; *Autocracy,* 170–203.
12. David Ransel, "Bureaucracy and Patronage: The View from an Eighteenth-Century Russian Letter Writer," in *The Rich, the Well Born, and the Powerful,* ed. Frederic Cople Jaher (Urbana: University of Illinois Press, 1973), 163.
13. Ransel, "Bureacracy and Patronage," 164, 166.
14. Evgenii Anisimov, *The Reforms of Peter the Great,* trans. with an introduction by John T. Alexander (Armonk, NY: M. E. Sharpe, 1993), 60–65.
15. *PSZ* 5: 2775.

16. Raeff, *Origins,* 38–42.
17. Meehan-Waters, *Autocracy,* 22.
18. Ibid., 164.
19. Ibid., 21.
20. Nikolai Gogol, *Dead Souls,* trans. Bernard Guilbert Guerney (New Haven and London: Yale University Press, 1996), 15.
21. Ibid., 176–77.
22. Blum, 349.
23. Ransel, "Bureaucracy and Patronage," 155; Theodore Taranovskii, "Nobility in the Russian Empire: Some Problems of Definition and Interpretation," review of *The Crisis of the Old Order in Russia,* by Roberta T. Manning, and *Nobility and Privilege in Late Imperial Russia,* by Seymour Becker, *Slavic Review* 47, 2 (Summer 1988): 314–18; Michel Confino, "Histoire et psychologie: A propos de la noblesse russe au XVIII siecle," *Annales* 6 (November–December 1967), 1195–99.
24. Elise Kimerling Wirtschafter, *Social Identity in Imperial Russia* (Dekalb: Northern Illinois University Press, 1997), 22–37.
25. See the examples of Alexander Ivanovich Rumiantsev, the Lopukhins, and the Dolgorukiis described in chapter 7; Soloviev, *Istoriia Rossii s drevneishikh vremen: v piatnadtsati knigakh* (Moscow, 1959–63), X, vol. 19: 265–67; XI, vol. 21: 133.
26. Blum, 375–76.
27. D. A. Korsakov, *Votsarenie imperatritsy Anny Ioannovny* (Kazan, 1880), 10; Raeff, *Plans for Political Reform, 1730–1905* (Englewood Cliffs, NJ: Prentice Hall, 1966), 46–50; V. Kashpirev, ed., *Pamiatniki novoi russkoi istorii: Sbornik istoricheskikh statei i materialov* (St. Petersburg, 1871–73), 5–7.
28. N. Kalachov, ed., *Materialy dlia istorii russkogo dvorianstva,* 3 vols. in 1 (St. Petersburg, 1885), 11, 20.
29. *Sbornik Imperatorskago russkago istoricheskago obshchestva* (St. Petersburg, 1874–1916), 4: 245–46, 287–88; hereafter referred to as *SIRIO,* followed by volume and page number.
30. Gogol, 213.
31. Roosevelt, 159.
32. Salaries for state and military service were notoriously low and irregularly paid, and most nobles were not sufficiently engaged in any type of industry or trade to reap substantial income from these sources.
33. This phrase is translated as "slaves" by Hellie in his English translation of the Ulozhenie.
34. Ulozhenie 17: 41.
35. *PSZ* 6: 3711.
36. *PSZ* 8: 5633. It can be assumed that the law was not universally heeded, since in 1758 Elizabeth found it necessary to repeat the prohibition and the threat of confiscation for noncompliance; *PSZ* 15: 10796.
37. *PSZ* 15: 10796. This demand that persons sell their illegal immovable property in six months was reiterated in 1758.
38. Arcadius Kahan, "The Costs of 'Westernization' in Russia: The Gentry and the Economy in the Eighteenth Century," *Slavic Review* 25, 1 (1966): 57.
39. *PSZ* 15: 11490; 16: 11638.
40. *PSZ* 11: 8145.

41. RGADA, f. 248, op. 106, d. 659, l. 4.
42. Ia. E. Vodarskii, *Dvorianskoe zemlevladenie v Rossii v XVII-pervoi polovine XIX v.* (Moscow: Nauka, 1988), 219–40.
43. Ia. L. Barskov, "Pisma imperatritsy Ekateriny II k graf P. V. Zavodovskomy," *Russkii istoricheskii zhurnal,* book 5 (1918), 241.
44. Lindsey Hughes, *Sophia, Regent of Russia, 1657–1704* (New Haven and London: Yale University Press, 1990), 107.
45. Soloviev, X, vol. 19: 262.
46. Ibid., XI, vol. 21: 134.
47. *SIRIO* 8: 442; 14: 390; 68: 104–5; 327.
48. William R. Augustine, "Notes toward a Portrait of the Eighteenth-Century Russian Nobility," *Canadian-Slavic Studies* 4, 3 (Fall 1970): 394.
49. This important point about the role of land as the center of social relations has been noted by Augustine in his article cited in note 48.
50. Blum, 247, 254.
51. Denis Fonvizin, "Nedorosl," in *The Government Inspector and Other Russian Plays,* trans. with an introduction by Joshua Cooper (London: Penguin Books, 1972; repr., 1990), 53.
52. Blum, 219–35, 456, 367. For discussions of the social and economic relationships that evolved under the institution of serfdom see Stephen Hoch, *Serfdom and Social Control in Russia: Petrovskoe, a Village in Tambov* (Chicago: University of Chicago Press, 1986) and Edgar Melton, "Enlightened Seigniorialism and Its Dilemma in Serf Russia, 1750–1830," *Journal of Modern History* 62, 4 (December 1990): 675–708.
53. Augustine, "Notes," 387.
54. Blum, 428–41.
55. Augustine, "Notes," 407. Peter Kolchin, in his comparison of Russian serfdom and American slavery, has argued that the paternalistic element was lacking in the Russian case. Edgar Melton, however, has argued that the relationship of the Russian noble landowner to his serfs was much more complex, combining both goals of paternalism and order and a desire for economic improvement; Peter Kolchin, *Unfree Labor: American Slavery and Russian Serfdom* (Cambridge, MA: Belknap Press, 1987); Melton, "Enlightened Seignorialism," 675–708.
56. October 3, 1755; P. Baranov, ed., *Opis' vysochaishim ukazam i poveleniiam, khraniashchimsia v S-Peterburgskom senatskom arkhive za XVIII vek* (St. Petersburg, 1872–78), 3: 312.
57. Melton, "Enlightened Seignorialism," 696–99.
58. See John Bushnell, "Did Serf Owners Control Serf Marriage? Orlov Serfs and Their Neighbors, 1733–1861," *Slavic Review* 52, 3 (Fall 1993): 419–45.
59. Blum, 370; O. A. Shvatchenko, "Razmeshchenie i struktura votchinnogo zemlevladeniia v pervoi treti XVII v.," *Istoricheskie zapiski* 115 (1987): 303.
60. See, for example, Judith J. Hurwich, "Inheritance Practices in Early Modern Germany," *Journal of Interdisciplinary History* 23, 4 (Spring 1993): 699–718; Andrés Barrera-González, "Eldest and Younger Siblings in a Stem-Family System: The Case of Rural Catalonia," *Continuity and Change* 7, 3 (1992): 335–55; Lloyd Bonfield, "Property, Settlements on Marriage in England from the Anglo-Saxons to the Mid-Eighteenth Century," in *Marriage, Property and Succession,* ed. Lloyd Bonfield (Berlin: Duncker and Humblot, 1992):

287–308, and "Affective Families, Open Elites and Strict Family Settlements in Early Modern England," *Economic History Review,* 2nd ser., 39, 3 (1986): 341–54; J. P. Cooper, "Patterns of Inheritance and Settlement by Great Landowners from the Fifteenth to Eighteenth Centuries," in *Family and Inheritance, Rural Society in Western Europe, 1200–1800,* ed. Jack Goody, Joan Thirsk, and E. P. Thompson (Cambridge: Cambridge University Press, 1976): 192–327; Barbara English and John Saville, *Strict Settlement: A Guide for Historians* (Hull, UK: University of Hull Press, 1983).

61. Jonathon Powis, *Aristocracy* (Oxford: Basil Blackwell, 1984), 39–40. E. P. Karnovich notes the absence of this European practice in Russia; E. P. Karnovich, *Rodovye prozvaniia i tituly v Rossii* (St. Petersburg, 1886).

62. Raeff, *Origins,* 46; Seymour Becker, *Nobility and Privilege in Late Imperial Russia* (Dekalb: Northern Illinois Press, 1985), 29–31; A. Romanovich-Slavatinskii, *Dvorianstvo v Rossii ot nachala XVIII veka do otmeny krepostnago prava* (St. Petersburg, 1870), 165–67.

63. Michel Confino, *Domaines et seigneurs en Russie vers la fin du XVIII siecle: Etude de structures agraires et de mentalities economiques* (Paris: Institute d'etudes slaves de l'Universite de Paris, 1963). This idea is also supported by S. A. Korf, *Dvorianstvo i ego soslovnoe upravlenie za stoletie 1762–1855 godov* (St. Petersburg, 1906),13–14, and Romanovich-Slavatinskii, 198.

64. John Halit Brown, "A Provincial Landowner: A. T. Bolotov (1738–1833) (Ph.D. diss., Princeton University, 1977), 59, 72, 83.

65. Melton, "Enlightened Seigniorialism," 675–708.

66. Roosevelt, 3. See also, John Randolph, "The Bakunins: Family, Nobility, and Social Thought in Imperial Russia, 1780–1840," (Ph.D. diss., University of California, Berkeley, 1997).

Chapter 3. "Everyone sees the world . . ."

Epigraph at the beginning of the chpater is from J. Aylmer, *An Harborowe for faithfull and Trewe Subiectes* (Strausbourg, 1559), cited in J. P. Cooper, "Patterns of Inheritance," in *Family and Inheritance.*

1. *PSZ* 4: 2471.
2. LeDonne, *Absolutism,* 226.
3. RGADA, f. 1209, kn. 14640, d. 19, l. 78.
4. RGADA, f. 1209, op. 84, ch. 14, d. 1710, l. 22.
5. Sales: RGADA, f. 1209, kn. 9971, d. 1, l. 2; f. 1209, kn. 14640, d. 11, l. 35; d. 13, ll. 68–69; d. 19, l. 78; d. 25, ll. 100–101; f. 1209, kn. 14649, d. 34, l. 162; f. 1209, op. 83, d. 366, no. 1, ll. 1 ob-2; no. 2, ll. 1 ob-2; no. 5, ll. 20 ob-21 ob; no. 12, l. 1 ob; no. 13, l. 1 ob; f. 1209, op. 84, ch. 14, d. 232, ll. 66, 94; d. 401, 11. 25 ob-26; d. 582, l. 3 ob; d. 607, ll. 39– 40, 40–41; d. 770, ll. 1 ob-2; d. 927, l. 5; d. 1010, ll. 12 ob-13 ob, 13–15; d. 1181, ll. 538; d. 1690, l. 2; d. 1710, l. 22; f. 1209, op. 83, d. 366, no. 1, no. 3, no. 5, no. 12, no. 13, no. 15.
6. RGADA, f. 1209, kn. 9971, d. 8, l. 295.
7. RGADA, f. 1209, kn. 14640, d. 4, l. 22. For other examples of this phrase in mortgages, see, RGADA, f. 1209, op. 83, d. 223, ll. 3 ob-4; d. 366, no. 15, l. 1 ob; f. 1209, op. 84, ch. 14, d. 401, ll. 11–13; d. 423, l. 2; d. 582, l. 5 ob; d. 607, ll. 12 ob-14; d. 770, ll. 10–11 ob.

8. *PSZ* 4: 2471.
9. O. Chistiakov, ed., *Rossiiskoe zakonodatel'stvo X–XX vekov v deviati tomakh* (Moscow: Iuridicheskaia literatura, 1986), 4: 295–96. Peter's law applied not only to noble estates but also to shops and other forms of immovable property. Clearly, however, the law was aimed primarily at the nobility.
10. Raeff, *Origins,* 35–37.
11. *Rossiiskoe zakonodatel'stvo* 4: 295. See also Romanovich-Slavatinskii, 249. For a discussion of the expenses involved in aristocratic life see Kahan, "The Cost of 'Westernization.'"
12. *PSZ* 5: 3294; L. R. Lewitter, "Commentary," in Ivan Pososhkov, *The Book of Poverty and Wealth* (London: Athlone Press, 1987), 307.
13. Russkaia Pravda, art. 92.
14. The 1731 statute repealing Peter's law says that land would henceforth be divided equally among children "according to the Ulozhenie." Archival sources also support this interpretation; RGADA, f. 22, op. 1, d. 156; f. 1209, op. 83, d. 108.
15. *Rossiiskoe zakonodatel'stvo,* 4: 295–96.
16. Jerome Blum has presented data from the cadastral survey of Tver', which in 1540 listed 318 votchiny as belonging to 659 owners. Eight years later the same votchiny were held by 771 owners. Over the same period of time the average holding decreased in size as well, in one district from 970 chetverts per individual to 176 chetverts; Blum, 172.
17. Kivelson, "The Effects of Partible Inheritance," 205–6.
18. *PSZ* 7: 4722, art. 9, dok. 2, res 3.
19. RGADA, f. 1209, op. 84, ch. 14, d. 1151, l. 14; see also, f. 1209, op. 80, d. 209, l. 3; f. 1209, op. 83, d. 148, l. 1; f. 1209, op. 84, ch. 14, d. 249, l. 9; d. 1337, l. 4-4 ob.
20. RGADA, f. 1209, kn. 9971, d. 7, ll. 245–94; see also, f. 1209, op. 83, d. 76; d. 117, l. 1; d. 366; f. 1209, f. 1209, op. 84, ch. 14, d. 871, l. 3; f. 1209, op. 84, ch. 14, d. 1003, l. 12; f. 1209, op. 84, ch. 14, d. 529, l. 6.; f. 1209, kn. 9971, d. 6, ll. 36–244; *PSZ* 20: 14535.
21. Dukes, *Catherine the Great,* 100; A. B. Anikin, *Muza i mamona: Sotsial'no-ekonomicheskie motivy u Pushkina* (Moscow: Mysl', 1989), 196–97.
22. *Rossiiskoe zakonodatel'stvo,* 4: 296.
23. Ibid.
24. See art. 15, ibid., 299.
25. Levin, "The Role and Status of Women," 11.
26. *Rossiiskoe zakonodatel'stvo,* 4: 297.
27. Marc Raeff, "La noblesse et le discours politique sous le regne de Pierre le grand," *Cahiers du monde russe et sovietique* 34 (January–June 1993): 35–36.
28. RGADA, f. 1209, op. 84, ch. 14, d. 176.
29. RGADA, f. 22, op. 1, d. 133. For an example of this argument see, V. B. El'iashevich, *Istoriia prava pozemel'noi sobstvennosti v Rossii,* 2 vols. (Paris, 1951), 231–33, 251.
30. *PSZ* 4: 2471.
31. Later, after Peter's death, the supplemental law of 1725 strengthened this point, adding that if no eligible parties would consent to the addition of the family name, then the property would be considered escheated and written to Her Majesty; *PSZ* 7: 4722, art. 7.
32. Art. 9, *Rossiiskoe zakonodatel'stvo,* 4: 298.

33. Pskov Charter, articles 88 and 89.

34. In an apparent oversight, Peter did not define such specifications in the earlier article of the law that established inheritance rules for a childless landowner. Here he did not specify that the immovable estate pass to an heir, but simply ordered that it remain within the family. Thus, as we will see in other instances, despite Peter's apparent attention to detail, there were many inconsistencies in the law.

35. See, for example, the case of Prince Anikita Ivanovich Repnin discussed earlier in this chapter; RGADA, f. 22, op. 1, d. 133, ll. 1–2.

36. Art. 14, *Rossiiskoe zakonodatel'stvo,* 4: 299.

37. N. A. Voskresenskii, *Zakonodatel'nie akty Petra I* (Moscow-Leningrad: Akademii nauk, 1945), 40; *PSZ* 5: 3294. These orders undermine Kliuchevskii's argument that Peter intended his law as a temporary measure.

38. Art. 5, *Rossiiskoe zakonodatel'stvo,* 4: 297.

39. Commentary in ibid., 304.

40. Art. 6, ibid., 297.

41. Art. 9, ibid., 298.

42. *PSZ* 5: 3013. See also K. Pobedonostsev, *Kurs grazhdanskago prava* (St. Petersburg, 1875), 274.

43. Although the article of 1716 does not specifically prohibit a widow from alienating her ukaznaia chast, this was likely the case given the fact that Art. 9 had clearly stated this restriction and that such a restriction, by serving to keep lands intact and within a family, embodied one of the major goals of Peter's law. It would appear that this rule applied for childless widows and widows with children from a subsequent marriage. That is, I have found no cases or laws that indicate that between 1714 and 1731 a widow could leave property that she had received as her one-fourth portion to children from a successive marriage. These children, after all, would belong to a different clan.

44. Meehan-Waters cites the complex lawsuit between Prince Konstantin Kantemir and his stepmother as evidence of the conflicts that arose out of this new order of inheritance for widows; *Autocracy and Aristocracy,* 120–21.

45. RGADA, f. 1209, op. 84, ch. 14, d. 171.

46. Russkaia Pravda, art. 103; Pskov Charter, art. 88, *Pamiatniki,* 297. See also Levin, "The Role and Status of Women," 12.

47. Kleimola, "Muscovite Dowries," 205, 208.

48. Art. 8, *Rossiiskoe zakonodatel'stvo,* 4: 298. This article has been briefly described by Meehan-Waters, *Autocracy and Aristocracy,* 232.

49. Kivelson, "The Effects of Partible Inheritance," 207–8.

50. Kaiser, "Women, Property and the Law," 16.

51. RGADA, f. 1209, op. 84, ch. 14, d. 14.

52. Ulozhenie, 17: 2, 4; Kivelson, "The Effects of Partible Inheritance," 207.

53. RGADA, f. 1209, op. 84, ch. 14, d. 58.

54. Art. 7, *Rossiiskoe zakonodatel'stvo,* 4: 297–98; Meehan-Waters, *Autocracy and Aristocracy,* 121.

55. There are several notable studies examining the question of opposition to Peter. See, for example, Paul Bushkovitch, "Aristocractic Faction and the Opposition to Peter the Great," *Forschungen zur osteuropaischen Geschichte* 50 (1995): 80–120, and *Peter the Great: The Struggle for Power, 1671–1725* (Cambridge: Cambridge University Press, 2001); James Cracraft, "Opposition to

Peter the Great," in *Peter the Great Transforms Russia,* ed. James Cracraft (Lexington, MA: D.C. Heath, 1991), 258–71.

56. Romanovich-Slavatinskii, 251–52; Lewitter, 132.

57. *PSZ* 8: 5653.

58. *PSZ* 4: 2796; Eevgenii Anisimov, *Vremia Petrovskikh reform* (Leningrad: Lenizdat, 1989), 312.

59. *PSZ* 7: 4722, art. 2, dok. 1, res. 1, 2, 3.

60. Ibid., 7: 4722, art. 2, dok. 2, res. 1.

61. Ibid., art. 2, dok. 3, res. 1, 2, 3.

62. Ibid., art. 2, dok. 6, res. 1, 2, 3.

63. Ibid., 7: 4722.

64. Korsakov, 147.

65. RGADA, f. 3, d. 4, ll. 49–50; Kashpirev, 1: 6–7.

66. RGADA, f. 3, d. 4, ll. 47–48; f. 3, d. 6, ll. 16–24; f. 3, d. 6, l. 25.

67. Korsakov, 161.

68. Kashpirev, 1: 7–8; this project is called the "Summary" by Korsakov; Raeff, *Plans for Political Reform,* 46–50. For a recent discussion of the 1730 crisis see David L. Ransel, "The Government Crisis of 1730," in *Reform in Russia and the USSR: Past and Prospects,* ed. Robert O. Crummey (Urbana: University of Illinois, 1989), 45–71.

69. Crummey, *Aristocrats,* 116.

70. Mikhail Vasilevich Danilov, *Zapiski artillerii maiora* (Moscow, 1842), 14; Vasilii Aleksandrovich Nashchokin, *Zapiski Vasiliia Aleksandrovicha Nashchokina (1758–59),* ed. D. Iazykov (St. Petersburg, 1842), 196.

71. Kollman, *Kinship and Politics;* Kivelson, "The Effects of Partible Inheritance," 198, 211. See also, Gustave Alef, "The Origins of Muscovite Autocracy: The Age of Ivan III," *Forschungen zur osteuropaischen Geschichte* 39 (1986): 77–109; Crummey, *Aristocrats and Servitors;* John LeDonne, "Ruling Families in the Russian Political Order, 1689–1725," *Cahiers du monde russe et sovietique* 18 (July–December, 1987): 233–322.

72. Bisha, "The Promise of Patriarchy," 143–44; Elizabeth Fox-Genovese, *Within the Plantation Household: Black and White Women of the Old South* (Chapel Hill: University of North Carolina Press, 1988).

73. This difference between wealthier and poorer nobles both in the way the law affected them and in the way they perceived the law, has been noted by several historians. See Romanovich-Slavatinskii, *Dvorianstvo v Rossii,* 251–52; Soloviev, X, vol. 19: 225; and Dukes, *Catherine the Great,* 8. Moreover, the same distinction can be found among the nobilities of Western Europe; see, Cooper, 213.

74. *PSZ* 8: 5653.

75. Ibid.

76. Ibid.

77. RGADA, f. 1209, op. 84, ch. 14, d. 529.

78. RGADA, f. 1209, op. 80, d. 929.

79. RGADA, f. 1209, op. 84, ch. 14, d. 225.

80. *PSZ* 8: 5717. It is important to note that a widow's right to one-seventh of her husband's immovable property meant one-seventh of each village of each estate. As we shall see, this type of fragmentation would be problematic and would elicit complaints later in the century.

81. *PSZ* 16: 12194; 21: 15364; 27: 20128; 34: 26762.

82. RGADA, f. 1209, op. 84, ch. 14, d. 903; see also, f. 1209, kn. 14649, d. 34, ll. 292–93.

83. RGADA, f. 1209, op. 84, ch. 14, d. 228; see also, dd. 153, 158, 171.

84. RGADA, f. 1209, op. 84, ch. 14, d. 1069; see also, f. 1209, op. 84, ch. 14, d. 638.

85. RGADA, f. 1209, op. 84, ch. 14, d. 737; see also, f. 1209, op. 84, ch. 14, dd. 375, 627, 1091, 1254.

86. *PSZ* 11: 8190.

87. Ibid., 8: 5880.

88. RGADA, f. 1209, op. 84, ch. 14, d. 568; f. 1209, kn. 14640, d. 2, ll. 16–17.

89. Ibid., 8: 5653.

90. Kliuchevskii, *Kurs russkoi istorii,* 4: 82.

Chapter 4. Fool's Gold

1. O. A. Omel'chenko, *"Zakonnaia monarkhiia" Ekateriny II* (Moscow, 1993), 70–73.

2. Isabel de Madariaga, *Russia in the Age of Catherine the Great* (New Haven: Yale University Press, 1981), 7, 9, 279, 292; John T. Alexander, *Catherine the Great: Life and Legend* (New York and Oxford: Oxford University Press, 1989), 68.

3. Alexander, 69–71. For a thorough discussion of the Imperial Council project, see David Ransel, *The Politics of Catherinian Russia* (New Haven: Yale University Press, 1975), 73–98. Panin's project for the council can be found in *SIRIO* 7: 202–17. For an English translation see, Raeff, ed., *Plans for Political Reform in Russia,* 54–68.

4. Alexander, 71; de Madariaga, *Russia,* 83–87. For a thorough discussion of the Commission and its final report see, Ransel, *Catherinian Russia,* 153–61. Catherine's instructions to the Commission can be found in *SIRIO* 7: 232–33.

5. Robert L. Givens, "Servitors or Seigneurs: The Nobility and the Eighteenth-Century Russian State" (Ph.D. diss., University of California, Berkeley, 1975), 175; de Madariaga, *Russia,* 83–85.

6. de Madariaga, *Russia,* 86–87; Alexander, 71. The report of the Commission on the Freedom of the Nobility can be found in *SIRIO* 7: 238–66.

7. Alexander, 100–101; de Madariaga, *Russia,* 151–53.

8. Chap. 2, art. 9 of the Nakaz, in W. F. Reddaway, ed., *The Documents of Catherine the Great: The Correspondence with Voltaire and the Instruction of 1767 in the English Text of 1768* (New York: Russell and Russell, 1971), 216.

9. Ibid., ch. 18, art. 405, 407, 408, and 410.

10. Ibid.

11. Ibid., ch. 18, art. 416, 417, and 419.

12. Ibid., ch. 18, art. 425.

13. de Madariaga, *Russia,* 139–40; Alexander, 102.

14. Alexander, 112–14; de Madariaga, *Russia,* 164–168.

15. The noble nakazy of 1767 can be found in the *SIRIO,* volumes 4, 8, 14, and 68.

16. Augustine, "Economic Attitudes," 21, 35–39.
17. Augustine, "Economic Attitudes," 39.
18. de Madariaga, *Russia,* 169. A. V. Florovsky investigated the possibility of pressure or influence from above in preparation of the local nakazy and concluded that it was insignificant; A. V. Florovsky, *Sostav zakonodatel'noi komissii, 1767–1774 gg.* (Odessa, 1915).
19. *SIRIO* 4: 245–46, 287–88, 298–99.
20. *SIRIO* 68: 28–29, 34, 113.
21. *SIRIO* 68: 104, 327, 443; 14: 390.
22. *SIRIO* 4: 416; 8: 442; 491.
23. *SIRIO* 68: 447, 454. See also, *SIRIO* 68: 434–35.
24. *SIRIO* 4: 342; 8: 489–90, 556; 68: 327, 545.
25. *SIRIO* 68: 25.
26. *SIRIO* 68: 660. See also, *SIRIO* 68: 25.
27. *SIRIO* 68: 112–13, 431.
28. *SIRIO* 68: 373.
29. *SIRIO* 4: 246–47; translated in Augustine, "Notes," 383.
30. *SIRIO* 68: 25–26.
31. *SIRIO* 4: 324–25, 333, 345, 406–7; 8: 444–45, 458, 514–15, 520–21, 534, 563–64; 14: 419, 489; 68: 105, 264, 383, 428, 502–3, 514, 541–42, 550–51, 573–74, 604, 634, 651.
32. *SIRIO* 4: 324, 342, 345, 364, 388; 8: 526–27, 539, 547; 14: 270, 428–29, 464–65; 68: 16, 382, 402–3, 405, 431, 439, 507–8, 542, 601, 647.
33. Augustine, "Notes," 380–81.
34. *SIRIO* 68: 647.
35. *SIRIO* 68: 13, 439.
36. *SIRIO* 4: 275–76, 342, 364, 377–79; 8: 549–51; 68: 458–59.
37. *SIRIO* 68: 106–7.
38. *SIRIO* 4: 275; translated in Augustine, "Notes," 398.
39. *SIRIO* 68: 496–97, 589.
40. *SIRIO* 8: 481.
41. *SIRIO* 4: 275, 423.
42. *SIRIO* 4: 326.
43. *SIRIO* 4: 228–29.
44. *SIRIO* 68: 623–25; 8: 496.
45. Dukes, *Catherine the Great,* 161.
46. See Romanovich-Slavatinskii, 251–52; Soloviev, X, vol. 19: 225; and Dukes, *Catherine the Great,* 8.
47. *SIRIO* 68: 7, 115; 4: 227. See also, the nakaz from Pereslavskii-Zalesskii uezd, *SIRIO* 8: 496.
48. *PSZ* 8: 5717.
49. *SIRIO* 68: 346–47. See also, *SIRIO* 68: 368–69, 429, 471–72, 493–94, 532, 654.
50. *SIRIO* 68: 488–89. See also, *SIRIO* 68: 516, 602–3; 4: 283.
51. *SIRIO* 68: 108, 440–41, 532.
52. *SIRIO* 4: 252; 68: 31–32, 98, 115, 330, 411, 440, 459, 471, 479, 489, 493, 516, 533, 551–52, 611–12, 654.
53. *SIRIO* 68: 435. See also, 68: 331, 489, 493–94.
54. *SIRIO* 68: 612. See also, *SIRIO* 8: 514, 553; 14: 345.

55. *SIRIO* 4: 284. A woman's right to carry out transactions on her own land had been established by law as early as 1715; *PSZ* 5: 2952. This right was reaffirmed and further clarified by a law of 1753, which added that the wife was not obliged to obtain her husband's permission; *PSZ* 13:10111. The noble nakazy also addressed the issue of whether a woman's dowry servants who were married to her husband's servants should be counted as part of her dowry or as part of her one-seventh portion; see, *SIRIO* 68: 118, 362, 456. A law of 1744 had established that, upon her husband's death, the wife should receive those female servants in return as part of her dowry, along with their husbands and children, and that these servants were not to be counted as part of the one-seventh allotment; *PSZ* 12: 9095.

56. *SIRIO* 4: 388.

57. *SIRIO* 68: 441, 532.

58. *SIRIO* 68: 6, 16. Jones states that twelve instructions called for full ownership and control; Robert Jones, *The Emancipation of the Russian Nobility, 1762–1785* (Princeton: Princeton University Press, 1973), 75.

59. *SIRIO* 68: 342. See also, *SIRIO* 4: 462; 8: 508–9; 14: 398, 459, 481.

60. de Madariaga, *Russia,* 281–82; Jones, *Emancipation,* 87–88; Omel'chenko, 266–71.

61. Dukes, *Catherine the Great,* 224–25, 233; *PSZ* 20: 15074.

62. *PSZ* 19: 14089.

63. *PSZ* 38: 29511; V. N. Latkin, *Uchebnik istorii russkago prava perioda imperii* (St. Petersburg, 1909), 461; Rozhdestvenskii, 77.

64. *PSZ* 20: 14535.

65. *PSZ* 19: 14117. For a discussion of the formation of entails in Russia in the eighteenth and nineteenth centuries, see A. M. Anfimov, "Maioratnoe zemlevladenie v tsarskoi Rossii," *Istoriia SSSR* 5 (1962): 151–59. According to the guidelines of 1845, the minimum amount of land required to establish an entail was set at 10,000 desiatiny, a number too high for most nobles. As a result, between 1845 and 1905 only sixty entails were established; Becker, 70–71.

66. de Madariaga, *Russia,* 296–98; Alexander, 193–96; Dukes, *Catherine the Great,* 227–28.

67. Jones, *The Emancipation,* 283–84.

68. Pipes, *Russia under the Old Regime,* 69; Pipes, "Was There Private Property?" 530; Latkin, 468; Wortman, 26. In a similar vein, L. G. Beskrovnyi has described the Charter as the pinnacle in the formation of noble privilege; L. G. Beskrovnyi, *Khrestomatiia po istorii SSSR, XVIII v.* (Moscow, 1963), 296.

69. de Madariaga recognizes these limitations; 296–98.

70. *PSZ* 22: 16187. For an English translation of Catherine's Charter, see David Griffiths and George E. Munro, trans. and eds., *Catherine II's Charters of 1785 to the Nobility and the Towns* (Bakersfield: Charles Schlacks, Jr., 1991).

71. Art. 33; quoted from Griffiths's translation, 7–8. The law being referred to here can be found in *PSZ* 21: 15447.

72. In fact, this distinction had existed in medieval Novgorod; Levin, 10.

73. *PSZ* 8: 5880.

74. Ibid., 16: 12140; see also, ibid., 16: 11740.

75. See, for example, *PSZ* 18: 12830; 19: 13875, 13995, 14208; 26: 19955. See also, RGADA, f. 22, op. 1, d. 156 and *Senatskii arkhiv,* 15: 131–32.

76. Levin, 10.

77. This right was supported by law in subsequent years. See, for example, *PSZ* 25: 18381; 28: 21310.

78. Art. 24, quoted from Griffiths's translation.

79. Art. 23, quoted from Griffiths's translation.

80. RGADA, f. 22, op. 1, d. 136. See also, f. 22, op. 1, d. 104.

81. *Senatskii arkhiv,* 12: 409–15.

82. Ibid., 15: 137–38. See also, ibid., 12: 276.

83. See, for example, RGADA, f. 22, op. 1, d. 104 and f. 248, op. 106, d. 1542.

84. An owner had greater freedom when it came to his acquired property, but "even here the vagueness and frequent silences of statutory law limited his options and often rendered his arrangements insecure." Statutory law did not clearly define the workings of a will, for example, when it took effect and whether it included property acquired after it was drawn up; Wagner, 230.

85. Wagner, 228–29.

86. Ibid., 258.

87. Art. 6, in Griffiths and Munro, 5.

88. Even this exception had legal precedent. In 1780, for example, the Senate decided that the noble Vasilii Grigorov should be stripped of his rank and noble status, branded, and sent to Siberia for the murder of Captain Rodion Skoriatin; *PSZ* 20: 15032.

89. *PSZ* 23: 16901.

90. *PSZ* 24: 17916.

91. *PSZ* 23: 17033.

92. Roderick E. McGrew, *Paul I of Russia, 1754–1801* (Oxford: Clarendon Press, 1992), 223. See also, *PSZ* 26: 19756.

93. Griffiths and Munro, xxii.

94. Ch. 2, art. 9 of the Nakaz, in Reddaway, 216; Omel'chenko, 76–101.

95. Wagner, 3, 240–42, 263.

Chapter 5. Women, Inheritance

1. For a thorough study of women and property, see Marrese, *A Woman's Kingdom,* and "The Enigma of Married Women's Control of Property in Eighteenth-Century Russia," *Russian Review* 58, 3 (July 1999): 380–95.

2. Marrese, "Enigma," 380–95.

3. *Every Saturday: A Journal of Choice Reading,* vol. 1 (January 6, 1872), 27.

4. *SIRIO* 4: 284.

5. *PSZ* 16: 11764.

6. Levin, 21; see, RGADA, f. 1209, op. 84, ch. 14, dd. 1539, 1772; *Senatskii arkhiv,* 14: 160–63.

7. RGADA, f. 1209, op. 84, ch. 14, d. 14; see also, f. 1209, op. 84, ch. 14, dd. 52, 193, 1129; *Doklady i prigovori,* t. 2, kn. 2, nos. 716 and 865. Once a woman's pomest'e was registered to her groom, the extent to which her family maintained a claim to that land depended on the time and circumstances of her death. If the female died childless prior to 1681, her family had no claims to this land. If, however, the female died after 1681, three shares of the pomest'e would

be returned to her family while one-fourth remained with the groom; *PSZ* 2: 860.

8. *PSZ* 2: 650; *PSZ* 2: 803; RGADA, f. 1209, kn. 14649, d. 34, l. 204.

9. *PSZ* 2: 675.

10. Art. 8, *Rossiiskoe zakonodatel'stvo,* 4: 298.

11. Art. 7, *Rossiiskoe zakonodatel'stvo,* 4: 297–98.

12. *PSZ* 8: 5880.

13. RGADA, f. 1209, op. 84, ch. 14, d. 171. See also, f. 1209, op. 84, ch. 14, d. 228.

14. RGADA, f. 1209, op. 84, ch. 14, d. 193. See also, f. 1209, op. 84, ch. 14, dd. 14, 52, 58, 171, and 228; f. 248, op. 13, kn. 687, d. 14, ll. 104–10; *Doklady i prigovori,* t. 2, kn. 1, nos. 343, 484; t. 2, kn. 2, nos. 716, 823, and 865.

15. RGADA, f. 248, op. 13, kn. 687, d. 14, ll. 104–10.

16. RGADA, f. 1209, op. 84, ch. 14, d. 352; f. 1209, kn. 14640, d. 2, ll. 16–17. Fathers, mothers, and brothers would also petition on behalf of the bride; see, f. 1209, op. 83, d. 168; f. 1209, op. 84, ch. 14, dd. 568, 638, and 1356.

17. RGADA, f. 1209, op. 84, ch. 14, d. 1467; see also, dd. 545, 630, 636, 642, 876, 710, and 1069. Marrese has other archival examples; "Enigma," 388–89.

18. RGADA, f. 248, op. 13, kn. 691, d. 95, l. 427.

19. RGADA, f. 22, op. 1, d. 149.

20. *PSZ* 5: 3204.

21. RGADA, f. 248, op. 13, kn. 740, d. 125, ll. 1076–1117; see also, f. 248, op. 13, kn. 745, d. 35, ll. 540–847.

22. Art. 9.

23. *PSZ* 5: 3013. See also Pobedonostsev, 274. Although the article of 1716 does not specifically prohibit a widow from alienating her ukaznaia chast, this was likely the case given the fact that article 9 had clearly stated this restriction and that such a restriction, by serving to keep lands intact and within a family, embodied one of the major goals of Peter's law. It would appear that this rule applied for childless widows and widows with children from a subsequent marriage. That is, I have found no cases or laws that indicate that between 1714 and 1731 a widow could leave property that she had received as her one-fourth portion to children from a successive marriage. These children, after all, would belong to a different clan.

24. *Doklady i prigovory,* t. 6, kn.1, no. 529.

25. RGADA, f. 1209, op. 84, ch. 14, d. 185, l. 1.

26. RGADA, f. 1209, op. 84, ch. 14, d. 129; see also, f. 1209, op. 84, ch. 14, d. 187.

27. *PSZ* 8: 5717. It is important to note that a widow's right to one-seventh of her husband's immovable property meant one-seventh of each village of each estate.

28. *PSZ* 16: 12194; 21: 15364; 27: 20128; 34: 26762.

29. RGADA, f. 248, op. 13, kn. 745, d. 24, ll. 464–67; see also, f. 1209, op. 84, ch. 14, dd. 296, 451.

30. RGADA, f. 22, op. 1, d. 167.

31. *PSZ* 12: 9217.

32. RGADA, f. 1209, op. 84, ch. 14, d. 1345.

33. *PSZ* 2: 700, sec. 2, art. 9.

34. *PSZ* 3: 1428.

35. Rozhdestvenskii, 53.
36. *PSZ* 13: 9728.
37. *PSZ* 16: 12193.
38. RGADA, f. 248, op. 13, kn. 691, d. 84, ll. 382–85. See also, *PSZ* 21: 15110.
39. RGADA, f. 1209, op. 83, d. 144. See also, a case from 1749: RGADA, f. 22, op. 1, d. 127.
40. *PSZ* 23: 17185.
41. *PSZ* 7: 4722, art 7.
42. RGADA, f. 1209, op. 84, ch. 14, d. 137.
43. RGADA, f. 1209, op. 83, d. 144.
44. Levin, 165.
45. RGADA, f. 248, op. 106, d. 659, l. 7–8.
46. Bisha, 130–32. Michelle Marrese discusses this dilemma in her book, 32–39.
47. *PSZ* 13: 9728; RGADA, f. 1209, op. 4, d. 114/5759, l. 195.
48. RGADA, f. 1209, op. 84, ch. 14, d. 235.
49. RGADA, f. 1209, op. 79, d. 27, l. 162, cited in Marrese, 36.
50. RGADA, f. 1209, op. 83, d. 110.
51. RGADA, f. 1209, op. 84, ch. 14, d. 226, ll. 2–3. See also, f. 1209, op. 84, ch. 14, d. 238; f. 12–0, op. 80, d. 144, l. 82; f. 1209, kn. 14649, d. 34, l. 206; f. 22, op. 1, d. 94, ll. 1, 13.
52. RGADA, f. 1209, op. 84, ch. 14, d. 249, ll. 8, 11; f. 1209, op. 84, ch. 14, d. 255, ll. 25–26. Marrese cites more archival examples in her book, 32–39.
53. RGADA, f. 1209, kn. 9971, d. 6, ll. 87–88. See also, *Senatskii arkhiv,* 14: 160–63; *PSZ* 13: 9728.
54. *PSZ* 16: 12031.
55. *SIRIO* 4: 326; RGADA, f. 1209, op. 4, d. 114/5759, ll. 195–97.
56. *PSZ* 19: 13520.
57. Ibid., 19: 13750.
58. Marrese, 38.
59. RGADA, f. 1209, op. 84, ch. 14, d. 1772.
60. Ibid., d. 1539.
61. *PSZ* 23: 16769.
62. *PSZ* 32: 25576; Marrese, 39.
63. *PSZ* 12: 8936.
64. *PSZ* 17: 12782.
65. *PSZ* 33: 25833; *Sobranie zakonov o nasledstve, razdele imenii i vykup onykh* (Moscow, 1818), 58–68.
66. PSZ 38: 29357.
67. Crummey, 68–69.

Chapter 6. The Best-Laid Plans

1. Jack Goody, "Strategies of Heirship," *Comparative Studies in Society and History* 15 (1973): 16. M. L. Bush gives much higher percentages, but agrees that lack of a viable heir and family extinction was a significant problem; M. L. Bush, *Rich Noble, Poor Noble* (Manchester: Manchester University Press, 1988),

97–98. I have not, however, conducted any true statistical examination of the question.

2. *Sobranie zakonov o nasledstve,* 26–27.
3. Ulozhenie 17:1.
4. *PSZ,* 2: 634, art. 8.
5. Ibid., 2: 634, art. 11.
6. Ibid., 2: 700, sec. 2, art. 11.
7. *PSZ* 11: 8127.
8. RGADA, f. 1209, op. 84, ch. 14, d. 1195. See also, f. 1209, op. 84, ch. 14, d. 232 and f. 1209, op. 80, d. 213. See also, RGADA, f. 1209, op. 80, d. 213.
9. RGADA, f. 1209, op. 84, ch. 4, d. 232. Although this case contained no conclusion, we can assume that the will was upheld by the courts since Ivan was not the last in his clan.
10. *PSZ* 23: 16993.
11. *PSZ* 28: 21170; *Sobranie zakonov o nasledstve,* 12–13.
12. *PSZ* 31: 24835.
13. *PSZ* 35: 27468
14. *Doklady i prigovory,* t. 6, kn.1, no. 35.
15. RGADA, f. 1209, op. 84, ch. 14, d. 181.
16. *Doklady i prigovory,* t. 6, kn. 1, no. 492.
17. RGADA, f. 1209, op. 83, d. 129.
18. *Doklady i prigovory,* t. 5, kn. 2, no. 982.
19. *PSZ* 18: 12866.
20. *PSZ* 16: 11783; 18: 12830. See also, *PSZ* 16: 12140.
21. *Doklady i prigovory,* t. 6, kn. 1, no. 510.
22. RGADA, f. 1209, op. 83, d. 147. See also, *Doklady i prigovory,* t. 6, kn. 1, no. 108.
23. RGADA, f. 1209, op. 84, ch. 14, d. 259.
24. *PSZ* 2: 700, sec. 2, art. 8, art. 10, art. 11; *PSZ* 2: 634, art. 10, art. 11.
25. RGADA, f. 1209, op. 83, d. 253.
26. *Sobranie zakonov o nasledstve,* 30; *PSZ* 28: 21687.
27. PSZ 37: 28270.
28. *PSZ* 16: 12194. See also, *Doklady i prigovory,* t. 6, kn. 1, no. 542.
29. *Senatskii arkhiv,* 14: 341–42, 398–400; see also, *Senatskii arkhiv,* 14: 170. For other examples of escheated land, see, RGADA, f. 1209, op. 84, d. 1339; f. 1209, op. 84, ch. 14, d. 1456; f. 340, op. 2, d. 130, l. 300 ob.
30. F. C. Weber, *The Present State of Russia,* 2 vols. (London, 1722–23), 1: 200.
31. *PSZ* 7: 4722, art 7.
32. *PSZ* 19: 13428; Marrese, 56.
33. *PSZ* 17: 12720.
34. RGADA, f. 22, op. 1, d. 122.
35. See, for example, *PSZ* 16: 11740, 12140; 19: 13875, 13995, 14208; 26: 19955.
36. Ulozhenie 17: 3, *PSZ* 2: 634, art. 2.
37. RGADA, f. 1209, kn. 14649, d. 34, ll. 162–294.
38. *SIRIO* 68: 411; 14: 287–88. See also, *SIRIO* 4: 252; 14: 447, 481, 493; 68: 31–32; 68: 98; 68: 511; 68: 330; 68: 344; 68: 440; 68: 459; 68: 471; 68: 479; 68: 489; 68: 493; 68: 516; 68: 533; 68: 551–52; 68: 611–12; 68: 654.
39. *PSZ* 19: 14089.

CHAPTER 7. THE LONG ARM OF THE LAW

1. It is important to recognize that redemption also occurred among members of the merchantry; see, for example, *PSZ* 20: 15100.

2. The subject of redemption has rarely been treated in Russian studies, particularly for the eighteenth century. There are, however, a few brief discussions of this practice; see, for example, Oswald P. Backus III, "Mortgages, Alienations, and Redemptions: The Rights in Land of the Nobility in Sixteenth-Century Lithuanian and Muscovite Law and Practice Compared," *Forschungen zur osteuropaischen Geschichte* 18 (1973): 139–67; Latkin, 472–73. A lengthier treatment can be found in *Sobranie zakonov o nasledstve,* 51–86.

3. RGADA, f. 1209, op. 84, ch. 14, d. 1303; see also, f. 1209, op. 80, d. 397.

4. Ulozhenie 17: 31; *PSZ* 26: 19243.

5. V. I. Sergeevich, *Lektsii i izsledovaniia po drevnei istorii russkago prava,* 4th ed. (St. Petersburg, 1910), 536–38.

6. 1550 Sudebnik, art. 85, in Michigan Slavic materials, no. 7. *Muscovite Judicial Texts 1488–1556,* comp., trans., and ed., with annotation and selected glossary by H. W. Dewey (Ann Arbor, MI: Department of Slavic Languages and Literatures, 1966); Sergeevich, 541.

7. *Zakonodatel'nye akty,* ed. N. E. Nosov, no. 145.

8. Ulozhenie 17: 30.

9. *PSZ* 3: 702.

10. Ulozhenie 17: 27, 30. A law of February 1679 also reaffirmed the term of forty years; *PSZ* 2: 752. On acquired property, see Ulozhenie 17: 31; *PSZ* 22: 16463; 26: 19243.

11. *PSZ* 3: 753; *PSZ* 3: 1662.

12. *PSZ* 2: 702; Ulozhenie 17:38.

13. Art. 13; *Rossiiskoe zakonodatel'stvo,* 4: 299.

14. *Doklady i prigovory,* t. 1, no. 536.

15. Martyn Rady, *Nobility, Land and Service in Medieval Hungary* (London and New York: Palgrave, 2000), 97.

16. Paul Ourliac, "Le Retrait Lignager dans le Sud-Ouest de la France," *Revue historique de droit français et létranger* 30, no. 4 (1952): 328–55.

17. The right of first refusal was called *retrait lignager* in France, *prawo retraktu* in Poland, *recht van naasting* in the Netherlands, *Losungsrecht, Vorkaufsrecht,* or *Näherrecht* in the German states or resumption in England. The right to take land in the absence of a male heir was called *mainmorte* in France. See, M. L. Bush, *Noble Privilege* (New York: Holmes & Meier Publishers, 1983), 167.

18. RGADA, f. 1209, op. 84, ch. 14, d. 828, d. 163, and d. 401.

19. RGADA, f. 1209, op. 84, ch. 14, d. 56.

20. Ibid., d. 850, d. 1596.

21. According to the law of 1737; *PSZ* 10: 7339. Later, a law of 1800 gave a mortgager six months to redeem expired mortgaged property, and in 1849, the time period was extended to a year; PSZ 26: 19692; Konstantin Nevolin, *Istoriia rossiskikh grazhdanskikh zakonov* (St. Petersburg), 1851, 3: 96.

22. RGADA, f. 1209, op. 84, ch. 14, d. 1278.

23. RGADA, f. 22, op. 1, d. 130, l. 3

24. RGADA, f. 1209, op. 84, ch. 14, d. 69.
25. *Doklady i prigovory,* t. 5, kn. 2, no. 1159.
26. RGADA, f. 1209, op. 84, ch. 14, d. 122.
27. RGADA, f. 1209, op. 84, ch. 14, dd. 69, 210.
28. Ibid., d. 122.
29. Ibid., d. 1571.
30. RGADA, f. 1209, op. 83, d. 298.
31. RGADA, f. 1209, op. 84, ch. 14, d. 2017.
32. See, for example, RGADA, f. 1209, op. 83, d. 232 and op. 84, ch. 14, d. 223.
33. RGADA, f. 1209, op. 84, ch. 14, d. 349. For other examples of how the redemption process worked, see RGADA, f. 1209, op. 84, ch. 14, d. 445.
34. RGADA, f. 1209, op. 80, d. 514; see also, f. 1209, op. 83, d. 297, d. 645; f. 1209, op. 84, ch. 14, d. 1124.
35. RGADA, f. 1209, op. 84, ch. 14, d. 251. For other examples of redemption see, f. 1209, op. 84, ch. 14, dd. 69, 210, 223, 298, 349, 445.
36. RGADA, f. 1209, op. 83, d. 299; f. 1209, op. 84, ch. 14, d. 582.
37. *PSZ* 10: 7339.
38. *PSZ* 26: 19692; Nevolin, 96.
39. *SIRIO* 4: 469.
40. RGADA, f. 1209, op. 84, ch. 14, d. 2073 and d. 434.
41. RGADA, f. 1209, op. 84, ch. 14, d. 850; f. 1209, op. 80, d. 675, ll. 2 ob-4 ob. See also, f. 1209, op. 84, ch. 14, d. 828. The law of 1737 cited this as a method used by lenders to avoid giving back mortgaged property; *PSZ* 10: 7339.
42. RGADA, f. 1209, op. 84, ch. 14, d. 69.
43. *PSZ* 2: 753.
44. RGADA, f. 1209, op. 84, ch. 14, d. 607; see also, f. 1209, op. 83, d. 209.
45. RGADA, f. 1209, op. 83, d. 206.
46. *PSZ* 10: 7339; *Senatskii arkhiv,* t. 14: 344–45; RGADA, f. 1209, op. 84, ch. 14, d. 1278; *PSZ* 28: 21127.
47. RGADA, f. 1209, op. 84, ch. 14, d. 2073; see also, f. 1209, op. 84, ch. 14, dd. 472 and 1178, f. 1209, op. 83, d. 150, ll. 1–3, and d. 547. *PSZ* 28: 21973.
48. *PSZ* 12: 8936. This rule that family land that was sold or mortgaged to another family member was not eligible for redemption was in subsequent laws, such as the redemption law of 1766; *PSZ* 17: 12782.
49. *PSZ* 12: 8936.
50. RGADA, f. 1209, op. 84, ch. 14, d. 1339.
51. *PSZ* 14: 10461.
52. RGADA, f. 1209, op. 84, ch. 14, d. 1172; see also, f. 1209, op. 84, ch. 14, d. 401.
53. *PSZ* 17: 12782. The law of 1766 also made some slight alterations to the list of eligible redeemers; for example, it was added that in the absence of sons, daughters and granddaughters (daughters of deceased sons) would equally be eligible for redemption. The law also added that when the line of eligible redeemers had reached uncles and nephews, in the absence of these eligibility would be extended first to the seller's sisters and nieces (daughters of deceased brothers), and then to the sisters' sons and daughters.
54. Augustine, "The Economic Attitudes," 102.
55. *SIRIO* 14: 477–78.

56. *SIRIO* 4: 333. This complaint was answer by a law of 1815; Nevolin, 105–6.
57. *SIRIO* 4: 326, 393.
58. *SIRIO* 68: 342–43.
59. *SIRIO* 14: 450, 493; 68: 472.
60. *PSZ* 22: 16463; 26: 19243; 33: 25833; *Sobranie zakonov o nasledstve,* 58–68.
61. Wagner, 258.
62. RGADA, f. 1209, op. 84, ch. 14, d. 770.
63. *SIRIO* 4: 333, 379; 14: 466, 469–74, 486.
64. RGADA, f. 1209, op. 84, ch. 14, d. 1181.
65. Nevolin, 112.
66. Ibid. 112.
67. Blum, 80–81, 170–71.
68. J. L. Fennell, *Ivan the Great of Moscow* (London: Macmillan, 1963), 58–60.
69. Ulozhenie 2: 5, 7: 20; 16: 51; 17: 39, 42, 4. Also punishable by confiscation was the act of falsely claiming a piece of land was deserted in order to petition for it as a grant (16: 60), concealing the amount of land owned (16: 25), and failing to serve the tsar (17: 37).
70. *PSZ* 2: 1175, 1165, 1102; see also, *PSZ* 1: 260, 365, 489, 616; 2: 694, 724, 784, 934, 957, 1154, and 1189.
71. *Zakonodate'lnye akty,* ed. N. E. Nosov, nos. 10; 241; 14; 252, 81, 367, 394, 395; 275; 323; see also, nos. 244, 284, 340, 371, 381.
72. Ibid., no. 401; see also, *PSZ* 3: 1414, 1524, 1538, 1554, 1555, 1590; 4: 1761, 1960, 2008, 2033, 2330, 2385; 5: 2625, 2652, 2663, 2749, 2845, 2859, 2871, 2915, 2920, 2925, 2929, 2954, 2980, 3060, 3134, 3618, 3433; 6: 3509, 3586, 3599, 3601, 3631, 3676, 3687, 3707, 3709, 3762, 3772, 3803, 4007, 4028, 4091, 4113; 7: 4178, 4267, 4295, 4343, 4431, 4460, 4505.
73. PSZ 8: 5348, 15: 10898; 9: 6436, 10: 7987, 12: 8934, 9167, 15: 11421, 11555; 8: 5554, 17: 12542, 9: 6928, 10: 7755, 13: 9705, 9833, 9855, 9889, 10128, 10193; 14: 10653, 15: 1158.
74. *PSZ* 8: 5601.
75. "Kantseliariia konfiskatsii," in Brokgauz-Efron, 14: 342–43. See also, I. E. Andreevskii, "Kantselariia konfiskatsii, 1729–80 gg.," *Russkaia starina* 6 (1881):167–86.
76. *PSZ* 8: 5601.
77. RGADA, f. 340, op. 2, d. 71, ll. 82–83.
78. RGADA, f. 1209, op. 80, d. 451; see also, f. 340, op. 2, d. 150, l. 68 ob; d. 120, l. 277, 235 ob.; d. 130, l. 124 ob; f. 1209, op. 80, d. 416; d. 448, nos. 128, 131, 133, 141, 142, 144; d. 253; d. 316.
79. RGADA, f. 340, op. 2, d. 1200, ll. 1–13.
80. RGADA, f. 248, op. 13, kn. 737, d. 29, ll. 303–6, d. 37, ll. 356–59, d. 234, ll. 316–19; kn. 740, d. 24, ll. 147–48.
81. *PSZ* 10: 7151.
82. *PSZ* 11: 8506.
83. *PSZ* 11: 8775.
84. Soloviev, X, vol. 19: 265–66.
85. Ibid., 267; XI, vol. 21: 133.

86. *Doklady i prigovory,* t. 5, kn. 1, no. 645.

87. RGADA, f. 248, op. 13, kn. 691, d. 60, ll. 333.

88. RGADA, f. 248, op. 5, d. 273, d. 274.

89. Kahan, "The Costs of 'Westernization' in Russia," 40–66. See also, *Senatskii arkhiv,* t. 11: 287–28; t. 12: 271, 289.

90. RGADA, f. 248, op. 106, d. 793; f. 340, op. 2, d. 71, l. 117, f. 248, op. 106, d. 1559. See also, for example, f. 248, op. 13, kn. 691, d. 8, ll. 53–63; f. 248, op. 106, d. 378 and *Doklady i prigovory,* t. 5, kn. 1, no. 33.

91. "The Manifesto on the Freedom of the Nobility, 1762," in *Russia under Catherine the Great, vol. 1, Select Documents on Government and Society,* trans. and intro. Paul Dukes (Newtonville, MA: Oriental Research Partners, 1978), 28–35.

92. *PSZ* 20: 14750.

93. *PSZ* 22: 16187.

94. Art. 6, in Griffiths and Munro, 5.

95. *PSZ* 24: 17916.

96. Even this exception had legal precedent. In 1780, for example, the Senate decided that the noble Vasilii Grigorov should be stripped of his rank and noble status, branded, and sent to Siberia for the murder of Captain Rodion Skoriatin; *PSZ* 20: 15032.

97. *PSZ* 23: 16901.

98. *PSZ* 23: 17033.

99. McGrew, 223. See also, *PSZ* 26: 19756.

100. *PSZ* 26: 19756.

101. Valerii I. Mil'don, "Petr Vladimirovich Dolgorukov," in *Russkie pisateli 1800–1917, biograficheskii slovar',* tom 2 (Moscow, 1992), 151–53.

102. Ibid., "Iz niotkuda v nikuda (k metabiografii V. C. Pecherin)," in *Litsa biograficheskii al'manakh,* tom 4 (Moscow, 1994), 355–72.

103. *Senatskii arkhiv,* t. 14: 18, 187–91; Kashpirev, 1: 307–11.

104. Of the fifty-seven members who were granted estates, half (twenty-eight) of them received confiscated properties; Meehan-Waters, *Autocracy,* 92–93.

105. E. I. Indova, "K voprosi o dvorianskoi sobstvennosti v Rossii v pozdnii feodal'nyi period," in *Dvorianstvo i krepostnoi stroi Rossii XVI–XVIII vv.,* ed. A. A. Novosel'skii (Moscow: Nauka, 1975), 272–92. A collection of documents in *Materialy po istorii krest'ianskogo i pomeshchichego khoziaistva pervoi chetverti XVIII v.,* comp. K. B. Sivkov (Moscow: Akademii Nauk, 1951) supports and elucidates the circumstances of confiscation for a number of the people on Indova's list.

106. Baranov, ed., *Opis' vysochaishim ukazam i poveleniiam, khraniashchimsia v S-Peterburgskom senatskom arkhive za XVIII vek.*

107. Givens, "Servitors," 172, 175. See also, V. N. Tatishchev, "The Voluntary and Agreed Dissertation of the Assembled Russian Nobility about the State Government, c. 1730," in *Russia under Catherine the Great, vol. 1, Select Documents on Government and Society,* trans. and intro. Paul Dukes 26; Omel'chenko, 199.

108. *SIRIO* 4: 462.

109. *PSZ* 5: 3204; RGADA, f. 248, op. 13, kn. 740, d. 125, ll. 1076–1117; f. 248, op. 106, d. 1542; f. 248, op. 13, kn. 745, d. 35, ll. 540–847. See also, f. 22, op. 1, d. 124.

110. *PSZ* 15: 11450; see also, *PSZ* 16: 11693, *PSZ* 23: 16901; RGADA, f. 22, op. 1, d. 104.

111. Art. 23, quoted from Griffiths's translation.

112. RGADA, f. 248, op. 13, kn. 740, d. 138, ll. 1265–1265 ob. See also, Anna Iushkova's petition for a home in Moscow confiscated from one of Menshikov's men in RGADA, f. 248, op. 13, kn. 740, d. 85, l. 671.

113. RGADA, f. 248, op. 13, kn. 738, d. 7, ll. 109–23.

114. RGADA, f. 340, op. 2, d. 1200, ll. 1–20.

115. RGADA, f. 248, op. 13, kn. 737, d. 29, ll. 303–6; d. 34, ll. 316–19; d. 37, ll. 356–59; kn. 740, d. 23, ll. 135–45.

116. Claude Rulhiere, *The History, or Anecdotes, of the Revolution in Russia, in the Year 1762* (London, 1797), 38–39. An interesting comparison can be found in the descriptions of Donald Renshaw, an American who distributed famine relief through the American Relief Administration between 1921–23. When ARA members arrived in Moscow to set up headquarters, they were taken to a warehouse of items confiscated by the government from the homes of affluent bourgeoisie where they were allowed to pick rugs, furniture, and other items to furnish their office; Lee Farrow, "From Jackson Square to Red Square: Donald Renshaw and Famine Relief in Russia, 1921–1923," *Louisiana History* 43, 3 (Summer 2002): 270.

117. Fonvizin, "Rassuzhdenie o nepremennykh gosudarstvennykh zakonakh," 257.

118. Meehan-Waters, *Autocracy,* 94.

Chapter 8. Many Dimensions

1. Sergei Aksakov, *A Russian Gentleman,* trans. J. D. Duff (Westport, CT: Hyperion Press, 1977), 1.

2. RGADA, f. 1209, op. 84, ch. 14, d. 529.

3. Ibid., d. 318.

4. *Trudy vol'nago ekonomicheskago obshchestva,* II (St. Petersburg, 1801), 162–63, 165–67.

5. *Senatskii arkhiv,* t. 14: 19–22.

6. *PSZ* 19: 14117.

7. Anfimov, 151–52; *PSZ* 20: 19202.

8. Becker, 71.

9. Confino, *Domaines et seigneurs,* 115–16.

10. N. P. Zalomanov, *Dvorianskoe zemlevladenie i mery k ego sokhraneniiu i razvitiiu* (St. Petersburg, 1899); cited in Becker, 37.

11. August von Haxthausen, *Studies on the Interior of Russia,* ed., with an introduction by S. Frederick Starr, trans. Eleanore L. M. Schmidt (Chicago: University of Chicago Press, 1972), 257.

12. Givens, "Servitors," 215–16.

13. RGADA, f. 248, op. 13, kn. 752, d. 34, ll. 329–53.

14. *SIRIO* 8: 449; 526–27;14: 464–65; 68: 8–9; 335–37; 402–3, 405–6; 621–22; 647.

15. Jones, *Provincial Development in Russia* (New Brunswick: Rutgers University Press, 1984), 109; Jones, *The Emancipation of the Russian Nobility,* 77–78; Givens, "Servitors," 103.

16. Raeff, *Origins,* 47.

17. Aksakov, *Years of Childhood,* trans. J. D. Duff (Westport, CT: Hyperion Press, 1977), 82, 104–5, 152, 154.

18. RGADA, f. 1209, op. 84, ch. 14, d. 166. According to the noble nakazy of 1762 contained in *SIRIO,* these uezds were located in at least three guberniia; *SIRIO* 8: xxii; 68: viii; 14: xi; 4: xvi.

19. RGADA, f. 1209, op. 84, ch. 14, d. 927; *SIRIO* 4: xvi; 8: xxii; 68: viii.

20. For other examples see, RGADA, f. 1209, op. 84, ch. 14, dd. 129, 166, 185, 228, 260, 1091, 1264; f. 22, op. 1, d. 167.

21. Hughes, 106.

22. *PSZ* 2: 926, 938.

23. Ibid., 2: 1013.

24. Ibid., 2: 1192.

25. "Generalnoe mezhevanie," in Brokgauz-Efron, 8: 318; *PSZ* 14: 10237.

26. Robert L. Givens, "To Measure and to Encroach: The Nobility and the Land Survey," in *Russia and the World in the Eighteenth Century,* ed. R. P. Bartlett, A. G. Cross, and Karen Rasmussen (Columbus, OH: Slavica, 1986), 535.

27. *PSZ* 17: 12474.

28. Givens, "To Measure and to Encroach," 535–36.

29. Jones, *Provincial Development in Russia,* 110.

30. de Madariaga, 110.

31. Givens, "To Measure and to Encroach," 537, 542.

32. Brown, " Provincial Landowner," 80.

33. Givens, "To Measure and to Encroach," 537; Brown, "Provincial Landowner," 80.

34. Raeff, *Origins,* 45–46, 50.

35. Varvara Nikolaevna Golovina, *Memoirs of Countess Golovine,* trans. G. M. Fox-Davies (London, 1910), 14.

36. Aksakov, *Years of Childhood,* 281.

37. RGADA, f. 1209, op. 84, ch. 14, d. 69, l. 2.

38. RGADA, f. 1209, op. 83, d. 232, l. 12.

39. RGADA, f. 1209, op. 84, ch. 14, d. 238, l. 33; *Doklady i prigovory,* t. 2, kn. 2, no. 823. For similar complaints see, RGADA, f. 1209, op. 84, ch. 14, dd. 226, 375; f. 1209, op. 83, d. 206; t. 2, kn. 2, no. 716; t. 5, kn. 1, no. 566; t. 6, kn. 1, no. 295, 527.

40. Raeff, *Origins,* 29–30, 45–47. There are, of course, some exceptions. Brown, for example, argues that Bolotov had quite strong ties to his family estate, and that Bolotov was not alone in this attachment; Brown, "Provincial Landowner," 22, 25.

41. Kahan, "The Costs of 'Westernization' in Russia," 40–66; Daniel Kaiser, "Forgive Us Our Debts . . . : Debts and Debtors in Early Modern Russia," *Forschungen zur osteuropaischen Geschichte* 50 (1995): 155–84. See also, *Senatskii arkhiv,* t. 11: 287–28; t. 12: 271, 289.

42. William Doyle, *The Old European Order, 1660–1800* (Oxford: Oxford University Press, 1992), 87–88; Powis, 28.

43. E. P. Karnovich, *Zamechatel'nye bogatstva chastnykh lits v Rossii* (St. Petersburg, 1874; repr., The Hague, 1965), 259; quoted in Roosevelt, 18.
44. For a thorough description of estate culture, including its lavish excesses, see Roosevelt, *Life on the Russian Country Estate.*
45. Romanovich-Slavatinskii, *Dvorianstvo,* 64–65.
46. Ibid., 64; *PSZ* 19: 13743.
47. K. V. Sivkov, "Biudzhet krupnogo sobstvennika-krepostnika pervoi treti XIX v.," *Istoricheskie zapiski* 9 (1940): 140–41.
48. Blum, 379–80.
49. Ekaterina Dashkova, *Zapiski, 1743–1810* (Leningrad: Nauka, 1985), 70, 168, 175–76.
50. J. V. Beckett, *The Aristocracy in England, 1600–1914* (Oxford: Basil Blackwell, 1986), 296.
51. William Tooke, *View of the Russian Empire,* 3 vols. (London: Bye and Law; repr., New York: Arno Press, 1970), 2:379.
52. 8 February 1810, in W. C. Ford, ed., *Writings of John Quincy Adams,* 7 vols. (New York: Macmillan, 1913–17), 3: 396; cited in Powis, 28–29.
53. RGADA, f. 1209, op. 4, ch. 1, ll. 205–6.
54. *Senatskii arkhiv,* t. 12: 289. For other examples of noble requests for assistance, see RGADA, f. 22, op. 1, d. 158.
55. RGADA, f. 1209, kn. 9971, d. 7, l. 274.
56. *PSZ* 8: 5462.
57. *PSZ* 8: 5817; *PSZ* 8: 6458. See also, *PSZ* 8: 5975, *PSZ* 11: 8363, and 8637.
58. Soloviev, X, vol. 20: 496; Kahan, *The Plow,* 312.
59. Kliuchevskii, *Kurs russkoi istorii,* 4: 332; Kahan, *The Plow,* 313. This situation can be distinguished from that in England where, in the eighteenth century, nobles borrowed money from private sources. It was only in the nineteenth century that institutional borrowing became common among English aristocrats; Beckett, 309.
60. *Senatskii arkhiv,* t. 12: 271.
61. Ibid., 382; Kahan, *The Plow,* 314.
62. Blum, 383.
63. Blum, 383–84; Kahan, *The Plow,* 313.
64. Kahan, "The Costs of 'Westernization,'" 46.
65. Blum, 385.
66. RGADA, f. 1209, op. 83, d. 92.
67. *Senatskii arkhiv,* t. 12: 294–95.
68. *SIRIO* 68: 526–27.

Conclusion

1. See Bushkovitch, *Peter the Great.*
2. The Spanish historian Charles Jago makes the same link between noble indebtedness in Castile and the advantageous position this gave the Spanish monarchy; Charles Jago, "The Influence of Debt on the Relations between Crown and Aristocracy in Seventeenth-Century Castile," *Economic History Review* 26 (1973): 218–36.

3. Meehan-Waters found that, "The crown dispensed an estate to eleven of the fifty-four judges in the elite within one year of their having sat on a political trial. Rarely, however, did a judge receive an estate confiscated from an official in whose trial he had participated. Only five of the fifty-four judges received such blatant remuneration"; *Autocracy,* 158.

4. Wagner, 258.

5. Griffiths and Munro, 5.

6. McGrew, 223.

7. Pipes, "Was There Private Property in Muscovite Russia?" 525.

8. Meehan-Waters, *Autocracy,* 95.

9. Jeremy Bentham, "Principles of the Civil Code," in *The Works of Jeremy Bentham,* ed. John Bowring (New York: Russell and Russell, 1962), 1: 308.

10. "Project for a Charter to the Russian People," in Raeff, ed., *Plans for Political Reform,* 75–84.

11. Note the difficulty that Russia has had since the fall of communism with establishing private property; Patrick Henry and Michael Gulyalev, "President to Decree the Right to Buy Land," *Moscow Times,* February 21, 1996; Anton Zhigulsky, "Official: Land Decree is a Boost for Reform," *Moscow Times,* March 12, 1996; Katy Daigle, "Helping the Land Transform," *Moscow Times,* May 16, 1996; Peter Baker, "Experiment in Land Ownership Has Few Takers in Rural Russia," *Washington Post,* March 25, 2001; "Land for Sale," *Economic Newsletter,* Davis Center, Harvard University 27, 7 (March 11, 2002): 2; Amy Ridenour, "Lack of Respect for Law and Private Property Rights Undermines Future of Democratic Capitalism in Russia," *National Policy Analysis: A Publication of the National Center for Public Policy Research,* #410 (May 2002).

Bibliography

Archival Sources

Rossiiskii gosudarstvennyi arkhiv drevnikh aktov (RGADA) [Russian State Archive of Ancient Acts], Moscow:

fond 3, Dela, otnosiashchiesia do vnytrennei i vneshnei politiki Rossii

fond 22, Dela sudnye, opis' 1.

fond 248, Senat i ego uchrezhdeniia, opis' 5, 13, 106.

fond 340, Kantseliariia konfiskatsii, opis' 2.

fond 1209, Arkhiv prezhnikh votchinnykh del, opis' 4, 80, 83, 84; books 9971, 14640, 14649.

Published Primary and Secondary Sources

Aksakov, Sergei. *A Russian Gentleman.* Translated by J. D. Duff. Westport, CT: Hyperion Press, 1977.

———. *Years of Childhood.* Translated by J. D. Duff. Westport, CT: Hyperion Press, 1977.

———. *A Russian Schoolboy.* Translated by J. D. Duff. Westport, CT: Hyperion Press, 1977.

Alef, Gustave. "Aristocratic Politics and Royal Policy in the Late Fifteenth and Early Sixteenth Centuries." *Forschungen zur osteuropaischen Geschichte* 27 (1980): 77–109.

———. "The Crisis of Muscovite Aristocracy: A Factor in the Growth of Monarchical Power." *Forschungen zur osteuropaischen Geschichte* 15 (1970): 15–58.

———. "The Origins of Muscovite Autocracy: The Age of Ivan III." *Forschungen zur osteuropaischen Geschichte* 39 (1986): 7–362.

Alexander, John T. *Catherine the Great: Life and Legend.* New York and Oxford: Oxford University Press, 1989.

Alexandrov, V. A. *Sel'skaia obschina v Rossii (XVII–nachalo XIX v.).* Moscow, 1976.

Andreevskii, I. E. "Kantselariia konfiskatsii, 1729–1780 gg." *Russkaia starina* 6 (1881): 167–186.

———, K. K. Arsen'er, and F. F. Petnishevskii. *Entsiklopedicheskii slovar.* 82 vols. St. Petesby, 1895.

Anfimov, A. M. "Maioratnoe zemlevladenie v tsarskoi Rossii." *Istorii SSSR* 5 (1962): 151–59.

Anikin, A. B. *Muza i mamona: Sotsial'no-ekonomichskie motivy u Pushkina.* Moscow: Mysl', 1989.

Anisimov, Evgenii. *The Reforms of Peter the Great.* Translated with an introduction by John T. Alexander. Armonk, NY: M. E. Sharpe, 1993.

———. *Vremia Petrovskikh reform.* Leningrad: Lenizdat, 1989.

Augustine, William R. "The Economic Attitudes and Opinions Expressed by the Russian Nobility in the Great Commission of 1767." Ph.D. diss., Columbia University, 1969.

———. "Notes toward a Portrait of the Eighteenth-Century Russian Nobility." *Canadian-Slavic Studies* 4, 3 (Fall 1970): 373–425.

Backus III, Oswald P. "Mortgages, Alienations, and Redemptions: The Rights in Land of the Nobility in Sixteenth-Century Lithuanian and Muscovite Law and Practice Compared." *Forschungen zur osteuropaischen Geschichte* 18 (1973): 139–67.

Baker, Peter. "Experiment in Land Ownership Has Few Takers in Rural Russia." *Washington Post,* March 25, 2001.

Banac, Ivo, and Paul Bushkovitch, eds. *The Nobility in Russia and Eastern Europe.* New Haven: Yale Concilium of International and Area Studies, Columbus, OH: Distributed by Slavica, 1983.

Baranov, P., ed. *Opis' vysochaishim ukazam i poveleniiam, khraniashchimsia v S-Peterburgskom senatskom arkhive za XVIII vek.* 3 vols. St. Petersburg, 1872–78.

Barrera-González, Andrés. "Eldest and Younger Siblings in a Stem-Family System: The Case of Rural Catalonia." *Continuity and Change* 7, 3 (1992): 335–55.

Barskov, Ia. L. "Pisma imperatritsy Ekateriny II k graf P. V. Zavodovskomy." *Russkii istoricheskii zhurnal,* book 5 (1918): 223–57.

Bartlett, R. P., A. G. Cross, and Karen Rasmussen, eds. *Russia and the World in the Eighteenth Century.* Columbus, OH: Slavic, 1986.

Becker, Seymour. *Nobility and Privilege in Late Imperial Russia.* DeKalb: Northern Illinois University Press, 1985.

Beckett, J. V. *The Aristocracy in England, 1600–1914.* Oxford: Basil Blackwell, 1986.

Beloff, Max. "Russia." In *The European Nobility in the Eighteenth-Century Studies of the Nobilities of the Major European States in the Pre-Reform Era,* ed. A. Goodwin. London: A. & C. Black, 1953.

Bentham, Jeremy. *The Works of Jeremy Bentham.* 11 vols. Edited by John Bowring. New York: Russell and Russell, 1962.

Beskrovnyi, L. G. *Khrestomatiia po istorii SSSR, XVIII v.* Moscow, 1963.

Bisha, Robin. "The Promise of Patriarchy: Marriage in Eighteenth-Century Russia." Ph.D. diss., Indiana University, 1993.

Black, Henry. *Black's Law Dictionary.* 5th ed. St. Paul, MN: West, 1979.

Bloch, Marc. *Feudal Society.* 2 vols. Translated by L. A. Manyon. Chicago: University of Chicago Press, 1971.

Blum, Jerome. *Lord and Peasant in Russia from the Ninth to the Nineteenth Century.* Princeton: Princeton University Press, 1961.

Bogoslovskii, M. *Byt i nravy russkogo dvorianstva v pervoi polovine XVIII veka.* Petrograd, 1918.

Bonfield, Lloyd. "Property Settlements on Marriage in England from the Anglo-Saxons to the Mid-Eighteenth Century." In *Marriage, Property, and Succession,* ed. Lloyd Bonfield, 287–308. Berlin: Duncker and Humblot, 1992.

———. "Affective Families, Open Elites and Strict Family Settlements in Early Modern England." *Economic History Review,* 2d. ser., 39, 3 (1986): 341–54.

Brewer, Holly. "Entailing Aristocracy in Colonia Virginia: A Reconsideration of 'Ancient Feudal Restraints' and Revolutionary Reform." *William and Mary Quarterly* (April 1997): 307–46.

Brown, A. H. "S. E. M. Desnitsky, Adam Smith and the Nakaz of Catherine II." *Oxford Slavonic Papers,* new series, vol. 7. Oxford, 1974.

Brown, John Halit. "The Free Economic Society and the Nobility, 1765–96: Some Observations." *Canadian-American Slavic Studies* XIV14, 3 (Fall): 427–35.

———. "A Provincial Landowner: A. T. Bolotov (1738–1833)." Ph.D. diss., Princeton University, 1977.

Bulygin, I. A. "Votchina College." In *Modern Encyclopedia of Russian and Soviet History.* 60 vols. Gulf Breeze, FL: Academic International Press, 1976–2000.

Bush, M. L. *Noble Privilege.* New York: Holmes & Meier Publishers, 1983.

———. *Rich Noble, Poor Noble.* Manchester: Manchester University Press, 1988.

Bushkovitch, Paul. "Aristocractic Faction and the Opposition to Peter the Great." *Forschungen zur osteuropaischen Geschichte* 50 (1995): 80–120.

———. *Peter the Great: The Struggle for Power, 1671–1725.* Cambridge: Cambridge University Press, 2001.

Bushnell, John. "Did Serf Owners Control Serf Marriage? Orlov Serfs and Their Neighbors, 1733–1861." *Slavic Review* 52, 3 (Fall 1993): 419–45.

Cherniavsky, M. *Tsar and People.* New Haven: Yale University Press, 1961.

Chistiakov, O. I., ed. *Rossiiskoe zakonodatel'stvo X–XX vekov v deviati tomakh.* Moscow: Iuridicheskaia literatura, 1986.

Confino, Michel. *Domaines et seigneurs en Russie vers la fin du XVIIIe siecle: Etude de structures agraires et de mentalities economiques.* Paris: Institut d'etudes slaves de l'Universite de Paris, 1963.

———. "Histoire et psychologie: A propos de noblesse russe au XVIII siecle." *Annales* 6 (November–December 1967): 1163–1205.

Cooper, J. P. "Patterns of Inheritance and Settlement by Great Landowners from the Fifteenth to Eighteenth Centuries." In *Family and Inheritance, Rural Society in Western Europe, 1200–1800,* ed. Jack Goody, Joan Thirsk, and E. P. Thompson, 192–327. Cambridge: Cambridge University Press, 1976.

Coquin, Francois-Xavier. *La Grande Commission Legislative (1767–1768), Les Cahiers de doleances urbains.* Paris-Louvain: Nauwelaerts, 1972.

Cracraft, James. "Opposition to Peter the Great." In *Peter the Great Transforms Russia,* ed. James Cracraft, 258–71. Lexington, MA: D.C. Heath, 1991.

Crummey, Robert O. *Aristocrats and Servitors.* Princeton: Princeton University Press, 1983.

———. *The Formation of Muscovy, 1304–1613.* London and New York: Longman, 1987.

Danilov, M. V. *Zapiski artillerii maiora Mihailova Vasilievicha Danilova.* Moscow, 1842.

Dashkova, Ekaterina. *Zapiski, 1743–1810.* Leningrad: Nauka, 1985.

de Madariaga, Isabel. "Catherine II and the Serfs: A Reconsideration of Some Problems." *Slavonic and East European Review* 52, 126 (January 1974): 34–62.

———. *Russia in the Age of Catherine the Great.* New Haven: Yale University Press, 1981.

Demidova, N. F. "Pomestnyi Prikaz." In *Modern Encyclopedia of Russian and Soviet History.* 60 vols. Gulf Breeze, FL: Academic International Press, 1976–2000.

de Toqueville, Alexis. *Democracy in America.* Edited by J. P. Mayer. Translated by George Lawrence. Garden City, NY: Doubleday and Company, 1969.

Dewey, Horace W. "The 1497 Sudebnik—Muscovite Russia's First National Law Code." *The American Slavic and East European Review* 15 (1956): 325–38.

———. "The 1550 Sudebnik as an Instrument of Reform." In *Government in Reformation Europe,* ed. by Henry J. Cohn, 284–309. London: Macmillan, 1971.

———, comp., trans., and ed. *Muscovite Judicial Texts, 1488–1556.* Michigan Slavic Materials, no. 7. Ann Arbor, MI: Department of Slavic Languages and Literatures, 1966.

Doyle, William. *The Old European Order, 1660–1800.* Oxford: Oxford University Press, 1992.

Druzhinin, N. M. *Gosudarstvennye krest'iane i reforma P. D. Kiseleva.* 2 vols. Moscow, 1958.

Dukes, Paul, *Catherine the Great and the Russian Nobility.* Cambridge: Cambridge University Press, 1967.

———. ed. and trans. *Select Documents on Government and Society: Russia under Catherine the Great.* Newtonville, MA: Oriental Research Partners, 1978.

Economic Newsletter. Davis Center, Harvard University.

El'iashevich, V. B. *Istoriia prava pozemel'noi sobstvennosti v Rossii.* 2 vols. Paris, 1951.

Emmons, Terence. *The Russian Landed Gentry and the Peasant Emancipation.* Cambridge: Cambridge University Press, 1968.

English, Barbara, and John Saville. *Strict Settlement: A Guide for Historians.* Hull, UK: University of Hull Press, 1983.

Eskin, Iurii M. "Mestnichestvo v sotsial'noi strukture feodal'nogo obshchestva." *Otechestvennaia Istoriia* 5 (1993): 39–53.

Every Saturday: A Journal of Choice Reading. Vol. 1 (January 6, 1872).

Farrow, Lee. "From Jackson Square to Red Square: Donald Renshaw and Famine Relief in Russia, 1921–1923." *Louisiana History* 43, 3 (Summer 2002): 261–79.

Feldbrugge, F. J. M. "The Law of Land Tenure in Kievan Russia." In *Russian Law: Historical and Political Perspectives,* ed. William E. Butler, 1–28. Leyden: A.W. Sijthoff, 1977.

Fennell, J. L. I. *Ivan the Great of Moscow.* London: Macmillan, 1963.

Florovsky, A. V. *Sostav zakonodatel'noi komissii, 1767–1774 gg.* Odessa, 1915.

Fonvizin, Denis. "A Discourse on Permanent Laws of State." Translated by Ronald Hingley. In *Russian Intellectual History, An Anthology,* ed. Marc Raeff, 96–105. New Jersey: Humanities Press, 1978.

———. "Nedorosl." In *The Government Inspector and Other Russian Plays.* Translated with an introduction by Joshua Cooper, 47–124. London: Penguin Books, 1972; repr., 1990.

———. "Rassuzhdenie o nepremennykh gosudarstvennykh zakonakh." In *Sobranie sochinenii,* 2 vols., ed. G. P. Makogonenko, 254–67. Moscow, 1959.

Ford, Franklin. *Robe and Sword.* New York: Harper and Row, 1965.

Ford, W. C., ed. *Writings of John Quincy Adams.* 7 vols. New York: Macmillan, 1913–17.

Forster, Robert. *The Nobility in Toulouse in the Eighteenth Century: A Social and Economic Study.* Baltimore: Johns Hopkins University Press, 1960.

Fox-Genovese, Elizabeth. *Within the Plantation Household: Black and White Women of the Old South.* Chapel Hill: University of North Carolina Press, 1988.

Freeze, Gregory. "Bringing Order to the Russian Family: Marriage and Divorce in Imperial Russia, 1760–1860." *Journal of Modern History* 62, 4 (December 1990): 709–46.

———. *From Supplication to Revolution.* New York: Oxford University Press, 1988.

"Generalnoe mezhevanie." In *Entsiklopedicheskii Slovar' VIII,* by Brokgauz-Efron, 318. St. Petersburg, 1895.

German, I. E. *Istoriia mezhevogo zakonodatelstv ot Ulozheniia, do Generalnogo mezhevaniia 1649–1765 gg.* Moscow, 1893.

———. *Istoriia russkogo mezhevaniia.* Moscow, 1914.

———. *Materialy k istorii generalnogo mezhevaniia v Rossii.* Moscow, 1911.

Giesey, Ralph E. "Rules of Inheritance and Strategies of Mobility in Prerevolutionary France." *The American Historical Review* 82, 2 (April 1977): 271–89.

Givens, Robert L. "Servitors or Seigneurs: The Nobility and the Eighteenth-Century Russian State." Ph.D. diss., University of California, Berkeley, 1975.

———. "Supplication and Reform in the Instructions of the Nobility." *Canadian-American Slavic Studies* 11(1977): 483–502.

———. "To Measure and to Encroach: The Nobility and the Land Survey." In *Russia and the World of the Eighteenth Century,* ed. R. P. Bartlett, A. G. Cross, and Karen Rasmussen, 533–47. Columbus, OH: Slavica, 1986.

Gibson, Ralph, and Martin Blinkhorn, eds. *Landownership and Power in Modern Europe.* New York: HarperCollins Academic, 1991.

Gogol, Nikolai. *Dead Souls.* Translated by Bernard Guerney. New Haven and London: Yale University Press, 1996.

Golovina, Varvara Nikolaevna. *Memoirs of Countess Golovine.* Translated by G. M. Fox-Davies. London, 1910.

Goody, Jack. "Strategies of Heirship." *Comparative Studies in Society and History* 15 (1973): 3–20.

Goody, Jack, Joan Thirsk, and E. P. Thompson, eds. *Family and Inheritance: Rural Society in Western Europe,1200–1800.* Cambridge: Cambridge University Press, 1976.

Griboedov, Alexander. "Woe from Wit." In *The Government Inspector and Other Russian Plays.* Translated with an introduction by Joshua Cooper, 47–124. London: Penguin Books, 1972; repr., 1990.

Griffiths, David. "Catherine II: The Republican Empress." *Jahrbucher fur Geschichte osteuropas* 21, 3 (1973): 323–44.

Griffiths, David and George Munro, trans. and eds. *Catherine II's Charters of 1785 to the Nobility and the Towns.* Bakersfield, CA: Charles Schlacks, Jr., 1991.

Halperin, Charles J. "Muscovy as a Hypertrophic State: A Critique." *Kritika* 3, 3 (Summer 2002): 501–7.

Hassel, J. "Implementation of the Russian Table of Ranks During the Eighteenth Century." *Slavic Review* 29 (1970): 273–95.

Haxthausen, August von. *Studies on the Interior of Russia.* Edited with an introduction by S. Frederick Starr. Translated by Eleanore L. M. Schmidt. Chicago: University of Chicago Press, 1972.

Hellie, Richard. "In Search of Ivan the Terrible." In *Ivan the Terrible* by S. F. Platonov, ed. and trans. by Joseph L. Wieczynski, ix–xxxiv. Gulf Breeze, FL: Academic International Press, 1974.

———, trans. and ed. *The Muscovite Law Code (Ulozhenie) of 1649. Part I: Text and Translation.* Irvine, CA: Charles Schlacks, Jr., 1988.

———. *Serfdom and Military Change in Muscovy.* Chicago: University of Chicago Press, 1971.

———. "Sudebniki." In *Modern Encyclopedia of Russian and Soviet History,* vol. 38. Gulf Breeze, FL: Academic International Press, 1976–2000.

Herrup, Cynthia. *A House in Gross Disorder: Sex, Law and the 2nd Earl of Castlehaven.* Oxford: Oxford University Press, 1999.

Hoch, Stephen. *Serfdom and Social Control in Russia: Petrovskoe, a Village in Tambov.* Chicago: University of Chicago Press, 1986.

Hughes, Lindsey. *Sophia, Regent of Russia, 1657–1704.* New Haven and London: Yale University Press, 1990.

Humphreys, L. J. "The Vorontsov Family: Russian Nobility in a Century of Change, 1725–1825." Ph.D. diss., University of Pennsylvania, 1969.

Hurwich, Judith J. "Inheritance Practices in Early Modern Germany." *Journal of Interdisciplinary History* 23, 4 (Spring 1993): 699–718.

Indova, E. I. "K voprosi o dvorianskoi sobstvennosti v Rossii v pozdnii feodal'nyi period." In *Dvorianstvo i krepostnoi stroi v Rossii XVI–XVIII vv.,* ed. A. A. Novosel'skii. Moscow: Nauka, 1975.

Iushkov, S. V., ed. *Pamiatniki russkogo prava.* Moscow, 1953.

Ivinoi, L. I., ed. *Sobornoe Ulozhenie 1649 goda.* Leningrad: Nauka, 1987.

Jago, Charles. "The Influence of Debt on the Relations between Crown and Aristocracy in Seventeenth-Century Castile." *Economic History Review* 26 (1973): 218–36.

Jones, Robert. *The Emancipation of the Russian Nobility, 1762–1785.* Princeton: Princeton Univerity Press, 1973.

———. *Provincial Development in Russia.* New Brunswick: Rutgers University Press, 1984.

Kahan, Arcadius. "The Costs of 'Westernization' in Russia: The Gentry and the Economy in the Eighteenth Century." *Slavic Review* 25, 1 (1966): 40–66.

———. *The Plow, the Hammer and the Knout.* Chicago: University of Chicago Press, 1985.

Kaiser, Daniel. "Forgive Us Our Debts . . .: Debts and Debtors in Early Modern Russia." *Forschungen zur osteuropaischen Geschichte* 50 (1995): 155–84.

———. "Women, Property and the Law in Early Modern Russia." Unpublished paper. Grinnell, IA. 1988.

Kalachov, N., ed. *Materialy dlia istorii russkogo dvorianstva.* 3 vols. in 1. St. Petersburg, 1885.

Kalachov, N., and N. Dubrovin, ed. *Doklady i prigovory, sostoiavshiesia v Pravitel'stvuiushchem Senatie v tsarstvovanie Petra Velikogo.* 6 vols. In 10. St. Petersburg, 1880–1901.

"Kantseliariia konfiskatsii." In *Entsiklopedicheskii slovar,* by Brokgauz-Efron, 14: 342–43. St. Petersburg, 1895.

Karnovich, E. P. *Zamechatel'nye bogatstva chastnykh lits v Rossii.* St. Petersburg, 1874; repr., The Hague, 1965.

———. *Rodovye prozvaniia i tituly v Rossii.* St. Petersburg, 1886.

Kashpirev, V., ed. *Pamiatniki novoi russkoi istorii: Sbornik istoricheskikh statei i materialov.* 3 vols. St. Petersburg, 1871–1873.

Khodnev, A. I. *Istoriia imperatorskago vol'nogo ekonomicheskago obshchestva.* St. Petersburg, 1865.

Kiem, C. Ray. "Primogeniture and Entail in Colonial Virginia." *William and Mary Quarterly* 25 (October 1968): 545–86.

Kivelson, Valerie. *Autocracy in the Provinces.* Stanford: Stanford University Press, 1996.

———. "The Devil Stole His Mind: The Tsar and the 1648 Moscow Uprising." *American Historical Review* 98 (June 1993): 733–56.

———. "The Effects of Partible Inheritance: Gentry Families and the State in Muscovy." *Russian Review* 53 (April 1994): 197–212.

———. "On Words, Sources, and Historical Method: Which Truth about Muscovy?" *Kritika* 3, 3 (Summer 2002): 487–99.

Kleimola, Ann. "'In accordance with the canons of the Holy Apostles': Muscovite Dowries and Women's Property Rights." *Russian Review* 51 (April 1992): 204–29.

———. "Up Through Servitude: The Changing Condition of the Muscovite Elite in the Sixteenth and Seventeenth Centuries." *Russian History* 6, 2 (1979): 210–29.

Kliuchevskii, V. O. *Boiarskaia duma drevnei Rusi.* Moscow, 1909; repr., The Hague: European Printing, 1965.

———. *Kurs russkoi istorii: Sochineniia v deviati tomakh.* 10 vols. Moscow, 1989.

Kolchin, Peter. *Unfree Labor: American Slavery and Russian Serfdom.* Cambridge, MA: Belknap Press, 1987.

Kollman, Nancy Shields. *Kinship and Politics: The Making of the Muscovite Political System, 1345–1547.* Stanford: Stanford University Press, 1987.

Korf, S. A. *Dvorianstvo i ego soslovnoe upravlenie za stoletie 1762–1855 godov.* St. Petersburg, 1906.

Korsakov, D. A. *Votsarenie imperatritsy Anny Ioannovny.* Kazan, 1880.

Kucherov, Samuel. "Indigenous and Foreign Influences on the Early Russian Legal Heritage." *Slavic Review* 31, 2 (June 1972): 257–82.

Kuznetsov, Ia., ed. "Iz perepiski pomeshchika s krest'iananom vo vtoroi polovine XVIII st." *Trudy Vladimirskoi uchenoi arkhivnoi komissii* vol. 4 (1904).

Latkin, V. N. *Uchebnik istorii russkago prava perioda imperii.* St. Petersburg, 1909.

LeDonne, John. *Absolutism and Ruling Class.* New York: Oxford University Press, 1991.

———. "Ruling Families in the Russian Political Order, 1689–1725." *Cahiers du monde russe et sovietique* 18 (July–Dec. 1987): 233–322.

———. *Ruling Russia.* Princeton: Princeton University Press, 1984.

Lektonen, U. L. *Die polnischen Provinzen Russlands unter Katherina II in den Jahren, 1772–1782.* Berlin, 1907.

Levin, Eve. "The Role and Status of Women in Medieval Novgorod." Ph.D. diss., Indiana University, 1983.

Levy, Sandra. "Women and the Control of Property in Sixteenth-Century Muscovy." *Russian History* 10, 2 (1983): 201–12.

Lewitter, L. R. "Commentary." In *The Book of Poverty and Wealth,* by Ivan Pososhkov. London: Athlone Press, 1987.

Lipski, Alexander. "A Re-examination of the 'Dark Era' of Anna Ioannovna." *The American Slavic and East European Review* 15, 4 (December 1956): 477–88.

Lotman, Iurii. *Besedy o russkoi kulture: Byt i traditsii russkogo dvorianstva (XVIII–nachalo XIX veka).* St. Petersburg: Iskusstvo, 1994.

———. "Concerning Khlestakov." In *The Semiotics of Russian Cultural History,* ed. Alexander D. Nakhimovsky and Alice Stone Nakhimovsky, 150–87. Ithaca and New York: Cornell University Press, 1985.

———. "The Poetics of Everyday Behavior in Eighteenth-Century Russian Culture." In *The Semiotics of Russian Cultural History,* ed. Alexander D. Nakhimovsky and Alice Stone Nakhimovsky, 67–94. Ithaca and New York: Cornell University Press, 1985.

Marasinova E. N. *Psikhologiia elity rossiiskogo dvorianstva poslednei treti XVIII veka (Po materialiam perepiski).* Moscow: ROSSPEN, 1999.

Marrese, Michelle. "The Enigma of Married Women's Control of Property in Eighteenth-Century Russia." *Russian Review* 58, 3 (July 1999): 380–95.

———. *A Woman's Kingdom: Noblewomen and the Control of Property in Russia, 1700–1861.* Ithaca: Cornell University Press, 2002.

Martin, Janet. *Medieval Russia, 908–1584.* Cambridge: Cambridge University Press, 1995.

McGrew, Roderick. *Paul I of Russia, 1754–1801.* Oxford: Clarendon Press, 1992.

———. "The Politics of Absolutism: Paul I and the Bank of Assistance for the Nobility." *Canadian-American Slavic Studies* 7 (1973): 15–38.

McNally, Susanne. "From Public Person to Private Prisoner: The Changing Place of Women in Medieval Russia." Ph.D. diss., SUNY-Binghamton, 1976.

Meehan-Waters, Brenda. *Autocracy and Aristocracy: The Russian Service Elite of 1730.* New Brunswick: Rutgers University Press, 1982.

———. "The Development and the Limits of Security of Noble Status, Person and Property in Eighteenth-Century Russia." In *Russia and the West in the Eighteenth Century,* ed. A. G. Cross, 294–305. Proceedings of the Second International Conference organized by the Study Group on Eighteenth-Century Russia and held at the University of East Anglia, Norwich, England, July, 17–22, 1981.

———. "Russian Convents and the Secularization of Monastic Property." In *Russia and the World of the Eighteenth Century,* ed. R. P. Bartlett, A. G. Cross, and Karen Rasmussen, 112–24. Proceedings of the Third International Conference organized by the Study Group on Eighteenth-Century Russian and held at Indiana University at Bloomington, USA, September 1984.

Melton, Edgar. "Enlightened Seigniorialism and Its Dilemma in Serf Russia, 1750–1830." *Journal of Modern History* 62, 4 (December 1990): 675–708.

———. "Proto-Industrialization, Serf Agriculture and Agrarian Social Structure: Two Estates in Nineteenth-Century Russia." *Past and Present* 115 (May 1987): 69–106.

Mil'don, Valerii. "Iz niotkuda v nikuda (k metabiografii V. C. Pecherin)." In *Litsa biograficheskii al'manakh,* t. 4, 355–72. Moscow, 1994.

———. "Petr Vladimirovich Dolgorukov." In *Russkie pisateli 1800–1917, biograficheskii slovar',* t. 2, 151–53. Moscow, 1992.

Morrison, Kerry R. "Catherine II's Legislative Commission: An Administrative Interpretation." *Canadian Slavic Studies* 4, 3 (Fall 1970): 464–84.

Moscow Times.

Nashchokin, Vasilii Aleksandrovich. *Zapiski Vasiliia Aleksandrovicha Nashchokina (1758–59).* Edited by D. Iazykov. St. Petersburg, 1842.

Nevolin, Konstantin A. *Istoriia rossiskikh grazhdanskikh zakonov.* 3 vols. St. Petersburg, 1851.

Nosov, N. E., ed. *Zakonodatel'nye akty russkogo gosudarstva vtoroi poloviny XVI–pervoi poloviny XVIII veka.* Leningrad: Nauka, 1986.

Omel'chenko, O. A. *"Zakonnaia monarkhiia" Ekateriny II.* Moscow, 1993.

Oreshkin, V. V. *Vol'noe ekonomicheskoe obshchestvo v Rossii, 1765–1917.* Moscow, 1963.

Ostrowski, Donald. "The Facade of Legitimacy: Exchange of Power and Authority in Early Modern Russia." *Comparative Studies in Society and History* 44 (2002): 534–63.

———. *Muscovy and the Mongols: Cross-Cultural Influences on the Steppe Frontier, 1304–1589.* Cambridge: Cambridge University Press, 1998.

Ourliac, Paul. "Le Retrait Lignager dans le Sud-Ouest de la France." *Revue historique de droit français et létranger* 30, no. 4 (1952): 328–55.

Ozment, Steven. *The Bürgermeister's Daughter: Scandal in a Sixteenth-Century German Town.* New York: St. Martin's Press, 1996.

Palmer, Francis H. E. *Russian Life in Town and Country.* New York and London: G. P. Putnam's Sons, 1905.

Papmehl, K. A. "The Problem of Civil Liberties in the Records of the Great Commission." *Slavonic and East European Review* 42, 99 (June 1964): 274–91.

Pavlov-Silvanskii, Nikolai P. *Feodalizm v Rossii.* Moscow, 1988.

———. *Gosudarevy sluzhilye liudi—proiskhozhdenie russkogo dvorianstvo.* St. Petersburg, 1898.

Pipes, Richard. *Property and Freedom.* New York: Alfred A. Knopf, 1999.

———. *The Russian Revolution.* New York: Vintage Books, 1991.

———. *Russia under the Old Regime.* New York: Collier Books, 1974.

———. "Was There Private Property in Muscovite Russia?" *Slavic Review* 53, 2 (Summer 1994): 524–38.

Platonov, S. F. *Ivan Groznyi.* Leningrad, 1923.

Pobedonostsev, K. *Kurs grazhdanskago prava.* St. Petersburg, 1875.

Poe, Marshall. "The Truth about Muscovy." *Kritika* 3, 3 (Summer 2002): 473–86.

Polnoe sobranie zakonov. Moscow, 1830.

Powis, Jonathon. *Aristocracy.* Oxford: Basil Blackwell, 1984.

Pratt, Joan K. "The Russian Free Economic Society, 1765–1915." Ph.D. diss., University of Missouri, 1983.

Presniakov, A. E. *The Formation of the Great Russian State.* Translated by A. E. Moorhouse. With an introduction by Alfred J. Rieber. Gulf Breeze, FL: Academic International Press, 1993.

Pushkin, Alexander. "Dubrovsky." In *The Government Inspector and Other Russian Plays.* Translated with an introduction by Joshua Cooper, 61–150. London: Penguin Books, 1972; repr., 1990.

Rady, Martyn. *Nobility, Land and Service in Medieval Hungary.* London and New York: Palgrave, 2000.

Raeff, Marc. "The Domestic Policies of Peter III and His Overthrow." *American Historical Review* 75, 5 (June 1970): 1289–1310.

———. "La noblesse et le discours politique sous le regne de Pierre le grand." *Cahiers du monde russe et sovietique* 34 (January–June 1993): 33–46.

———. *Origins of the Russian Intelligentsia.* New York: Harcourt Brace Jovanovich, 1966.

———. *Plans for Political Reform in Imperial Russia, 1730–1905.* Englewood Cliffs, NJ: Prentice-Hall, 1966.

———. *Political Ideas and Institutions in Imperial Russia.* Boulder, CO: Westview Press, 1994.

———. "The Russian Nobility in the Eighteenth and Nineteenth Centuries: Trends and Comparisons." In *The Nobility in Russia and Eastern Europe,* ed. Ivo Banac and Paul Bushkovitch, 99–121. New Haven: Yale Concilium on International and Area Studies, 1983.

———. "State and Nobility in the Ideology of M. M. Shcherbatov." *Slavic Review* 19 (October 1960): 363–79.

———. *The Well-Ordered Police State: Social and Institutional Change through Law in the Germanies and Russia, 1600–1800.* New Haven: Yale University Press, 1983.

Randolph, John. "The Bakunins: Family, Nobility and Social Thought in Imperial Russia, 1780–1840." Ph.D. diss., University of California, Berkeley, 1997.

Ransel, David. "Bureaucracy and Patronage: The View from an Eighteenth-Century Russian Letter Writer." In *The Rich, the Well Born, and the Powerful,* ed. Frederic Cople Jaher, 154–78. Urbana: University of Illinois Press, 1973.

———. "The Government Crisis of 1730." In *Reform in Russia and the USSR: Past and Prospects,* ed. Robert O. Crummey, 45–71. Urbana: University of Illinois, 1989.

———. "Political Perceptions of the Russian Nobility: The Constitutional Crisis of 1730." *Laurentian University Review* 4 (1972): 20–38.

———. *The Politics of Catherinian Russia.* New Haven: Yale University Press, 1975.

Reddaway, W. F., ed. *Documents of Catherine the Great: The Correspondence with Voltaire and the Instruction of 1767 in the English Text of 1768.* New York: Russell and Russell, 1971.

Ridenour, Amy. "Lack of Respect for Law and Private Property Rights Undermines Future of Democratic Capitalism in Russia," *National Policy Analysis: A Publication of the National Center for Public Policy Research,* #410 (May 2002).

Robinson, Geroid T. *Rural Russia under the Old Regime.* Berkeley: University of California Press, 1932.

Romanovich-Slavatinskii, A. *Dvorianstvo v Rossii ot nachala XVIII veka do otmeny krepostnago prava.* St. Petersburg, 1870.

Roosevelt, Priscilla. *Life on the Russian Country Estate.* New Haven and London: Yale University Press, 1995.

Rozhdestvenskii, Nikolai. *Istoricheskoe izlozhenie russkago zakonodatel'stva o nasledstve.* St. Petersburg, 1839.

Rulhiere, Claude. *The History, or Anecdotes, of the Revolution in Russia, in the Year 1762.* London, 1797.

Sacke, George. *Die Gesetzgebende Kommission Katherinas II.* Breslau: Verlag Priebatchs Buchhandlung, 1940; repr., New York and London: Johnson Reprint Corporation, 1966.

Sbornik Imperatorskago russkago istoricheskago obshchestva. 136 vols. St. Petersburg, 1874–1916.

Schmidt, S. O. "Mestnichestvo i absoliutizm (postanovka voprosa)." In *Absoliutizm v Rossii,* ed. N. M. Druzhinin, 168–205. Moscow, 1964.

Scott, James. *Weapons of the Weak.* New Haven: Yale University Press, 1985.

Senatskii arkhiv. St. Petersburg, 1888–1913.

Shvatchenko, O. A. "Razmeshchenie i struktura votchinnogo zemlevladeniia v pervoi treti XVII v." *Istoricheskie zapiski* 115 (1987): 286–307.

Sivkov, K. V. "Biudzhet krupnogo sobstvennika-krepostnika pervoi treti XIX v." *Istoricheskie zapiski* 9 (1940): 125–53.

———, comp. *Materialy po istorii krest'ianskogo i pomeshchichego khoziaistva pervoi chetverti XVIII veka.* Moscow, 1951.

Sergeevich, V. I. *Lektsii i izsledovaniia po drevnei istorii russkago prava.* 4th ed. St. Petersburg, 1910.

Skrynnikov, Ruslan. *Ivan Groznyi.* Moscow: Academii nauk, 1975.

Sobranie zakonov o nasledstve, razdele imenii i vykup onykh. Moscow, 1818.

Soloviev, S. *Istoriia Rossii s drevneishikh vremen: v piatnadtsati knigakh.* 29 vols. in 15 bks. Moscow, 1959–63.

Stone, Lawrence. *The Family, Sex and Marriage in England, 1500–1800.* New York: Harper and Row, 1979.

Szeftel, Marc. "Personal Inviolability in the Legislation of the Russian Absolute Monarchy." *American Slavic and East European Review* 17 (1958): 1–24.

Taranovski, Theodore. "Nobility in the Russian Empire: Some Problems of Definition and Interpretation." *Slavic Review* 47, 2 (Summer 1988): 314–18.

Taranovsky, F. "Politicheskaia doktrine v nakaze Inperatritsy Ekateriny II." In *Sbornik statei po istorii russkogo prava posviashchennii prof. M. F. Vladimirskomu Budanovu.* Kiev, 1904.

Tillyard, Stella. *Aristocrats.* New York: Noonday Press, 1994.

Tolstoi, Lev. *Voina i mir.* Riga: Latgoizdat, 1951.

Tooke, William. *View of the Russian Empire.* 3 vols. London: Bye and Law; repr., New York: Arno Press, 1970.

Tovrov, Jessica. *The Russian Noble Family: Structure and Change.* New York: Garland Publishing, 1987.

Trudy vol'nago ekonomicheskago obshchestva. 30 vols. St. Petersburg, 1801.

van Zwieten, Adriana E. "The Orphan Chamber of New Amsterdam." *The William and Mary Quarterly,* 3d. series, 53, 2 (April 1996): 319–40.

Vernadsky, George. *Kievan Russia.* New Haven and London: Yale University Press, 1976.

———, trans. *Medieval Russian Laws.* New York: Octagon Books, 1965.

———. "Studies in the History of Muscovite Private Law of the Sixteenth and Seventeenth Centuries: The Case of the Childless Wife." In *Studi in Memoria de Aldo Albertoni.* 3 vols. Padova, 1938.

Veselovskii, S. B. *Issledovaniia po istorii oprichniny.* Moscow, 1963.

Vodarskii, Ia. E. *Dvorianskoe zemlevladenie v Rossii v XVII–pervoi polovine XIX v.* Moscow: Nauka, 1988.

Voskresenskii, N. A. *Zakonodatel'nie akty Petra I.* Moscow-Leningrad: Akademii nauk, 1945.

Wagner, William. *Marriage, Property and Law in Late Imperial Russia.* Oxford: Oxford University Press, 1994.

Weber, F. C. *The Present State of Russia.* 2 vols. London, 1722–23.

Wirtschafter, Elise Kimerling. *Social Identity in Imperial Russia.* Dekalb: Northern Illinois Press, 1997.

Weickhardt, George G. "Due Process and Equal Justice in Muscovite Codes." *Russian Review* 51, 4 (October 1992): 463–80.

———. "Pre-Petrine Property Law." *Slavic Review* 52, 4 (Winter 1993): 663–79.

Wittram, Reinhard. *Peter I, Czar und Kaiser.* Gottingen, 1964.

Wortman, Richard S. *The Development of Russian Legal Consciousness.* Chicago: University of Chicago Press, 1976.

———. *Scenarios of Power: Myth and Ceremony in Russian Monarchy.* 2 vols. Princeton: Princeton University Press, 1995.

Yaney, George. *The Systematization of Russian Government: Social Evolution in the Domestic Administration of Imperial Russia, 1711–1905.* Urbana: University of Illinois Press, 1973.

Zapiski po delu o imenii Kniazia Kantemira. Moscow, 1835.

Index